2010
Saint
Paul
ALMANAC

DATEBOOK • ENTERTAINMENT
STORIES • EVENTS

Community editors: Richard Broderick, May Lee-Yang, Donna Legato, Chamath Perera, Uri-biia H. Si-Asar, Deborah Torraine, Libby Tschida, Diego Vázquez, Jr.

Copy editors: Jan Zita Grover and Sharon Parker

Cover designer: Kevin R. Brown

Designer and typesetter: Donna Burch

History facts researcher: Steve Trimble

Proofreaders: Jan Zita Grover and Sharon Parker

Publisher and managing editor: Kimberly Nightingale

Saint Paul city map on pages x–xi and

Saint Paul downtown map on pages xii–xiii © 2007 Ellen Dahl

ISBN 978-0-9772651-5-2

Printed by Friesens in Canada

Saint Paul Almanac
PO Box 16243
Saint Paul, MN 55116
saintpaulalmanac.com

Saint Paul Almanac is a subsidiary of Arcata Press, a nonprofit publisher.

ARCATA
PRESS

Acknowledgments

So what the heck is the *Saint Paul Almanac* anyway?

Here at the nonprofit we keep the theme to Saint Paul and our doors wide open, welcoming literary giants, everyday residents, snowbirds, students, new English-language learners, and lovers of Saint Paul who live in other corners of the world, to send us stories and poems about our small chunk of global real estate. In keeping with our commitment to civic engagement, we include a yearly events calendar of all things Saint Paul and the birthdays of notable people who have lived in our city and made a significant contribution to it or the larger world. We offer historical facts, quotations, and trivia about Saint Paul too. Listed in the back of the book are our favorite restaurants, along with the city's independent coffee shops, health and fitness events, museums and tours, music and dance venues, theaters, art galleries, bookstores, food co-ops, and sports.

So why build an almanac around a city?

We do this to remind ourselves of the sacredness of our place on earth—how we move, live, and exist here, how we reach out and support each other. At the *Saint Paul Almanac*, we're convinced that our city places, spaces, and people deeply affect each of us.

And it's to remind ourselves of our strong belief in democracy and community. In past years, we recruited volunteers from every part of the city to go into their communities and collect stories. This year, the *Almanac's* stories were selected through a new process we at Arcata Press call democratic editing. We recruited eight community editors, ranging from high schoolers on up, from many cultures and many corners of our city, who collected a record-breaking 400-plus stories and poems. Using anonymous judging, the community editors debated, rated, voted, and decided which of these stories and poems to include in this year's *Almanac*. Each of them gave time and care to every piece they read. Initially, they disagreed with each other often and heatedly. Eventually, they reached agreement based on their collective commitment to the democratic editorial process.

I dedicate the *2010 Saint Paul Almanac* to the eight community editors who so unstintingly gave themselves to the shaping of this *Almanac's* contents: Richard Broderick, May Lee-Yang, Donna Legato, Chamath Perera, Uribiia H. Si-Asar, Deborah Torraine, Libby Tschida, and Diego Vázquez, Jr.

We hope this year's experiment in democratic editing will continue, becoming yet another great Saint Paul story.

Thank you, Steve Trimble, our Saint Paul historian, for finding all the local birthdays, quotations, facts, and trivia interspersed throughout the book. Luckily for us, Steve is really good at it, and we now have a library of over 400 birthdays to include in future volumes.

At the Minnesota Literacy Council, Jen Ouellette-Schramm, Susan Godon, Melissa Martinson, Guy Haglund, and Andrea Echelberger helped us gather stories from writers. Jen and her East Side class were kind enough to invite me to their classroom for a civic-engagement writing discussion.

Jamela Pettiford and her class at New Foundations brought their strong, loving, creative energy to the writing classes Deborah Torraine and I participated in. Thank you, Jamela and New Foundations writers!

Michelle Bierman, our liaison with Saint Paul Public Schools, worked diligently to collect the charming stories we are publishing this year from Saint Paul Public School students. Thank you, Michelle.

Our thanks to CPA Bernard L. Brodkorb and accounting/bookkeeping specialist Dawn Trexel, who keep our nonprofit in financial order.

And then we have our spectacular *Saint Paul Almanac* production team: cover artist Kevin R. Brown, typesetter and designer Donna Burch, copy editors and proofreaders Jan Zita Grover and Sharon Parker, staff photographer Patricia Bour-Schilla, and illustrators Andy Singer and Kirk Anderson. May Lee-Yang improved the writing quality of the restaurant listings, Teri Dwyer wrote the Health and Fitness Events section, and Donna Legato, Libby Tschida, and Deborah Torraine fact-checked the rest of the listings. Nigel Parry kept our website in fine shape. I want to thank all of you for your heavy lifting.

Thank you to photographers Heatherjo Gilberston, Tobechi Tobechukwu, Steve Rouch, Beth Kainz, and Tom Conlon for contributing your artistry to the project. Thank you, Eric Mortenson, Patrick Blaine, and Nick Duncan of the Minnesota Historical Society Library, and Susan Hoffman and Julie Tarshish of the Jewish Historical Society of the Upper Midwest, for your help in locating photos for this year's edition.

Thank you to Ann Nelson and Ann McKinnon for organizing our publicity and marketing for 2010, Shelagh Connolly and Deb Fisher for assisting at our *2009 Saint Paul Almanac* party, Beth and Bob Burns for showing us how to apply for a National Endowment for the Arts grant, and Quinn Keller for managing our data entry.

Big thanks to Sue Zumberge, manager of Common Good Books, for her kind support, and to Ann Polacheck of Polly's Coffee Cove, and to Ron Zaine, who delivered books in his trusty truck for just a few cold ones.

The fine minds of the *Saint Paul Almanac's* board of directors keep us dreaming big. Thank you to board members Abdimalik Askar, Ilka Bird, Carol Connolly, Denise Fosse, Sooriya Foster, Dyane Garvey, Metric Giles, Cathie Hartnett, Ann McKinnon, Tim Nolan, Chamath Perera, Sara Remke, and Dan Tilsen.

Thank you to the City of Saint Paul Cultural STAR Program, Minnesota Regional Art Council, Lowertown Future Fund of the Saint Paul Foundation, Friends of the Saint Paul Public Library, KFAI Radio, the Black Dog Cafe, the online Twin Cities Daily Planet, and our individual donors for your kind support and generous contributions.

Last, I especially want to thank my mother, Jeannea Jordan, and my father, Denny Nightingale, for encouraging me to do whatever I set my mind to do.

—*Kimberly Nightingale*

This activity is made possible, in part, by funds provided by the Metropolitan Regional Arts Council from an appropriation by the Minnesota Legislature.

THE SAINT PAUL FOUNDATION

The Lowertown Future Fund of The Saint Paul Foundation

Contents

Listings 291

Introduction

Saint Paul Almanac is at once a historical archive and a resource of stories, recipes, poetry, and photographs. Each page reflects the muse inside each writer, telling a story about a deed well done, an adventurer gone renegade, or an opportunity stumbled upon.

When I first held a Saint Paul Almanac, I thought to myself, "Here's a handy little tome penned by wannabe writers." But oh! was I delighted to find that inside each book was a treasure chest of memories, ideas, laughter, sorrow, history, pictures, and a year-long calendar! (I love calendars. I keep one on Yahoo.)

I love short stories, and I enjoy history. So it was easy to accept the invitation to join seven other Saint Paul residents (and fellow writers) as a community editor. Together, we read hundreds of submissions. We clocked hours that turned into days in an effort to bring you the best Saint Paul Almanac to date. You will read stores about old Saint Paul; you will bear witness to the current cultural changes in our community and our landscape. There will be times when you may actually feel snow fall upon your brow or may want to shout for your home team! By the end of this book, I hope you feel as I do—that the world is a better place because of Saint Paul. Enjoy, Encourage—Engagee!

—Deborah A. Torraine, Saint Paul Almanac community editor

For information on events listed in the calendar section, see pages 292–311

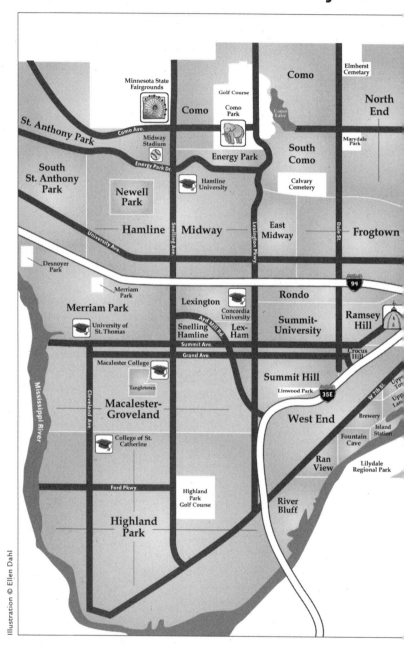

Saint Paul

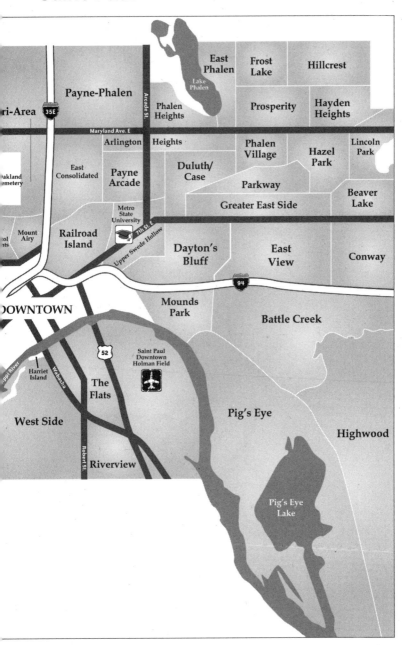

Downtown

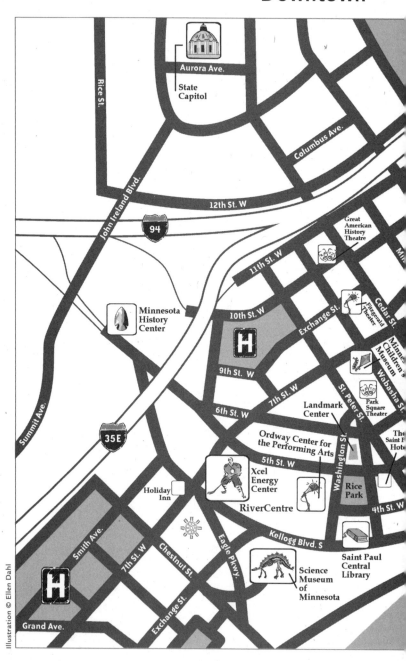

Illustration © Ellen Dahl

Saint Paul

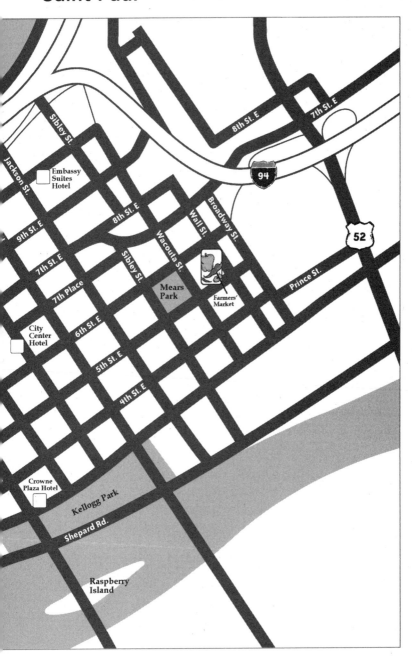

2010

JANUARY
S	M	T	W	T	F	S
27	28	29	30	31	1	2
3	4	5	6	7	8	9
10	11	12	13	14	15	16
17	18	19	20	21	22	23
24	25	26	27	28	29	30
31	1	2	3	4	5	6

FEBRUARY
S	M	T	W	T	F	S
31	1	2	3	4	5	6
7	8	9	10	11	12	13
14	15	16	17	18	19	20
21	22	23	24	25	26	27
28	1	2	3	4	5	6

MARCH
S	M	T	W	T	F	S
28	1	2	3	4	5	6
7	8	9	10	11	12	13
14	15	16	17	18	19	20
21	22	23	24	25	26	27
28	29	30	31	1	2	3

APRIL
S	M	T	W	T	F	S
28	29	30	31	1	2	3
4	5	6	7	8	9	10
11	12	13	14	15	16	17
18	19	20	21	22	23	24
25	26	27	28	29	30	1

MAY
S	M	T	W	T	F	S
26	27	28	29	30	31	1
2	3	4	5	6	7	8
9	10	11	12	13	14	15
16	17	18	19	20	21	22
23	24	25	26	27	28	29
30	31	1	2	3	4	5

JUNE
S	M	T	W	T	F	S
30	31	1	2	3	4	5
6	7	8	9	10	11	12
13	14	15	16	17	18	19
20	21	22	23	24	25	26
27	28	29	30	1	2	3

JULY
S	M	T	W	T	F	S
27	28	29	30	1	2	3
4	5	6	7	8	9	10
11	12	13	14	15	16	17
18	19	20	21	22	23	24
25	26	27	28	29	30	31

AUGUST
S	M	T	W	T	F	S
1	2	3	4	5	6	7
8	9	10	11	12	13	14
15	16	17	18	19	20	21
22	23	24	25	26	27	28
29	30	31	1	2	3	4

SEPTEMBER
S	M	T	W	T	F	S
29	30	31	1	2	3	4
5	6	7	8	9	10	11
12	13	14	15	16	17	18
19	20	21	22	23	24	25
26	27	28	29	30	1	2

OCTOBER
S	M	T	W	T	F	S
26	27	28	29	30	1	2
3	4	5	6	7	8	9
10	11	12	13	14	15	16
17	18	19	20	21	22	23
24	25	26	27	28	29	30
31	1	2	3	4	5	6

NOVEMBER
S	M	T	W	T	F	S
31	1	2	3	4	5	6
7	8	9	10	11	12	13
14	15	16	17	18	19	20
21	22	23	24	25	26	27
28	29	30		2	3	4

DECEMBER
S	M	T	W	T	F	S
28	29	30	1	2	3	4
5	6	7	8	9	10	11
12	13	14	15	16	17	18
19	20	21	22	23	24	25
26	27	28	29	30	31	1

Calendar

Plus Saint Paul
Stories,
Facts,
a Quiz,
and Poems

January

Photo © Patricia Bour-Schila

Ice

The geese were speaking, calling
From the lake, *Don't hold back love.*

Why don't you eat a little something?
One goose's wing was broken.

Hundreds faced the same direction.
The moon was falling on the ice.

The lake closed, then it opened
Like slow breathing.

Su Smallen

3

JANUARY

S	M	T	W	T	F	S
27	28	29	30	31	1	2
3	4	5	6	7	8	9
10	11	12	13	14	15	16
17	18	19	20	21	22	23
24	25	26	27	28	29	30
31	1	2	3	4	5	6

➪ "The writing of books is not easy.
. . . There must be reliance upon the
deeper sources of consciousness,
from which the best writing comes to
assure anything really worthwhile."
—Cornelia Cannon, Saint Paul writer

28 Monday

29 Tuesday

30 Wednesday

31 Thursday
New Year's Eve

Photo © Patricia Bour-Schilla

Landmark Center in Rice Park

1 Friday
New Year's Day

2 Saturday Saint Paul Winter Farmers' Market
Minnesota RollerGirls (Bout)

Alice Hugy, artist who started city's first art gallery, was born today in 1876

3 Sunday Minnesota Boychoir Winter Concert

Saint Paul's first McDonald's restaurant opens on West Seventh Street in 1964.

The Peaceable Kingdom

Norita Dittberner-Jax

"Nobody starts from scratch, especially in architecture."
—Ben Thompson, architect, Ordway Music Theatre

Start with the park
not the trees
but the arrangement of silence
that holds them.

With the library
the simplicity of windows
clear-eyed in daylight,
the balustrades on the walkway
slicing light like a sundial.

With Landmark Center,
the comic aspiration of its horns
the fabulous beast who feeds the souls
of merchants and secretaries
who know they are secretly royal.

Dream it.
Do not let your hands begin to draw
until they understand the task:
to keep the dream intact
that the bricks themselves
must be bent and sheathed in copper
curved like a great arm
sheltering music.

Make the doors large and mahogany
inviting all who enter to be the best
version of themselves,
wearing their colors like flags
brace for wind.

Start with the park
the trees tipping the wintry night
with the sky, which tires
of tenting the whole world
and comes to rest in Rice Park.

Clo-Spin Laundry

Tim Nolan

I remember carrying that giant green
laundry bag on my back—trudging

down St. Clair to the Clo-Spin
Laundry—in a sudden snow storm—

the sidewalks filling up with snow—
the streetlamps glowing—as I spilled

into the warm and friendly confines
of the Clo-Spin Laundry—all by myself—

with everything we owned—in terms
of clothes—agitating there in the hot

water—while the snow fell outside—
with some rushing urgency—

and the big dryer drum—turning—
like a great paddlewheel—mixing up

everything from our tender lives—
my sensible khaki work shirts—your

bras and panties—the red-striped
cotton socks I wore with those heavy

work boots—and the wild zebra sheets
we bought once at Montgomery Wards—

how did I get stuck in the rinse cycle?—
or stuck in the permanent press setting?—

I could have stayed there forever—
spinning—in the never-ending orbit

of the Clo-Spin Laundry—happy to be
in a city—where time—would go on and on—

JANUARY

⇨ "You have to understand that life and baseball is littered with all kinds of obstacles and problems along the way. You have to learn how to overcome them to be successful in life."
—Dave Winfield, Saint Paul
Hall of Fame baseball player

S	M	T	W	T	F	S
27	28	29	30	31	1	2
3	4	5	6	7	8	9
10	11	12	13	14	15	16
17	18	19	20	21	22	23
24	25	26	27	28	29	30
31	1	2	3	4	5	6

4 Monday

Saint Paul Almanac Reading Series

🏵 Diana (Kuske) Murphy, Minnesota's first female federal judge, was born today in 1934

5 Tuesday

January Morning on University Avenue
Outside the Job Center,
six men huddle against the wind,
some cupping cigarettes,
others paper cups of coffee,
all of them stamping their feet
to ward off the cold—
now as always, the ragtag
armies of the poor
marching endlessly in place.
Richard Broderick

6 Wednesday

🏵 Marisha Chamberlain, poet, playwright, and novelist, was born today in 1952

7 Thursday
Orthodox Christmas

Photo © Patricia Bour-Schilla

Clo-Spin Laundry at St. Clair Avenue and Albert Street

| 8 Friday | Land O' Lakes Kennel Club Dog Show |
| | Saint Paul Chamber Orchestra |

9 Saturday	Saint Paul Winter Farmers' Market
	Land O' Lakes Kennel Club Dog Show
	Saint Paul Chamber Orchestra

| 10 Sunday | Land O' Lakes Kennel Club Dog Show |

The Saint Paul Cemetery Association is formed in 1853.

History of My Life

Adán González

My name is Adán González. I am from Guatemala. When I was in my country I had a lot of problems because I had to work really hard and never had enough money to support my family.

One day I decided to make a future for my family. I decided to come to the U.S.A.

When I arrived in the U.S.A. I started to work really hard, seven days per week. I had to pay a lot of money but one day I finished paying everything. I began to buy stuff for my home and to save money.

I feel so good because my family is very good and I would like to give my daughters a better education. For that reason I want to learn English. I want my daughters to learn this language too. Maybe this way my daughters will have more opportunities to build their futures. That is my dream and my goal because they are my life.

Photo © Patricia Bour-Schilla

Adán González

Welcome to Mount Como

Aleli Balagtas

The sign mysteriously appears when the snow starts, at the foot of the golf club driveway, announcing the start of the ski season at Como Park: "Welcome to Mount Como." When my husband tells a friend visiting from Switzerland, a snowboard instructor, that his kids took downhill ski lessons there, the Swiss fellow looks puzzled. "But there are no hills," he says.

Now this is Minnesota, the land of understatement. Please don't flaunt your wealth, your worldliness, your peaks. Our hills are good enough. During the winter, the Como Park golf clubhouse becomes the Como Park Ski Chalet. At Mount Como, there's a snowmaker, a rope tow that shreds your ski mitts, and lots of very enthusiastic ski and snowboard instructors who come to the last, festive, balloon-festooned day of ski school dressed as clowns, wizards, and cows.

It's kind of a loud secret. The secret part is the fact of a long-running ski school in a place with such little change in elevation. Who would have guessed? What makes it loud is the organized mayhem on the first day of ski school: people lined up haphazardly to be fitted with highly experienced boots, bindings and skis; loose clumps of ski-ready kids waiting to hit the slope; parents on cell phones, a hand covering the nonphoned ear; all happening at high decibel.

The winter I took lessons, the school, in its infinite wisdom, segregated the adults from the children. Briefly, we were orphans until Paul, who managed the program, decided on the spot to be the adult instructor. He decided we didn't need to know how to snowplow and before I knew it I was paralleling down the hill sitting on my skis. If you live in Saint Paul and don't want people you know to see you learning to ski, *don't* take lessons here. My daughter's best friend's father shouted encouragement to his kindergartner and to me. Paul, my instructor, happened to be related to my kids' piano teacher.

Last week, the sign was gone. Once the ground stops squelching, the golfers will be out. But I know, come winter, that I'll slow the car down the day I see the sign again, and I'll remember the ski school at Como Park. My kids don't take lessons there anymore, they have bigger hills to ski. It makes me sigh. For every season, there is a mountain.

JANUARY

S	M	T	W	T	F	S
27	28	29	30	31	1	2
3	4	5	6	7	8	9
10	11	12	13	14	15	16
17	18	19	20	21	22	23
24	25	26	27	28	29	30
31	1	2	3	4	5	6

⇨ January 13, 1926: Local No. 3 of the Brotherhood of Sleeping Car Porters of Saint Paul, a predominately African American organization, holds its first meeting.

11 Monday

🌼 Izler Solomon, conductor and musicologist, was born today in 1910

12 Tuesday

Under Crystal Moonlight
under crystal moonlight
cold dreamers waken
in big warm shoes,
walking with
stars that are new,
creating light from past fires
where secrets burn
into explosions of
promise and hope.
Diego Vázquez, Jr.

13 Wednesday

🌼 William Mahoney, labor union activist and Saint Paul mayor, was born today in 1869

14 Thursday

Saint Paul Chamber Orchestra

Cross-country skiing on Pike Island

15 Friday

16 Saturday   Saint Paul Winter Farmers' Market

Saint Paul Chamber Orchestra

17 Sunday

🏵 Jacob Mannheimer, early department store owner, was born today in 1847

Red School House, which blended academics and Native
American culture, is founded in Saint Paul in 1971.

January 13

Photo © Patricia Bour-Schilla

January

The Best Place in the World

Maxine Lightfoot

I have lived in Saint Paul most of my life, and I'd say my favorite place in Saint Paul is the St. Anthony Park Public Library. With its many shelves and millions of stories, each one unique, each one special in its own way, there is no place like it in the world. I love going to the library after school for hours on end, looking at the books.

The St. Anthony Park Library is unique because of its architecture. The original library, now the adult-teen section, was part of a Carnegie Library built in 1917. It has been updated, and a children's section, built in the shape of a large dome, was attached to the old building. When I was little, I thought the library used to be a church because it was so fancy and so old.

On Mondays, instead of walking home from school, I walk to the St. Anthony Park Library. I eagerly climb up the double stairway, looking forward to the books I'll find when I open the door. I go inside, take a sip of water from the water fountain, dump my backpack on a window seat, and start looking for good books. I know where all of my favorite books are. I have many memories of just sitting there, book in hand, nose glued in stories of fantasy, adventure, and science fiction. The library is within walking distance of my house, but I rarely walk home from it because I usually have checked out a bagful of books. I call home to get picked up.

The St. Anthony Park Library is warm and friendly because of its librarians. They aren't just people who work there; they are people who love and care about the books, and this makes all the difference. They help me find books that are playing hide and seek with me, and they recommend books they think I might enjoy.

A luxury of the Saint Paul Public Library is that it has a very effective hold system. I can just go online, sign in using my PIN number and the number on my library card, and I can put any book on hold that is in any of the branches of the library system. When the book and I are ready, I can just go and pick it up. It's very efficient.

A year ago, I went to Namibia, a country in Africa with no public library. What I missed the most there, aside from friends, was having books. There were a few private libraries, but they weren't well stocked. There were a few bookstores, but they didn't have many books at my reading level that I hadn't already read. I missed my library so much. Sometimes I would just daydream of walking into the library and checking out "old friends" and

St. Anthony Park Library on Como Avenue

books I'd never seen before. Late at night, I would quiz myself about where my favorite books were in the St. Anthony Park Library.

When we returned after more than a year of being away from the library, I dramatically forced my mom to drive through the freezing winter winds to my much-missed St. Anthony Public Library. I was so happy! Books again! Mom thinks we checked out about twenty-five books; I think we checked out more.

To me, a good library feels as important as water and an exciting book feels like air. To me, the St. Anthony Park library feels like home.

JANUARY

S	M	T	W	T	F	S
27	28	29	30	31	1	2
3	4	5	6	7	8	9
10	11	12	13	14	15	16
17	18	19	20	21	22	23
24	25	26	27	28	29	30
31	1	2	3	4	5	6

⇨ "I'm not indecisive. Am I indecisive?"
—Jim Scheibel, Saint Paul mayor

18 Monday

Martin Luther King, Jr., Day

19 Tuesday

John Wozniak, alternative rock musician, was born today in 1971

20 Wednesday

21 Thursday   Saint Paul Winter Carnival

Photo © Patricia Bour-Schilla

Steam Engine no. 3985 in Saint Paul on Whistle Stop Tour—home base Wyoming

22 Friday	Saint Paul Winter Carnival

23 Saturday	Saint Paul Winter Farmers' Market
	Saint Paul Chamber Orchestra
	Saint Paul Winter Carnival
	Global Hotdish Variety Show
	Winter Carnival Orchid Show
	Saintly City Cat Show

24 Sunday	Saint Paul Chamber Orchestra
	Saint Paul Winter Carnival
	Winter Carnival Orchid Show
	Saintly City Cat Show

The 110-foot-high airway beacon in Indian Mounds Park, built in 1929, is the last of its kind still standing.

Yarusso Bros. Italian Restaurant sign

The Place

Joyce Garcia

Nineteen then, moved down from the north
living in a duplex on Railroad Island
it's May Savina's home
built by her husband with railroad wood
by that I mean the kitchen cabinets are from a rail car
this is Railroad Island
the neighbors are quick to offer whatever they can, it's its own world
with Morelli's down the block, good prices on Leinies
Yarusso's for lunch, hot dagos the best
Phil Korman's grocery, all the best meats totally fresh
It was a small town there in the middle of a big city
now May has passed
as has Phil
but on Railroad Island they're remembered
a small, safe place with all the best people
now twenty-eight years later
I still go to Morelli's
I still go to Yarusso's
I still think of May
and Phil
this is the place that made me want to stay
here in Saint Paul
and I must say, here has been a very good place to be

Cheesehead

Paul Bartlett

Conceived, born, and raised in Green Bay, Wisconsin—that's me, Paul Vincent Bartlett, a (displaced) cheesehead. And not of your typical Wisconsin lineage. Nope. Not one drop of German or Polish blood circulating in my body. With a Sicilian father (actual surname is Bartalatto, not Bartlett) and a Swedish mother, mine is a conflicted, confused DNA. My wife, Linda, is also a cheesehead, but she found her way to Wisconsin via Illinois. (I've never held that against her.)

I'm often asked, "What's it like, being a native Wisconsinite, living here in Minnesota?" It's a compare-and-contrast sort of question. So I answer with my standard litany: In Wisconsin, we cheer a pro football team that's won three SuperBowls. Our poor Minnesota brethren still lament four crushing SuperBowl defeats.

In Wisconsin, we cheer a university football team that's won three Rose Bowls in the past fifteen years. And poor Minnesotans—their team has not seen the inside of the Rose Bowl in recent memory.

In Wisconsin, we relish our fine artisan cheese. In Minnesota, Cheez Whiz (usually served on a slab of Spam) is a gourmet treat.

In Wisconsin, not only do we expect our churches to be open on Sundays, but we demand that our liquor stores also be open. Here, Minnesotans head to Wisconsin on Sundays to stock up on their libation du jour.

In Wisconsin (Green Bay, actually), our colloquial expressions include "deese" (these), "dem" (them), "dare" (their or there), and "dose" (those). In Minnesota, your major contribution to the English language is "Ya, you betcha."

Wisconsinites share an affinity for beer and brats (and lots of both). Here, a helping of lefse is a gastronomical delight.

But we do share more than a common border, healthy competition, and progressive history. Our men (mostly our men) take to such activities as deer hunting, snowmobiling, ice fishing, and, of course, falling through the ice (pickup truck and ice shanty in tow). In the fall, Wisconsin men don their Sunday-best Elmer Fudd attire and head "up nort" (up north, another Green Bay colloquialism) with the fervor of amorous bucks during rutting season. In Minnesota, Sven and Ole do the same.

But you know what? I'm no longer a Wisconsinite. I'm a Minnesotan. I'm a Saint Paulite. Everything I love about Green Bay I also love about Saint Paul: that small-city feeling, with kind, friendly, gracious people. (But I'm still a Packer fan!)

JANUARY

S	M	T	W	T	F	S
27	28	29	30	31	1	2
3	4	5	6	7	8	9
10	11	12	13	14	15	16
17	18	19	20	21	22	23
24	25	26	27	28	29	30
31	1	2	3	4	5	6

↪ "The law has a benevolent side to it, whether we wish to acknowledge it or not."—Judge Archie Gingold

25 Monday   Saint Paul Winter Carnival

26 Tuesday   Saint Paul Winter Carnival

⚜ S. Edward Hall, African American barber and activist, was born today in 1878

27 Wednesday   Saint Paul Winter Carnival

International Day of Commemoration in memory of the victims of the Holocaust

28 Thursday   Saint Paul Winter Carnival

Photo © Patricia Bour-Schilla

Schmidt's Brewery tower

29 Friday

Saint Paul Winter Carnival

Fourth Friday at the Movies

🏵 Oliver Crosby, businessman and inventor, was born today in 1856

30 Saturday

Saint Paul Winter Farmers' Market

Saint Paul Winter Carnival

Minnesota Opera, *Robert Devereaux*

Winter Flower Show begins

31 Sunday

Saint Paul Winter Carnival

Webster Magnet has the largest elementary school library
in Saint Paul, with over 40,000 books.

Afraid of Nothing

Andrew Hall

The dull crunch of snow underfoot fills the air as I make my way home after watching a play at St. Luke's Community Theater. I have a friend who works the lights. More snow swirls down from the white-saturated sky, further covering the blanketed landscape. Car engines hum as everyone drives slowly, wary of ice hidden under the snow. I bundle up in my coat, and adjust my hat to block as much snow from blowing into my face as possible. I trudge on, making slow progress. With the windchill, it's fourteen degrees below zero, the kind of cold that makes everyone lethargic.

I stop at Lexington Avenue. It's getting dark, but still light enough to easily see. I can either cut through an alley or stay on the lighted sidewalk. I know I should stay on Lexington all the way home, but doing so would add ten more minutes to my walk. Shrugging, I move into an alley.

It's dark in the alley, with only part of the light from the streetlights getting through. About halfway to the next street, I see a man up ahead. He looks menacing, although he hasn't noticed me. He has a hood trimmed with fur over his head, and a bulging coat, coupled with thick, baggy jeans. I walk faster with my head down, hoping to avoid his notice.

"Hey, kid!" So much for avoiding notice, I think to myself as I turn around. "Whatcha got? It's over if I have to search you." I consider my options. He looks faster than me, and all I have in my pockets are keys, and my wallet.

"I don't have anything worth taking." I say, hoping he'll give up.

"I'll be the judge of that. Empty your pockets." The thug gets closer, and my odds of escaping unscathed seem to be getting smaller and smaller. I slip my wallet into the sleeve of my jacket and pull out the keys.

"This is all I have, I promise." His eyes narrow at the bulge in my sleeve, but, thankfully, he seems to take no further notice. In times like these, I wish I could just turn invisible, or fly away, or do anything to escape. Unfortunately, I have but one way out of this, the only thing I can really do: talk.

"I don't suppose you're afraid of keys?" I ask hopefully. He spits.

"I ain't afraid of anything." He proclaims, walking closer. His breath crystallizes in the frozen air, only to dissipate as he breathes in again. The puffs of visible breath are getting uncomfortably close to my own clouds of carbon dioxide.

"So nothing frightens you?" I ask, trying to put a note of admiration in my voice.

"That's right, I'm scared of nothing." He answers, and stops.

"Why is nothing so terrifying to you?" I want to sound curious.

"What?" He asks, bewildered.

"Well," I start, making everything up as I go along. "You said that nothing scares you. Obviously, there is something about nothing that frightens you. I'm curious as to what it is. So, what is it about nothing that you find terrifying?"

"Uh, well, I . . . I don't know." He's rather sheepish for a man who was menacing not more than a minute ago.

"Unfortunately, all I have is nothing, would you like it anyway?" I take the tiniest of steps back, just in case he catches on.

"I . . . I guess not." He admits. The man turns, scratches his head, and walks away to ponder his brand new phobia. For a second, I'm afraid he's recovered his wits as he glances back, but he just continues to mutter to himself and looks away again as he trudges out of sight.

I walk fast out of the alley, and stick to the sidewalk the rest of the way home. As I round the last corner, I see my house. I double my pace, eager to get to its warmth, with the wood stove blazing merrily in the living room.

"How was the play?" Dad asks me, after I announce my return to the house.

"Oh, it was alright. Kind of boring, though." I say, as I start up the stairs to my bedroom.

Illustration © Kirk Anderson

Saint Paul: The Speaking Place

Angela Mack

I am a mother of three who moved to Saint Paul about a year ago from one of the meanest cities in the world, I think: Chicago. When I arrived at Saint Paul's Greyhound bus station, I was terrified. I did not know a soul and had nowhere to go, but I was determined to start a new life for me and my children.

I walked out of the station to flag down a cab, and this woman said hello. I looked at her like she was crazy. She didn't know me, and I kept moving. As my children and I got a little further down the street, people were speaking to us. I couldn't believe it—in Chicago, people didn't speak, and if they did, it was because they wanted something, like spare change or food. I told my kids, "Don't say a word—keep moving."

I was finally able to get a cab. The cabby pulled over, got out, and helped me with my bags and the kids. Cab drivers never did that for you in Chicago unless you were being picked up from a really expensive hotel or theater.

Once we were in the cab, he said "Where to?"

I started crying, telling him I had nowhere to go and very little money. He said, "Well, you have come to the right place. There are shelters that you can go to." He took me to a shelter that did not look like a shelter at all, it looked more like a mansion on a very nice street called Grand. I got out, walked up the stairs, and rang the doorbell. A lady answered the door. "May I help you?" she said.

I started to tell her my story. She told me to come in, fed us, then gave me and my children a room. Everyone at the shelter was friendly. Other women started telling me about different programs that would provide housing for us and what I needed to do. All in all, I was relieved my children and I had finally found a friendly place, a speaking place, someplace where it was okay to say hello to a stranger and not worry about what they were up to.

I love Saint Paul. I wouldn't change a thing about this place. So every morning when I wake up in my new place, I look forward to going outside just to say hello to all the wonderful strangers I meet.

A Trio of Saint Paul Storytellers

Steve Trimble

Groundbreaking urban historian Richard Wade always told his students, me included, that the true feel of cities was more likely to be found in literature than in scholarly works. That holds true for this metropolis and can be demonstrated through the works of three Jewish writers who grew up in Saint Paul. They had somewhat similar early experiences, but told their stories in different manners—humorous, serious, and nostalgic—and eventually traveled different paths. One thing the trio has in common, however, is the fact that they are still well worth reading.

William Hoffman: Neighborhood Nostalgia

When the people around us and the little worlds they live in are so real and so much a part of our everyday lives, all that is needed for those of us who write is to be able and willing to perceive with our heart as well as with the eye and to listen.

—William Hoffman

William Hoffman (1914–1990) was born in an attic apartment over a blacksmith shop, the middle of seven children of Russian Jewish immigrants. He was writing in seventh grade and edited his school's paper. After graduating from Humboldt High School, he went to the University of Minnesota and ended up with a journalism degree in 1935. He served in the Army from 1942 to 1946. Throughout life, he was engaged in social welfare and community work, crediting Miss Currie of Neighborhood House for fueling his compassionate nature.

Photo © Jewish historical Society of the Upper Midwest

West Side writer Wiliam Hoffman

The West Side neighborhood that Hoffman remembered was a self-contained community. As he put it, "Were it not for the lure of the Wilder Public Baths and a department store offering Green Stamps, no one would need to leave this area except to be buried."

Those Were the Days (1957), *Tales of Hoffman* (1961), *Mendel* (1969) and *West Side Story II* (1981) are collections of semiautobiographical vignettes about Jewish life in Saint Paul, mostly on the West Side. They often deal with intergenerational tensions and changing lifestyles. Typically, the Yiddish-speaking mothers live for their children and are hurt when those children stray from traditional ways. The older men are often portrayed through their involvement with religious rituals and the work needed to provide for their families.

In the West Side it was bad, too, but when had it been good? Here, though, the people did not look into garbage cans or buy canned mackerel, for buffalo and carp could still be had for the catching. But more important, the inhabitants thereof had known adversity before, as they had known terrible pogroms and suffering in the little villages thousands of miles away. So they girded their loins for the great depression which cast its shadow over the fair land of promise. . . . These were the proud and stubborn people of the West Side who labored valiantly to hide their despair and fear of unemployment and a lean table from their neighbors and from their children.

—William Hoffman, *Tales of Hoffman*

Max Shulman: Comedic Compositions

Facts are essential to comedy. . . . Recognizable facts and verifiable details give the appearance of reality you need to make comedy stand up . . . you've got all the rules of fiction to follow in humor writing—plus you've got to make somebody laugh too.
—Max Shulman

Some men love women, some love other men, some love dogs and horses, and occasionally you find one who loves his raincoat. Me, I love a hotel.
—Max Shulman

Humorist Max Shulman (1919–1988) was the son of an immigrant Russian house painter. One reviewer has suggested that he used humor as a way of making a life of poverty more bearable. He started writing as a child and graduated in 1936 from Central High School while living at 701 Selby. He majored in journalism at the University of Minnesota, received his degree in 1941, and served in the army during World War II.

One of Shulman's Minnesota Daily columns caught the attention of a Doubleday editor, who asked him to submit a novel. It became *Barefoot Boy With Cheek* (1943), a satirical look at life at the U of M. Its opening lines are characteristic of his style: "St. Paul and Minneapolis extend from the Mississippi River like the legs on a pair of trousers. Where they join is the University of Minnesota." It was later adapted for a Broadway play that ran for two years.

Some of his next novels—all of them humorous—were at least partially set in Minnesota, but the plots of later ones mostly occurred outside the state. Shulman consistently published short stories in magazines such as *Collier's, Esquire,* and *Playboy.* He is probably best known for a television series based on his 1953 novel, *The Many Loves of Doby Gillis.* His last book, *Potatoes are Cheaper* (1971), was a humorous yet sentimental look at his childhood and young adulthood in the Selby-Dale area.

On March the 14th, 1936, Pa went down to the St. Paul public library just like he did every day as usual. Not that he was such a great reader; in fact he could hardly read at all, not in English anyhow, except maybe for eviction and foreclosure notices. He could read Yiddish all right, but that didn't help since there were no Yiddish books in the St. Paul library. But Pa went every day anyhow. What else could he do? He didn't have a job to go to, and if he stayed at home Ma would give him the whammy all day long. So where else could he find that was (a) warm; and (b) free?"

—Max Shulman, *Potatoes Are Cheaper*

Norman Katkov: Noted Novels

Every Friday afternoon, after school, I walked to the branch library in St. Paul. I got four books—that was the limit. . . . On the way home there was a Goodwill store right near my house, and they had used pulp magazines. . . . I always had a nickel, so I'd buy two or three of those. . . . So, I was always reading, and I suppose the writing came from that.

—Norman Katkov

Norman Katkov was born near Kiev in the Ukraine in 1918 and came to Saint Paul with his parents around 1921. He graduated from the University of Minnesota in 1940 with a journalism degree. During World War wll, he was in the Army and put out a post newspaper, sometimes sending stories to the Pioneer Press. This connection later got him a job at the paper.

His first novel, *Eagle at My Eyes* (1948), set in Saint Paul and White Bear Lake, centered on the problems of intermarriage and anti-Semitism. His second, *A Little Sleep, A Little Slumber* (1949) is the story of a Jewish family on the West Side flats and includes the subtheme of illegal immigration. Scenes are also set in downtown and several neighborhoods. Katkov shifted focus in *Eric Mattson* (1964), a novel set in a hospital probably patterned after the one run by the University of Minnesota.

What chance did we have, even from the start? How fall in love with a woman who was actually verboten? She was a goy, and I knew all Gentiles were against us from the time I was ten. We lived on Colorado and Greenwood then, in a neighborhood of section hands, South St. Paul stockyards workers and still poorer Jews. Even at that age Ma had gotten her points across: I always had to be in shouting distance, and there were certain things I couldn't do. . . . Most of the kids slid on the hill which started on the dead end and ran down to near the railroad tracks. Not me. I had to slide behind the house and so did most of the Jew-boys in the neighborhood.

—Norman Katkov, *Eagle at My Eyes*

Katkov's later novels, which often had medical themes, were not set in Minnesota. He was a prolific magazine writer whose stories frequently appeared in *Saturday Evening Post*. After he moved to California, he started to write scripts for television shows and became well known for his work on the medical drama *Ben Casey*.

Katkov is in his early nineties, no longer actively writing, and lives in Los Angeles. You could send him a birthday card on July 26. His work and those of Hoffman and Shulman all appear to be out of print, but they are available in local libraries and used-book stores and are regularly listed on eBay.

February

Photo © Minnesota Historical Society

Dear Valentine

I want to tell you that I fell in love with your voice first, each word
I strung on a thread of silver,
(wear now criss-crossing my body, my own private rosary).

That because of you I listen
to the sound of want and loneliness the wind has gathered,

see how the sun lays on your jaw and cheekbone, how the air
curls itself around you, tucks itself in. Words flock, form letters
in the sky and I want to thank you, but I can hardly speak at all.

Julia Klatt Singer

☐ "My own personal and professional experiences have given me insight into the fleeting nature of life, and I strive to live each day with purpose."
—Anna Masellis, Saint Paul cancer researcher

FEBRUARY

S	M	T	W	T	F	S
31	1	2	3	4	5	6
7	8	9	10	11	12	13
14	15	16	17	18	19	20
21	22	23	24	25	26	27
28	1	2	3	4	5	6

1 Monday   *Saint Paul Almanac* Reading Series

2 Tuesday   Precinct caucuses
Groundhog Day   Minnesota Opera, *Robert Devereaux*

🐾 Thomas Disch, science fiction writer, was born today in 1940

3 Wednesday

4 Thursday

Minnesota Opera, *Robert Devereaux*

🐾 Elsie Shawe, Saint Paul music director, 1898–1933, was born today in 1866

First place winner "Hormel McSwine and Friends," carved by Scott, John, and Dick Mogren at the 2009 Winter Carnival snow sculpture competition

5 Friday	Saint Paul Chamber Orchestra
6 Saturday	Saint Paul Winter Farmers' Market
	Minnesota Opera, *Robert Devereaux*
	Minnesota RollerGirls (Bout)
7 Sunday	Saint Paul Chamber Orchestra
	Minnesota Opera, *Robert Devereaux*
	Urban Expedition: Korea

🎖 Heide Stefanyshyn-Piper, astronaut, was born today in 1963

The students in the Saint Paul school district come from homes in which 70 different languages are spoken.

25 Random Things About Me And Saint Paul

Michael Maupin

*R*ULES: *Once you've been tagged, you are supposed to write a note with 25 random things, facts, habits, or goals about you. At the end, choose 25 people to be tagged. You have to tag the person who tagged you. If I tagged you, it's because I want to know more about you. (I was tagged by Kimberly Nightingale, publisher of the* Saint Paul Almanac.)

1. The first thing I ever laid eyes on in Saint Paul was the used-car lot with the ski-chalet-looking office on University Avenue, in the early 1970s. While it's no longer there, I think it was on the avenue's north side, opposite the SuperTarget.

2. My second earliest memory of Saint Paul is waiting for the 16 bus to Minneapolis when it transferred from the White Bear Lake bus, coming back from college during the dismal winter of 1980. While standing at the corner of Sixth and St. Peter, I thought: "Saint Paul. What a dump."

3. By 1990, nearly all my friends were living in Saint Paul. So, I moved there on December 7, 1992. By 1999, all my friends had left.

4. I rented a room in a crappy old mansion on Summit Avenue owned by crazy people.

5. Saint Paul is "Grandpa in his garage." Grandpa doesn't want you touching his tools or cleaning up his garage—Grandpa doesn't want you messing around with his garage. Grandpa would prefer that you just go the hell back to Minneapolis, you with your hoity-toity ways, brown leather jackets, and moonshine over F. Scott Fitzgerald's birthplace.

6. I was an extra in *A Prairie Home Companion;* greeted John C. Reilly at the door, and was serenaded by Meryl Streep, whose affections I stole from some lurching tall guy in red tennis shoes.

7. I made the acquaintance of a tall, beautiful cottonwood tree in the back alley of the block bordering Milton and Chatsworth, Lincoln and Goodrich. Man, can that old girl sing!

8. Back when The Muddy Pig was Cognac McCarthy's, I attended a memorial service for the late poet John Engman. Between our tears and laughter, it was an unforgettable night.

9. I temped at Unity Unitarian Church under the late Rev. Roy Phillips, who constantly struggled with column deadlines for the church bulletin.

10. The best burger in Saint Paul (maybe the entire five-state area) is at Casper & Runyon's Nook on Hamline. Good luck getting a table or spot at the bar. And call your cardiologist first.

11. I once was offered a joint in Irvine Park.

12. Lenny Russo has transformed Highland Park with his wonderful Heartland restaurant. I still miss Merriam Park's Table of Contents.

13. Yes, I've been up the Highland Park Water Tower. You can see Minneapolis from there.

14. Every time I walk by St. Paul Academy and Summit School's spacious playground on Goodrich, I think of The Zombies' song "Beechwood Park."

15. Summit Avenue haunts me. A confluence of past, present, and future, it wends like an arrow toward the Mississippi, attended by tree giants who whisper of age and death and parting sad lovers who take final lunches under their shade.

16. I was a dramaturgy intern at the Great American History Theatre (now History Theatre) under Lynn Lohr and Lance S. Belville in 1991.

17. After six months of living in a one-bedroom behind the Chatterbox (now Costello's), hearing gang-related gunfire, and receiving infrequent freelance assignments, I moved from Cathedral Hill to Merriam Park, closer to Minneapolis.

18. I once ran into Paul Wellstone at the Hungry Mind. "What's the news from Washington, Senator?" "Good! Good!" he barked with a grin.

19. My friends Sheldon and Perin live on the East Side. We like to grill their garden veggies, drink Spanish wine, and play bocce in the back yard.

20. On the block where I now live, two blocks south of Grand Avenue, WCCO reporter Pat Kessler often stops to chat while he's walking his dogs, Shelby and Rupert.

21. I almost bought a co-worker's condo and moved to downtown Minneapolis.

22. If it came down to either Izzy's or Grand Ole Creamery, I'm sorry. The prize goes to Izzy's.

23. I have washed my clothes at the Laundromat on East Selby Avenue.

24. In 2008 I met an amazing woman, just across the courtyard from my place. She loves Saint Paul and seems to like me.

25. Think I'll stick around awhile longer.

FEBRUARY

S	M	T	W	T	F	S
31	1	2	3	4	5	6
7	8	9	10	11	12	13
14	15	16	17	18	19	20
21	22	23	24	25	26	27
28	1	2	3	4	5	6

⇨ Saint Paul celebrated Charles Darwin Day on February 12, 2009, the scientist's 200th birthday.

February

8 Monday

🐞 Katie McWatt, community activist who ran for City Council, was born today in 1931

9 Tuesday

🐞 Rick Cardenas, disability-rights activist, was born today in 1942

10 Wednesday

11 Thursday

Saint Paul Bouncing Team member Delores Weldon at the 2009 Winter Carnival

12 Friday   Saint Paul Chamber Orchestra

13 Saturday   Saint Paul Winter Farmers' Market
                                              Saint Paul Chamber Orchestra
                                                              Scottish Ramble

14 Sunday   Scottish Ramble
Chinese New Year (Tiger)
Valentine's Day

February 13, 1906: The botched hanging of William Williams
in Saint Paul is the last public execution in Minnesota.

Midnight Ruminator

for Katherine Whitcomb and the old Hungry Mind

Lonnie Howard

I found your poem "The Migration of Souls" taped
to the side of a bookshelf in the Ruminator
on Grand Avenue in St. Paul. One of the last independent
bookstores, it used to be the Hungry Mind.
Your poem mentioned Mr. Unowsky
        —how you saw him walk across the street
            to make his bank deposit and how you drove
            two blocks before remembering
            he was dead.
I stood there a long time, and wondered
if you meant this very
Mr. Unowsky, the bookstore owner,
standing behind the cash register?

I sat on the threadbare sofa for hours that day,
reading poems as I had for years. And that night
I came back with old friends to hear Robert Bly read.
The Iraq War—the second one—was well underway,
and he tossed free copies of his anti-war poems
into the audience, the thin books with red and black covers
spinning across the room. I didn't catch one, so I bought a copy,

and even though I couldn't afford it, I bought a broadside
by Li-Young Lee, with turquoise ink pressed
into a thick cream paper—the bookstore was trying to raise money.

It closed the next week after 34 years.
I ordered your book on the Internet
when I got home to Santa Fe.

        Mr. Unowsky didn't have a copy
        or I would have bought it from him.

I read all your poems—the one about John Berryman's
grave startled me most. I remember when he leapt
from the West Bank Bridge at the U. It was during the
Vietnam War. It was winter. It was night
when I heard. I hadn't known he was buried near my mother
and sister—in Resurrection Cemetery on the banks
of the Mississippi.

> I know what you mean, Katherine,
> I have to kick the leaves away to see their names too.

(This poem appeared in the Santa Fe Literary Review, *2009)*

FEBRUARY

S	M	T	W	T	F	S
31	1	2	3	4	5	6
7	8	9	10	11	12	13
14	15	16	17	18	19	20
21	22	23	24	25	26	27
28	1	2	3	4	5	6

⇨ "We all believe in Minnesota nice. An anarchist here still says, 'Have a nice day.'" —Tom Mischke, former KSTP-AM radio host

February

15 Monday
Presidents' Day

⚜ James F. O'Gara, founder of O'Gara's Bar and Grill, was born today in 1908

16 Tuesday
Mardi Gras

17 Wednesday
Ash Wednesday

February sucks
heat from my bones
shrouds the world in white.
Cupid chose the coldest month
to sling arrows toward my heart,
sly devil; breeding warmth
like compost, like spring
beneath a blanket of ice.
Diane Wilson

18 Thursday

⚜ Marty O'Neill, long-time sports announcer, was born today in 1908

Men and boys pushing a car at Dayton and Summit in winter of 1940

19 Friday	Saint Paul Chamber Orchestra

20 Saturday	Saint Paul Winter Farmers' Market

21 Sunday	Saint Paul Chamber Orchestra

February 19, 1914: The Saint Paul Federation of Men Teachers is chartered.

Lady Elegant's Tea Room

Amanda Baden

My favorite place in Saint Paul is Lady Elegant's tea room. Lady Elegant's tea room is special to me because that's where I had my first cup of tea.

It's fun to go there because in the back of the room is a wall lined with hooks. On each hook is a different hat. One hat in particular is special to me. That hat is red velvet with a fingertip veil in the front and three red bows on top of each other on the side. I wear it every time I have tea there with my mom, and it's my favorite.

Not only have I had good tea there, I've also had really good scones. I've had an apricot scone, a blueberry one, and a chocolate chip one. I have a memory associated with the blueberry scone: I had it with the first cup of tea I ever drank. It was Jane Austen tea, and I shared the pot with my mom. We both thought it was delicious.

When I go there with my mom, we always sit by the window so we can see the courtyard below us. The first thing my mom and I do when we go there is pick out a hat. I always pick out my favorite red one. Next, we sit down to a white tablecloth with a circle of candles at the side. The candles are for the teapot to rest on so it stays warm. On top of the tablecloth are white, frilly placemats. On each placemat is a goblet filled with water. Between the two placemats are a bowl filled with sugar cubes and a doily on top and a cup full of cream.

I like Lady Elegant's tea room because it's a nice, relaxing place where my mom and I can have fun. That's why Lady Elegant's tea room is my favorite place in Saint Paul.

Lady Elegant's Tea Room in St. Anthony Park

Photo © Patricia Bour-Schilla

Milagros *board at Our Lady of Guadalupe Church*

The *Milagros* of Our Lady of Guadalupe

D. D. Costandine

Our Lady of Guadalupe, a fixture on the West Side of Saint Paul since 1931, is steeped in Hispanic tradition. Its heavenly scent of incense and the warm light of its votive candles beckon me in. Kneeling worshippers light flickering candles that cast an ethereal golden glow about the church. Shadows dance to the backdrop of quiet reflection.

If not attentive, a worshipper may walk past the ex-voto board that holds tiny tin limbs dangling all akimbo. Ex-votos began as offerings many centuries ago in Italy. All traditions evolve, including that of the ex-voto. Tin was an abundant resource in Mexico, and folk artists there began to sculpt figures to represent hoped-for *milagros* (miracles). *Milagros* are offerings to help mend broken hearts or appendages, restore vigor, or rekindle lost love. Torn, pleading notes with stories of hope or despair are pinned to the board, along with wishes for mercy and miracles. Yellowed photographs of loved ones, tiny plastic doodads, and notes hoping for lottery wins: every kind of wish and desire is exposed in these very private yet very public offerings.

A photo of an infant is pinned to the board—the baby gravely ill. Later, the mother cuts her long dark hair and pins it, braided, to the board as testament to a miracle fulfilled. The infant lives! *Milagros* are indeed possible to the pious who believe in the power and mercy of Our Lady of Guadalupe Church on the West Side of Saint Paul.

FEBRUARY

S	M	T	W	T	F	S
31	1	2	3	4	5	6
7	8	9	10	11	12	13
14	15	16	17	18	19	20
21	22	23	24	25	26	27
28	1	2	3	4	5	6

⟳ February 24, 1985: An estimated 25,000 spectators gather up and down the Mississippi on a Sunday to watch the demolition of the old High Bridge.

22 Monday

23 Tuesday

🕸 John Camp (aka John Sanford), journalist and novelist, was born today in 1944

24 Wednesday

Minnesota State High School League
Girl's Hockey Tournament

🕸 Mitch Hedberg, comedian, was born today in 1968

25 Thursday

Minnesota State High School League
Girl's Hockey Tournament

Saint Paul Fire Department truck

26 Friday

Mawlid al-Nabi

Minnesota State High School League
Girl's Hockey Tournament
Fourth Friday at the Movies
World of Wheels

27 Saturday

Saint Paul Winter Farmers' Market
World of Wheels
Saint Paul Chamber Orchestra
Global Hot Dish Variety Show

28 Sunday

Purim

World of Wheels
Urban Expedition: Colombia

February 26, 1926: The Zonta Club of Saint Paul, a woman's service organization, is chartered.

Night Light Hockey at Groveland

Barbara Cox

During the cold winter months of Saint Paul, there is a mecca that kids of all ages flock to with religious fervor. Mecca is Groveland, the king of neighborhood ice rinks. Drive down St. Clair Avenue anytime day or night, and witness the packed rinks of pickup hockey, toddlers pushing plastic chairs in a circle, and packs of tween girls in huddles, observing packs of tween boys.

Each year the all-volunteer crew of the Groveland Booster Club erects three rinks on the elementary school playground, surrounded by a track of ice perfect for pulling a tiny skater on a sled. We went there one evening—two adults, our two young sons, and our two-year-old daughter. The boys, proud of their mini-mite moves, hoped to play with the "big guys" in one of the pickup games. They were in luck. Two junior high–aged girls approached the boys and asked if they'd like to make teams with the others gathered on the rink. They were elated, of course, and in the ancient tradition of hockey players everywhere, they placed their sticks on the ice. The girls divided the players into teams by selecting sticks by length, one by one. Our boys, ages five and six, became teammates of their father, one of the young women, and an adult couple. Both teams passed to the boys, and cheered them when they scored. The boys were in heaven. Or Mecca. Sometimes a sparkling night on the ice can be both.

Hockey at Groveland rink

Illustration © Andy Singer

Ten Years of Collecting, Preserving, and Serving

Marlin L. Heise

Hmong Archives was chartered on February 10, 1999, as a nonprofit with the mission to research, collect, preserve, interpret, and disseminate materials in all formats about or by Hmong. A dozen young Hmong professionals had this grand dream, but I credit Yuepheng Xiong of Hmong ABC with changing discussion into action by securing a charter and keys to a Metropolitan State University room. My role, and great joy as archivist, has been as chief volunteer recorder.

Hmong refugees from the Secret War in Laos first came to Saint Paul in 1975–1976 to an environment very unlike their tropical mountain villages. After fifteen years of war and relocation, they had lost or worn out most of their possessions. Very few were able to attend schools in the turmoil and poverty of Laos. Only in the 1960s did Hmong become a written language in Laos, using both Latin and Pahawm writing systems. Almost all Hmong knowledge was oral, passed down through the generations.

By 1999 the Hmong Saint Paul community had undergone dramatic changes. Hmong had become market gardeners, teachers, grocers, doctors, real estate agents, lawyers, and with Choua Lee's 1991 election, local government officials—while at the same time maintaining (or adapting) old traditions. Such changes lead to the loss of old knowledge and cultural materials, as well as developing new ones. Thus, Hmong Archives found its mission almost twenty-five years after the first refugee arrivals. Our inspiration came from the Minnesota Historical Society, and from the Norwegian-American Historical Association in Northfield, founded in 1925, a century after modern Norwegian immigration began.

Our volunteers have invested 13,000 hours in caring for the 115,000 items entrusted to Hmong Archives, now in six rooms above Hmong ABC. Our 750 donors and 2500 researchers and visitors are mostly from the U.S., but also from Australia, China, England, France, Germany, Japan, Laos, the Netherlands, Norway, Thailand, and Vietnam. Our collections of audio recordings, books, cards, files, maps, newspapers, objects, periodicals, photos, posters, videos, and works of art come from all parts of the Hmong world. What a great educational resource for students, teachers, researchers—locally and internationally! We are proud of connections with Hmong Cultural Center, Center for Hmong Arts and Talent (CHAT), *Hmong Today, Hmong Times,* Jackson Elementary, Phalen Lake Elementary,

Visit Hmong Archives at 298 1/2 University Avenue West

and individuals like Seexeng Lee, Kao Kalia Yang, Noah Vang, and many others who make Saint Paul the Hmong cultural capital of the U.S.

Daily archive work can be slow and tedious, processing a thousand donated items each month. There are, however, also exhilarating moments, such as when Grandma Yer discovered that a skirt she had discarded in Wat Tham Krabok is now a museum piece. Or when a Lao American researcher laid hands on Chairman Mao's Little Red Book in Lao. Or the proud high school student who donated her History Day DVD. Or Hmong veterans discovering their younger selves in Vang Xiong's Ban Vinai photos.

Hmong Archives is open to the public at 298½ University Avenue West, from 10 a.m. to 6 p.m. on Mondays, Wednesdays, and Fridays, and by appointment by calling 651.224.8754. Groups are very welcome, but please call first. Our website is www.hmongarchives.org, and we are on Facebook.

I wish to thank Chong Toua, Chia, Tong, Dang and Shoua, co-workers at Minnesota Historical Society in 1980–1981, for introducing me to the rich culture Hmong have brought with them and continue to develop in Saint Paul, a culture Hmong Archives has collected, preserved, and served for a decade.

Take the *Saint Paul Almanac* Coffee Shop Quiz

James McKenzie

"There's never two of anything," Truman Capote writes in his famous *A Christmas Memory*. Science has long proven Capote right about the uniqueness of every object: a doubting reader need look no further than the swirling tips of her own whorled fingers or the irises he sees looking back at him from a mirror. There's never two of anything.

The *Almanac* hereby invites readers to recognize and savor the unique features of Saint Paul's many coffee shops. A national survey of the country's burgeoning coffee house scene places the Twin Cities sixth in number of coffee houses, just behind Portland and ahead of Washington, D.C. No doubt the large chains swell these numbers considerably. But even in Saint Paul, despite corporate cultures, it is impossible to screen out the distinguishing influences of a particular neighborhood: a skyway-connected Starbucks, a Caribou near the nation's largest women's college, a downtown Dunn Brothers sharing space with an eyewear shop.

Still, the *Almanac* Coffee House Quiz concerns itself with independently owned shops. Test your Saint Paul coffee scene IQ with the following quiz. See if you can match the clue with the particular shop. Answers on page 358.

1. This shop helps sponsor owner's radio program, *Radio Café;* inside archway opens onto indoor court whose big stone fountain can be heard splashing from within the shop. Private room is available for a small fee.

Polly's Coffee Cove at 1382 Payne Avenue, a popular gathering place in Saint Paul

2. Large black-and-white photos of historic Saint Paul: huge, 1886 winter carnival ice palace; burial of Archbishop Ireland; many more. Brass mission statement on ceramic wall.

3. Ten pay computers; Pac Man, Atari, pinball machine, other games; garage in back alleged to have been Al Capone's hideout.

4. Nestled between homemade ice cream shop (east) and region's largest hobby train store (west); roomy, large-tabled, spacious backroom; couches too.

5. Named after colorful, historic Saint Paul figure; one-table second-story loft; Garrison Keillor describes some patrons as "intense young people with no clear prospects in life . . . genteel Bohemians dreaming of the Dead."

6. Integrated with connecting art gallery/frame shop whose varied work spills into its space; working piano; large painting of building with March Hare at that piano; live lute playing one Friday a month.

7. Caboose play area; toddler-height tables, too; orange boxcar for inside wall; working toy train visible in one window; huge outdoor jazz mural; parking lot marked for baby strollers.

8. Camels and palm trees; kilims and Persian rugs on the wall; brochures offering Persian language lessons; several dictionaries, thesaurus, atlas, mechanical pencil sharpener; hidden outdoor patio lined with plants on shelves.

9. Stained glass art and pottery in window; longest single coffee pew; witty signs with attitude (guns and cell phones); frequently changing art exhibits; beer and wine license; two muted TVs.

10. Jazz figures on the wall (Miles Davis, Billie Holiday); supports Selby Avenue Jazz Festival; working community meeting room; framed Obamas on the wall.

11. Occupies former longtime Swedish grocery store: whistling cockatiel named Spike; large Elvis cutout wearing a cross necklace; working TV in a sailboat.

12. American country furniture; wood-paneled wall space doubling as music stage or great meeting place (feels like a den); convenient drive-up parking lot; stepstool for kids to peek at ice cream flavors.

13. Five-sided room, no two sides the same length; proximity to history; best skyline view; Belgian waffles; Big Oops!: photos of building's fateful meeting (July 12, 1966) with a liquid sugar tanker.

14. Each cup weighed, ground, brewed before your eyes; detailed "Cupping Notes" on each blend posted, changing regularly; definitions of ristretto, machiatto, cappuccino, latte, and mocha on the wall.

15. Second-story operation; Saint Paul's tallest building visible through red neon coffee cup in window; Jamaican Blue Mountain available; genre books for sale by Maude & Blanche; check out bridge no. 31.

16. Surreal mural behind coffee bar: levitating meditator, old windmill, new wind farm; rocking chair in couch alcove; large dollhouse, ready for play.

17. One of three independent coffee shops in skyway; bar looking out on bridge no. 21; "friendship" in Korean over the door; teas without added tastes; four photo boards of loyal customers with the owner.

18. Recent name change; live old-time music jam Saturday mornings; a singing barista with an antique bike overhead. Saint Paul's westernmost independent shop.

19. Everything organic; large Van Gogh–inspired mural at entry; golden coffee cup painted on floor, spilling its brew deeper into shop; solar panels on roof; Saint Paul's highest coffee location.

20. Remodeled gas station; color photos of patrons' babies and pets; cut flower in vase on each table; money from refills goes to charity; free DVD, *In Search of the Divine*, available in extensive book shelf/bulletin board collection.

21. More than a century of Old World baking in this building; two eighty-year-old, working dough-mixing machines; three-tiered cakes; three walls of blackboard with colored chalk; Longfellow quotation painted on floor.

22. Coffee shop nearest to a movie theater; Sebastian Joe's ice cream; starred U.S. map showing the thirty-three states its coffee has been shipped to; colorful wildlife photos on wall; "A legend since 5 a.m."

23. "Coffee. Conversation. Community. Cause." Only nonprofit coffee shop, benefiting a job-training program for formerly homeless foster children; coffee cups in a fireplace; serves Starbucks.

24. Obama Blend (Kenyan and Kona, of course); carved bears in covered patio, one in a cup; Crow Creek Long Rider tee-shirts for sale; "the good stuff."

25. Seed store for ninth largest U.S. coffee shop chain, but remains independent; founded in 1987; watch, smell, hear the beans roasting; live music every night.

26. "Best of Twin Cities" plaque for brownies; cafeteria line (slide your tray); southwest-style fireplace; curved, tesseral coffee bar, inlaid with birds and vines; stone tile floor and walls.

27. City of Saint Paul planted this shop's namesake tree at its street corner location; branches in hospitals and Saints stadium; concert-format music series mentioned on MPR; goofy gifts: black nihilist mints, backward clocks, plastic flies and ants.

28. Farmer's Market outside the window; site of *Saint Paul Almanac* launch; robust music and art schedule, films on occasion; huge, exposed, pine beams reveal its past as Great Northern Railways storehouse; dog in lotus position.

29. Four free CD mix-and-burn units with thousands of tunes to choose from; thirty mounted vinyl album covers, including Duane Eddy, Nancy Sinatra, Scatman; watch yourself on security TV; one-page, irregular "Chronicle" bears this shop's new name.

30. Only shop with bilingual neon name in window; customers have donated many dozens of shop's namesake item in the four years since it opened; every seat looks out on busy, five-street intersection through curved sweep of windows.

31. Six floor-mounted, revolving, padded, red-seated ice cream chairs; fresh ground coffee each day, at five cents a cup, same price since 1923. More of a fountain than a coffee shop.

Ginkgo Coffee Shop on the corner of Snelling and Minnehaha avenues

March

Photo © Patricia Bour-Schilla

Bears shake off winter dust
Perennials stir
Earth
Softens
Shifts
May tulips
Begin their journey
upward.

Marcie Rendon

S	M	T	W	T	F	S
28	1	2	3	4	5	6
7	8	9	10	11	12	13
14	15	16	17	18	19	20
21	22	23	24	25	26	27
28	29	30	31	1	2	3

⇨ March 1, 1883: Gustav Svard, a poverty-stricken Swede, is the first person admitted to the new Bethesda Hospital at 1388 North Victoria.

March

1 Monday   *Saint Paul Almanac* Reading Series

2 Tuesday

✦ Clem Haupers, Minnesota artist, was born today in 1900

3 Wednesday   Minnesota State High School League
                                        Boys' Wrestling Tournament

4 Thursday   Minnesota State High School League
                                        Boys' Wrestling Tournament

Pigeon on the bank of the Mississippi River

5 Friday   Minnesota State High School League
Boys' Wrestling Tournament

Saint Paul Chamber Orchestra

🎖 Archibald Bush, 3M executive and philanthropist, was born today in 1887

6 Saturday   Saint Paul Winter Farmers' Market

Minnesota State High School League
Boys' Wrestling Tournament

Minnesota RollerGirls (Bout)

Minnesota Opera, *La bohème*

7 Sunday   Minnesota Opera, *La bohème*

Urban Expedition: Israel

March 1, 1881: Minnesota's first capitol building in Saint Paul
is destroyed by a fire.

Minnesota's *Crusaders For Justice*

Ann Cader

Arthur McWatt, a widely respected history teacher who retired after more than thirty years in the Saint Paul public school system, has written a moving and informative narrative that spans over a century of local and national history. *Crusaders for Justice: A Chronicle of Protest by Agitators, Advocates and Activists in their Struggle for Civil and Human Rights in St. Paul, Minnesota, 1802 through 1985* begins by telling us about the first noted African American in Minnesota, George Bonga in the late 1700s, then touches on

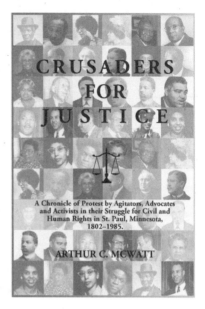

the great lawyers Frederick McGhee and W. T. Francis, who helped sow the seeds of the NAACP with W.E.B. Dubois, and profiles local newspaper publishing giants and civil rights activists, editors J.Q. Adams of *The Appeal* and Cecil Newman of the *Minneapolis Spokesman* and *St. Paul Recorder.* McWatt highlights the political elections and appointments of several key African American Saint Paulites, and leaves us with the current work of Nathaniel A. Khaliq of the Saint Paul NAACP, and community scholar-activist Mahmoud El-Kati. In the process, McWatt tells the story of Minnesota's struggle to expand civil and human rights, and shows how prominent Minnesotans, such as Whitney Young, Roy Wilkins, Carl Stokes, Hubert Humphrey, and Walter Mondale, influenced the national civil rights movement. A much-needed contribution to our understanding of the state's history, this book celebrates the sacred protest tradition of the African American community.

ISBN: 978-0-9675581-8-9: Hardcover, 236 Pages, $18.99
Published by Papyrus Publishing, Inc., in partnership with the St. Paul Chapter of the NAACP.

Available in Saint Paul at: Golden Thyme Coffee & Cafe and Common Good Books

From Nebraska, with Love

Hannah Kroonblawd

I thought about you today
as I stared out across the flat land
still brown from winter.
I thought of your lakes
because there are so few here,
and of your trees
because the plains lack them too

You know, when I first moved away
I didn't think of you so much.
I was enthralled by the expanse of blue
that could be seen when I gazed at the sky,
and the way the corn waved in the breeze
like a thousand ballerinas twirling their arms.

But now, months later and miles away,
I like to close my eyes and imagine the way
the snowplows came through the streets late at night,
the way the fishermen down at the lake would
meticulously cut their ice fishing holes,
the way the ice palace at the Winter Carnival
would light up in the glow of passing headlights,
and how Snoopy danced on nearly every corner.

I miss the river the most, I think.

The first time I came back from the headwaters
it was hard for me to understand how that tiny stream
could become the wide, gentle waterway
that cuts through the rolling hills.

Now I do understand.

Because leaving and coming back,
I am a part of that river too.
Sometimes I make it stronger,
other times I simply float along.

I'm always headed south.

But I'll always know
where I began.

☐ "As long as the children need me, I'll be there; and unless we mess up their minds and visions of the future as adults, they are our hope for the future."
—Mabel Cason, Saint Paul African American educator

MARCH

S	M	T	W	T	F	S
28	1	2	3	4	5	6
7	8	9	10	11	12	13
14	15	16	17	18	19	20
21	22	23	24	25	26	27
28	29	30	31	1	2	3

8 Monday

International Women's Day
United Nations Day for Women's Rights and International Peace

9 Tuesday

Minnesota Opera, *La bohème*

Phebe Hanson, poet, was born today in 1928

10 Wednesday

Minnesota Opera, *La bohème*

Minnesota State High School League Boys' Hockey Tournament

Emily Gilman Noyes, suffragist and birth control advocate, was born today in 1854

11 Thursday

Minnesota Opera, *La bohème*

Minnesota State High School League Boys' Hockey Tournament

Don Boxmeyer, newspaper columnist, was born today in 1941

March snow lays thick and heavy on a Saint Paul back yard

12 Friday

Minnesota Opera, *La bohème*

Minnesota State High School League
Boys' Hockey Tournament

13 Saturday

Saint Paul Winter Farmers' Market

Minnesota Opera, *La bohème*

Minnesota State High School League
Boys' Hockey Tournament

Saint Paul Chamber Orchestra

14 Sunday
Daylight Saving Time

Irish Music and Dance Association (IMDA)
Day of Irish Dance

Minnesota Opera, *La bohème*

March 11, 1884: Mary E. Jones of Saint Paul receives a patent
for her invention, a "bed spring fire escape."

Spooning

Camille Verzal

I rarely open the box. Mostly it stays on the bedroom shelf, gathering dust, carrying trinkets and love letters from my first significant relationship, remnants of escapes and journeys created by a four-year exhaustive memory shared with Jason, the first man I ever loved.

I often think I should just toss the box and its contents. But then I peek inside, and the memories flood. A tiny white bear looks up at me and triggers thoughts about the intangibles that exist only in the folds and curves of my mind, memories long since faded but not entirely forgotten.

* * *

Jason and I had only been dating a month. He declared his love a few weeks after our first kiss, followed by a statement that we would marry. Of course we would—Jason said so. He knew what he wanted. He could stare into my eyes for what seemed like forever. I was always the first to look away.

It's approaching midnight in early March; mild, but still winter in Minnesota. Jason says he has a surprise. We crawl into his decrepit brown car; I forget the make and model. It lacks style and a passenger-side seatbelt. But I'm not to worry about that—any sign of trouble, and Jason promises he will throw his arm out in front of me to keep me from going through the windshield.

We drive to Como Park. Jason tells me he has found an unlocked entrance to the zoo during his daily run that afternoon. Soon he maneuvers the car through the open gate, then a short distance to a large pit.

We stop, get out, walk to the pit. It's peaceful—we're in the middle of the city, but no cars, no voices. It begins to snow. I look around, trying to spot my surprise. Jason points down over the railing.

Far below, two polar bears sleep, cuddled up next to each other. I swear they are spooning. The larger one's front leg is an arm, protectively thrown over his mate's torso. Although they assume the position of all lovers before and those yet to come, I know they only represent two people—Jason and me—our love replicated in nature.

The male looks up sleepily at us, plenty annoyed, then falls back into silence.

I squeal with delight. I'm over the moon. I know Jason and I will grow old together.

Love and companionship at Como Zoo

* * *

I've since made new memories at the park: walking abandoned dogs at the Humane Society, running around the lake, meandering in the gardens. Yet I'm worried these new memories will smother the old, and I don't want them to. I want them to coexist peacefully.

Maybe that's why I keep the box. Jason and I haven't spoken in fourteen years, and I fear it's all beginning to fade. I'm losing what little remains of our history. And I know I'll never replicate that moment. I'll never steal into the zoo at night, nor would I want to. I've already done that, with a man I loved dearly but no longer, on a snowy evening in Saint Paul, believing then that my happy ending had finally arrived.

MARCH

S	M	T	W	T	F	S
28	1	2	3	4	5	6
7	8	9	10	11	12	13
14	15	16	17	18	19	20
21	22	23	24	25	26	27
28	29	30	31	1	2	3

▷ "Swell the great army of peace and production. . . . You are one of the spokes in this great wheel of progress and your absence will weaken the wheel by one member."
—J.P. McGaughey, Saint Paul labor leader (1880s)

15 Monday

🎖 Gil Elvgren, famed pin-up artist, was born today in 1914

16 Tuesday

17 Wednesday

Saint Patrick's Day

IMDA Saint Patrick's Day Celebration

Saint Patrick's Day Parade

Saint Patrick's Day Irish Ceili Dance

18 Thursday

Western Collegiate Hockey Association Men's Tournament

🎖 Constance Currie, Neighborhood House director, was born today in 1890

Saint Patrick's Day Parade 2009, downtown Saint Paul

19 Friday

Western Collegiate Hockey Association
Men's Tournament

20 Saturday

Spring Equinox

Saint Paul Winter Farmers' Market

Western Collegiate Hockey Association
Men's Tournament

21 Sunday

International Day for the Elimination
of Racial Discrimination

March 19, 1849: Benjamin Hoyt and others form the Saint Paul
Division No. 1 of the Sons of Temperance.

STP at SXSW

Matt Jackson

There are few social stages in Saint Paul for the young and hip to stand around and look cool, and even fewer venues to see cool live music. The Turf club and Big V's are the only two that really qualify; beyond that, illegal parties are the lone option. Can we then conclude Saint Paul is not a cool place? Yeah, sort of. Lack of cool spots has been the inherited complaint of Saint Paul's cool since F. Scott Fitzgerald left for New York. Our cool are forced to the coasts, to Europe, to—*gasp*—Minneapolis! There is one destination the cool from around the world have in common, the South by Southwest (SXSW) music festival in Austin, Texas. Could it possibly compete with the Turf Club? I decided to meet my friend's bands down there and find out.

Chris the "Peruvian Prince" and I made the twenty-hour drive to Austin in my Accord, which we named Killa B. We parked Killa B for the week and caught a cab into the heart of Indie Rock heaven. SXSW began in 1987 with 700 bands, and by 2008 had over 12,000. The festival's center is Sixth Street, a densely lined party strip of bars and clubs, but the whole city is a venue. Magazines like *Fader*, *Vice*, and *Rolling Stone* set up shop in empty warehouses, or prop up circus tents for throwing all-night parties. Bands play in furniture stores, fast-food restaurants, and on street corners.

After a wild first twenty-four hours of solid music, Chris and I took a tourism break and went to the Austin State Capitol building. When Chris pointed out a civil war monument in the front lawn, I was reminded of a high school trip my class took to Gettysburg—we felt proud then when we found a monument honoring the First Minnesota Regiment, the first in the country to answer Lincoln's call for 300,000 volunteer troops. The Texas monument honored their troops for defending "state's rights." The guitar-wielding army of Yankee Minnesotans currently invading Texas was surely more welcome. The Irongate and many other bars have entire days of Minnesota music. The big buzz bands often have a Minnesota connection, like Tapes 'n Tapes or The Hold Steady.

One of the Minnesota bands this year was Birthday Suits, fronted by Hideo of Saint Paul. Those who know him as the polite and reserved Japanese man who has tended bar at Saji Ya the last fifteen years are always shocked the first time they see him perform. He writhes on the ground, jumps from speakers, and snaps sweat at the crowd. I saw Birthday Suits play a bar called Head Hunters, a cavernous and sharp rock club. They set up out back in a structure for smokers, made of plywood and duct tape. There was no stage, so the crowd stood face-to-face with Hideo. Their slack expressions vanished as he began roaring like Godzilla through his guitar while Matt pounded like a beast on his drums. Half the crowd was awed two men could make this much noise, the rest grinned at each other knowing they had stumbled onto some good shit. It was the best show I saw in Texas.

At the other end of the showcase spectrum was Solid Gold. The lead singer, Zach Coulter, grew up in the Mac-Groveland neighborhood, and if magazines from there to England are correct, Solid Gold is the "next big thing." They have a dark British sound reminiscent of The Cure or Depeche Mode. When they weren't doing interviews, Solid Gold played three shows a day. On Friday, I saw them play the largest possible venue, the *Fader* stage. Kanye West played this stage Saturday night. Photographers lined up to take their pictures. We had to look up from behind crowd barricades. Saint Paul was headlining the biggest party at SXSW!

Saint Paul musicians certainly added to the coolness of SXSW, and those of us just standing around in tight jeans and V-necks didn't look too bad either. It's unfortunate our options at home are so limited. Maybe Saint Paul's coolness is destined to be an export product.

Photo courtesy Matt Jackson

Zach Coulter, Solid Gold's lead singer

⇨ "Whoever designed the streets must have been drunk. I think it was those Irish guys, you know what they like to do." —Jesse Ventura, former Minnesota governor, on *Late Night with David Letterman*

S	M	T	W	T	F	S
28	1	2	3	4	5	6
7	8	9	10	11	12	13
14	15	16	17	18	19	20
21	22	23	24	25	26	27
28	29	30	31	1	2	3

22 Monday
World Water Day

🐞 Jim Sazevich, Saint Paul's self-taught "House Detective," who helped popularize the investigation of the histories of Saint Paul houses, was born today in 1950

23 Tuesday

March Thaw in Mac-Groveland
Winter's run off again with water.
The south-facing slope of the roof
drains bitter night into the gutter.
The last heaps of snow count down
their lives one drip at a time.
The sun picks icy scabs up off the sidewalk.

24 Wednesday
No matter how many years in a row
this happens, we are, thankfully,
always surprised. Down the street now
skips this year's flock of children,
voices scattering like last fall's leaf-litter.
Richard Broderick

25 Thursday

Marjorie McNeely Conservatory—the place to go when winter is finally unbearable

26 Friday

Fourth Friday at the Movies

NCAA Division I Men's Hockey Championships

27 Saturday

Saint Paul Winter Farmers' Market

NCAA Division I Men's Hockey Championships

Global Hot Dish Variety Show

Spring Flower Show begins

❀ Thomas Tapeh, Liberian-born professional football player, was born today in 1980

28 Sunday

Palm Sunday

The Lao Family Community is established in 1977 as a nonprofit, mutual-assistance association for Hmong people.

Hastings Pond

Keith Sterner

All children need a place to explore their dreams and fantasies, a place where adults are not allowed. A sanctuary in the heart of Saint Paul's East Side, Hastings Pond and its surrounding area was once such a refuge for youth of all ages.

Hastings Pond, along with its two smaller neighboring ponds, was surrounded by thick brush, mature trees, a hilly terrain, and a scattering of trails. Salamanders slithering under rocks, frogs and toads camouflaged by the moist green groundcover, snakes squirming through the brush, and birds and insects harmoniously chirping were natural to this haven for wildlife. These living creatures, along with the stark beauty of the densely treed trails, contributed to the personality of this urban wilderness. The sweet fragrance of wildflowers, combined with the unmistakable odor of stagnant swamp water, provided my senses with all the contrasts nature can offer.

As a child, I didn't question the legends of Hastings Pond. One story described what happened on a cold and icy night in the early 1900s. Old man Hastings, who lived in a rundown shanty nestled amongst the trees at the pond's edge, was returning home on his horse-drawn wagon. When he descended the steep embankment leading to his homestead, he lost control of his team. Unable to regain control, he plunged through the pond's ice to a frigid death. Thereafter, a rumor persisted that the spirit of old man Hastings could be seen roaming his homestead at night.

Each of the three ponds had its own distinct appearance and personality. The largest, which was Hastings Pond, was a long and narrow band of relatively clean water spattered with lily pads and surrounded by thick jungles of cattails and marsh in summer. An observing eye could regularly see nesting waterfowl or the bobbing head of a muskrat gliding by. The pond next in size resembled a large oval crater surrounded by a steep incline and ringed by mature trees. Its water was covered by a stagnant, murky green crust that gave the appearance of a solid surface. The temperature was always cooler there because the sun's rays struggled to penetrate the massive canopy of trees. Only the most adventurous children frequented this pond, for it was reputed to be bottomless. The smallest pond resembled a large mud puddle, an inviting site on a hot summer day. In the early summer, thousands of miniature frogs could be seen hopping insistently through its brown muddy water.

Hasting's Pond, where a child's imagination reigned

Whether used for sledding and skating in the winter or rafting in the summer, Hastings Pond furnished an abundance of activities. Every day would bring a new challenge to a child's imagination. One could become a native in the jungles of the Amazon, an explorer on the frozen tundra of the polar ice cap, a soldier on the battlegrounds of World War II, or an American pioneer heading westward. Whatever the fantasy, Hastings Pond could embody it.

One summer morning in the early 1960s, unannounced to any children who frequented Hastings Pond, an army of yellow earthmovers and bulldozers began erasing this kingdom of nature from the earth's surface. During one summer season, the ponds were drained of their life and the beautiful terrain was graded smooth. Progress prevailed, and Hastings Pond and its many wonders became the site of Saint Paul's new Johnson High School and its athletic fields. Today, as I drive by, only my mind's eye can bring back the unforgettable memories of this urban oasis.

My Life

Sain Thin

I was born in Myanmar in 1972. I have one brother. My parents were farmers. My parents are dead. I started to go to school in 1978. I finished high school in 1991. My native town is Pah-an Division, Nong Lake Village. My country has many mountains, forests, and rivers. My country is very beautiful, so I like my country. But my government is very bad. They are always fighting near our village. The villagers ran quickly away from our village. So sometimes people got ill and died.

My brother was so ill that he couldn't eat or drink. His illness made him very unhappy. He tried all kinds of medicine and consulted all kinds of medicine men, yet day by day he grew weaker and weaker. At that time I was going from our village to Mae La refugee camp in Thailand. I lived in the camp years ago. I can't get information about my brother, I don't know exactly what happened to him. And then I came from Mae La to the U.S. on August 1, 2007.

Sain Thin

Vernal Equinox

Cahoots Coffee, Selby Ave., Saint Paul

Jim Heynen

We're here to taunt the deceptive smile of spring.
Through the winter-smudged window
I watch the fading snowbanks give way
to 60 degree sunlight. Dead sheep, I think.
The snowbanks are like decaying sheep, their entrails
curling out in the form of November twigs,
December Miller Lites, February dog droppings,
and last week's newspaper. Their inner skeleton
of ice glows, not like a sign of hope but of stony despair.

Minutes ago when I crossed those snowbanks they
crackled like crushed crystal, like winter's death rattle,
a giving up to what the robin on the bare branch says it knows.
One young woman (God, her blond hair is lovely,)
wears a flowered sun dress, but a woman across
from her wears a dark hooded sweatshirt and curses
French auxiliary verbs. At shoe level: sandals
on some and fur boots on others. We're all
confused about something, and we know it.
At least, I do. Spring is coming? Maybe.

No, it is not coming. I try to imagine green lawns,
earnest robin songs, lilacs, ripe tomatoes on bending vines.
I know better. Coffee shops are safe scenes
for denial, for ambivalence to parade as certainty.
I'm even drinking decaf. The robin outside revises
itself with a nervous twitch. Does it know that North Dakota's
Big White has awakened from Canadian slumber
and ambles toward us, sure-footed, determined to deliver
unto all of us, the bare armed and wool-clothed alike,
the inevitable truth? The robin knows. We all know.

Mickey's Diner

Mariela Consuela Cole

Have you ever been to Mickey's Diner? Well, I have. The first time was about four or five years ago. But I remember it clear as day. It looked like a house trailer. When we got there, I was amazed by how small but cool it was.

I went inside, and everyone was nice, joyful, polite, and seemed like they were always in a great mood. We got a booth by the window. Five minutes later, a woman came over, and I asked for a chocolate shake. It took only three minutes and it was ready. I'd never had a shake made so fast before, so I hesitated before I really tried it. *I loved it!!* It was the best milkshake I had ever had.

Then when I got the fries . . . Wow! They were hot, long, crispy, and completely delicious. It was so much fun that I'll never forget that day. I hope I can go there again really soon.

Half-Price Books

Kira Cronin-Hennessy

The smell of paper, the flickering lights, and the tall shelves. Where am I? Half-Price Books. This is a bookstore that sells used books. I like it there because it's nice and quiet. My favorite place is where all the chapter books are. There is a window that looks out on the parking lot, and the view is beautiful. I like it when it's dark and you can see the moon. Another thing I like is that the store has really good books. Half-Price Books is a good choice for readers.

Photo © Patricia Bour-Schilla

Half-Price Books on Ford Parkway

A Fanatic's Guide to Getting the Most out of the Weather in Saint Paul

Kenneth A. Blumenfeld

For those of us who think about, study, discuss, photograph, worship, and otherwise adore the weather, Saint Paul is a miniature atmospheric playground. Below is just a short list of some of my favorite places in Saint Paul to see, feel, and hear some of our weather.

Rapid temperature changes: Stroll down Kellogg Boulevard between Jackson and Broadway one to two hours before sunset or after sunrise. Experience the joyous micrometeorological condition known as thermal stratification, and feel the temperatures swing fifteen degrees Fahrenheit over that half-mile distance. You can have the same effect by walking or biking the Swede Hollow portion of the Bruce Vento Trail.

Clouds: Visit the high points of Cherokee Park or Indian Mounds Park (be respectful of the mounds!), or the south side of Lake Phalen. Just find a nice patch of grass, and on your back you go! Of course, if you have access to a high floor of a high-rise, take a peek out the windows from time to time.

Storm clouds, part I (when the storm is coming): On the observation platform adjoining the Smith Avenue Bridge (the High Bridge) on Cherokee Avenue, the power of the storm and the vulnerability of the city beneath are juxtaposed perfectly. Looking toward downtown from nearly any portion of Mounds Boulevard, or toward Minneapolis from Mississippi River Boulevard, also will do. But be careful—lightning kills!

Storm clouds, part II (when the storm is moving away): Try Linwood Park for storms to the south, or Arlington at Wheelock Parkway for storms to the east. Either one looks great with those magnificent purplish-blue clouds, and the sage-green undersides of the oak leaves contrast nicely with the stormy sky.

Thunderstorms: You are always safest being indoors during a thunderstorm, but if you are outside, the lower, the better; Crosby Farm Park is about as low as Saint Paul gets, and is a magical place to watch storms. The vegetation softens the thunder, the trees dampen the wind, and few things are more hypnotic than giant raindrops bouncing off the lily pads on marshy Crosby Lake.

Downpours: Ramsey Avenue hill and the Robert Street service roads on the West Side feature dramatic descents. When it rains furiously, every slope, no matter how shallow, becomes a temporary tributary, but these

Gathering clouds

outlandishly steep hills become raging cascades. Alternatively, watch the engineered segments of Battle Creek swell and rush as stormwater runs off the surrounding mini-canyon.

Rainbows: For rainbows, the sun must be behind you, about fifteen to thirty degrees above the horizon, with the rain in front of you. Thus, we see most of our rainbows to the east, in the evening. From West Seventh near Irvine Park, rainbows can straddle the High Bridge and/or have at least one foot planted in the river.

Snow, part I (snowfall): To really see the snow falling, you need contrast, and during the day, the dark bricks and short visual range of Lowertown can make snowfall seem even heavier than it is. At night, the intersection of Grand and Snelling illuminates in multiple directions, giving all snowflakes passing through ample opportunity to be seen and loved.

Snow, part II (snowcover): The trees in St. Anthony Park seem to hold on to the snow for a good long time, and the slopes can make it quite picturesque. Visit a day or two after a snowfall and walk along Commonwealth Avenue south of Como. Not to be outdone, the treacherous hill on Highwood Avenue off Point Douglas Road (on the far east side of town) offers excellent winter scenery as well.

Of course, the best advice may be to explore the city throughout the year, paying attention to the sky whenever possible. Soon, your own list of favorite places to see the weather will emerge.

April

April

Wait Long Enough and a Pattern Emerges

Today the river cannot decide
which course to take,
like a young woman rushing out
the door, then back again
to change her shoes.

Greg Watson

➮ "I don't tell the popular narratives, the commercial narratives, that one is supposed to tell as an African American writer, and there is a price to be paid for that."
—David Haynes, former Saint Paul writer and teacher

APRIL

S	M	T	W	T	F	S
28	29	30	31	1	2	3
4	5	6	7	8	9	10
11	12	13	14	15	16	17
18	19	20	21	22	23	24
25	26	27	28	29	30	1

29 Monday
Passover begins

30 Tuesday

✺ Denzil Carty, Episcopal priest and civil rights activist, was born today in 1904

31 Wednesday

1 Thursday
April Fools' Day

Downtown with First Bank in the distance

Photo © Patricia Bour-Schilla

2 Friday   Saint Paul Chamber Orchestra

Good Friday

3 Saturday   Saint Paul Winter Farmers' Market

Saint Paul Chamber Orchestra

Minnesota RollerGirls (Bout)

Eddie Benton Banai, a founder of the American Indian Movement
and Red School House, was born today in 1934

4 Sunday

Easter

Street Poetry
The worms have been up
all night writing long lines
of crazy, unintelligible
poetry in the street.
Drunk on spring,
they dry out in the sun.
Mike Hazard

April 1, 1929: The Hallie Q. Brown Center, created to serve the
city's African American community, is incorporated.

Can't Nobody Make a Sweet Potato Pie Like My Mama

Rose McGee

Every holiday, every barbecue, every church social, and Lord knows for every somebody or another's funeral, the unspoken expectation has always been that my mama makes the sweet potato pies. Calling her pies delicious is an understatement—they are heavenly.

Today, close to a hundred people are packed practically elbow to elbow in Mama's little five-room, tin-roof house in Jackson, Tennessee. None of her pies are being served because not a single one of us ever thought to keep a batch tucked away in the freezer. Instead, as is customary, everyone is waiting with a Southern style of patience for some of the church ladies to usher themselves into Mama's cozy little yellow-and-white gingham-accented kitchen, hauling in their own sweet potato pies. Each woman believes hers is the best and warrants first-to-be-served for today's special repast—Mama's funeral.

Peeking out the window and much to my surprise, I see seven distinguished elderly women, each wearing a white hat, a white dress, white shoes, and white gloves ceremoniously lined up on Mama's front porch, about to make some type of grand entrance. Looking closer, I realize these are Mama's cooking rivals and closest friends! A further cue of "All rise" becomes an unspoken command. Everyone stands to attention in stone military silence as the packed Red Sea living room begins parting, making way for the ladies' entrance. Each is carrying a colorful woven basket containing sweet potato pies.

Within minutes, sweet potato pie is being served. Definitely not hungry, but graciously, I nibble from a slice brought in to me by Mama's favorite niece, who now resides in Saint Paul, Minnesota. As Cousin Mary Louise continues serving slices of pie in a Northern sort of way, I am desperately wishing this whole funeral ordeal will hurry and come to closure. I'm given another slice of pie. I nibble a bit more. Not a bad flavor, but slightly too much nutmeg for my taste. Nothing like Mama's. Doesn't even come close. I only want Mama's pie. I only want Mama back.

Nobody could or ever will be able to make a sweet potato pie like my Mama.

Traditional Sweet Potato Pie

Rose McGee, *Owner of Deep Roots Gourmet Desserts*

Ingredients (makes two 9" pies):
1 stick of butter, softened
1 cup packed brown sugar
2 cups granulated sugar
4 medium to large sweet potatoes, cooked
2 eggs, lightly beaten
1 cup milk (whole, evaporated, or condensed)
1 teaspoon ginger
1 tablespoon nutmeg
1 tablespoon cinnamon
2 tablespoons vanilla extract
1 teaspoon lemon extract
2 unbaked pie shells

Directions:
Preheat oven to 400° F.
Use a hand or stand mixer.

1. In a large mixing bowl, blend cooked sweet potatoes with sugar. Blend in eggs.
2. Now blend in soft butter.
3. Add next 5 ingredients; mix well.
4. Pour into pie shells.
5. Reduce heat to 350° F and bake 60 minutes or until well set.
6. Remove from oven. Allow to cool and firm up before eating.

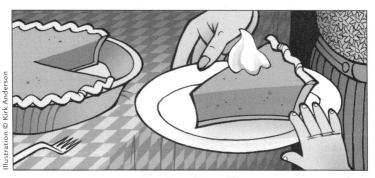

Yum: Sweet Potato Pie

Illustration © Kirk Anderson

"I have a feeling that when my ship comes in, I'll be at the airport."
—Charles M. Schulz, Saint Paul native and cartoonist

S	M	T	W	T	F	S
28	29	30	31	1	2	3
4	5	6	7	8	9	10
11	12	13	14	15	16	17
18	19	20	21	22	23	24
25	26	27	28	29	30	1

5 Monday

Saint Paul Almanac Reading Series

6 Tuesday

7 Wednesday

8 Thursday

Melvin Calvin, Nobel Prize–winning chemist, was born today in 1911

Red-winged blackbird on the Mississippi River bank in Saint Paul

9 Friday

10 Saturday   Saint Paul Winter Farmers' Market
Saint Paul Chamber Orchestra
Minnesota Opera *Salome*

11 Sunday   Urban Expedition: Ghana

The octagonal Highland Water Tower, built in 1927, is 134 feet high and holds 200,000 gallons of water in a steel tank.

Landmarks

For my parents

Ann Iverson

I. The Cathedral

After Mass she made pot roast and potatoes
and we sat in silence at the harvest table.
What I didn't know is that all of her life
she tucked away pieces of palm
inside of drawers and books,
pockets and glass knickknacks.
A certain kind of holiness
I keep finding years after her death
dusty, braided and frayed like the edges of a river.

II. Sanitary Farm Dairies

The last of the real milkmen slowly go out.
When my father lost 35 years of pension from the
merger, he slowly raked the yard.
A two hour job took him all day;
he stopped often to take long drags
from generic cigarettes.
After she died, he stopped
tending the yard altogether;
the weeds grew up
as he sat in the corner of his kitchen
memorizing the small portrait
offered by the window.

III. Downtown Saint Paul

Amazing then, at 47
I can wish myself
right back into her arms
as I did when she would leave
on Monday nights to shop
downtown Saint Paul.
From my bed, I would listen
for the click, click of her soft heels

on the sidewalk of an autumn night
the brush of packages against her coat.
In my life, have I ever felt more safe
than those evenings upon her return?

IV. Harriet Island

Some people climbed the fence
and scaled the slanted rock
that keeps the mighty water contained.
I was afraid of the rushing darkness;
the under currents which would
take me in and swallow.
My mother in her navy blue turban
told me this was so.

VI. Harriet Island, Spring 1965

When the others had gone to mass
at the Cathedral, shiny and domed
up off the hill,
we strolled the island
just the two of us
father and I
while the Mississippi
bent and lulled, groaned its size,
a giant woken from a deep, deep sleep.

I was too small to notice the high water
in that year of great flooding
how the edge of the familiar
is swallowed by what is never known.

He reached into his pocket
for pennies and nickels
secretly dropped them on the grass
where, with my keen eyes, I would find them.

All of this before the pain of our lives
rose above sea level.

A Century Ago: A special ceremony
is held on April 15, 1910, to open
the Saint Paul Hotel and its grand
ballroom, fine dining area, roof
garden, and elegant rooms.

APRIL

S	M	T	W	T	F	S
28	29	30	31	1	2	3
4	5	6	7	8	9	10
11	12	13	14	15	16	17
18	19	20	21	22	23	24
25	26	27	28	29	30	1

12 Monday

Billy "The St. Paul Thunderbolt" Miske, heavyweight boxer,
was born today in 1894

13 Tuesday

14 Wednesday

15 Thursday   Minnesota Opera *Salome*

April

Mississippi River bank and tree

16 Friday

Walter H. Deubener, inventor of grocery bag handles, was born today in 1885

17 Saturday

Saint Paul Farmers' Market

Minnesota Book Awards

18 Sunday

Minnesota Opera *Salome*

Saint Paul Conservatory for the Performing Arts

Day by Day Cafe on West Seventh is a nonprofit organization
that gives recovering addicts a place to learn skills.

Saints' Stadium

Sebastian Tippett

Wind up. Pitch. Crack. The smallest white speck in the stadium sails all 408 feet. The crowd screams in unison. Home run!

Sometimes I make it seem like it's not that exciting, but some things are more exciting unsaid. Every time I go to the Saints' stadium, there's a new feeling. On the opener, it's always exciting; playing a rival, it's always intense; but my favorite is when you're on the edge of your seat. Imagine this: 5–4, man on second base, two outs. The ball is hit, sailing into left field.

It drops in front of the fielder. He bare-hands it and whips the ball past the cutoff to ricochet in front of the catcher's glove, where it makes a strong bounce. Thousands of breaths are held while dust surrounds home plate. When it clears, he's touching the plate, and the ball is set lightly on his forearm. The call comes. Safe!

Of course, if you're excited now, imagine being at the game.

Another thing I love is being a family. For two hours, every single person in that stadium is a friend cheering his or her heart out. Saving seats, giving each other peanuts, talking friendly to strangers. At my first Saints game, I asked my mom, "Why are they all so nice?" and my mom said, "Because we're winning."

That made me even happier. Maybe if we all were at a Saints game, the world would be better. Maybe.

You should really go to a Saints game.

Poem for the State of the City
April 21, 2009

for Mayor Chris Coleman

Carol Connolly, *Saint Paul Poet Laureate*

Fire flood torture greed. Our world came close
to crashing in this avalanche of disasters.
Some man made. Some not.
We bid adieu now to what is past.
We stand here above sea level,
safe on ground solid for over a century.
Safe, we are, but not naïve. We know
tough times when we see them. We know
that greed, at last, has lost its gloss.
Workers arrive at just the right moment,
the sun pours light into the deep holes
they dig with the grace of an Andahazy,
the precision of a brain surgeon,
holes big enough to bury a dead horse.
This dig will deliver all sorts of new power soon
to this old neighborhood. Soon
these mighty excavations will be invisible
under a sidewalk of fresh concrete.
Somewhere in this city, someone is working
on a poem full of hope and resolve.
It will be stamped into this new concrete soon.
At noon on a sunny day, with his part
in delivering this new power nearly done,
a young man tips his hardhat,
lifts a small folding chair from his truck,
sits with his lunchbox, and for a while,
turns his face to the sun.
The trees, long out of leaf on this city street,
are beginning to green.
The decades-old lilac bushes are in bud
once more, and we know for certain.
We will keep our world moving.

⇨ "Because of our social circumstances, male and female are really two cultures and their life experiences are utterly different."—Kate Millett, Saint Paul native and writer

S	M	T	W	T	F	S
28	29	30	31	1	2	3
4	5	6	7	8	9	10
11	12	13	14	15	16	17
18	19	20	21	22	23	24
25	26	27	28	29	30	1

19 Monday

⚾ Joe Mauer, professional baseball player, was born today in 1983

20 Tuesday

Minnesota Opera *Salome*

21 Wednesday

22 Thursday

Earth Day

April

Photo © Patricia Bour-Schilla

Bridge joining Harriet and Raspberry islands

---

23 Friday

Fourth Friday at the Movies

Saint Paul Art Crawl

🌐 Arthur Farwell, noted composer, was born today in 1872

---

24 Saturday

Saint Paul Farmers' Market

Minnesota Opera *Salome*

Saint Paul Art Crawl

Saint Paul Chamber Orchestra

---

25 Sunday

Saint Paul Farmers' Market

Saint Paul Art Crawl

🌐 Father John A. Ryan, activist priest, teacher, and writer, was born today in 1869

Saint Paul's new Midway Stadium opens on April 25, 1957, with a
day-night doubleheader.

The Possibilities are Endless: To Include Typos

Suzanne Nielsen

I sit on the front steps of 761 East Third Street, waiting for the trolley to pull up to "experience the wonderful housing opportunities in Dayton's Bluff." The woman next door comes around the corner and I show her the ad in the Dayton's Bluff District Forum April issue; I even read her the bottom line in 22-point bold type: "This ad is no April Fool's joke! Don't miss this great tour!"

"It don't start here," she says.

I follow her to her back door; she goes inside, grabs a flyer, and hands it to me. THE POSSIBILITIES TOUR, it's titled, and it says the tour started at 798 East Seventh Street at noon. I run to my car, light a smoke, and race over a few blocks. My watch reads 12:03. There's the trolley, one seat left.

I hop on and sit next to Earl. No—wait, he lives on Earl; we ride right by his house, and then he points out Aunt Sally's house on Beech Street. Next to it is the first house on the tour, although the flyer says it's the third house (gotta love typos). 930 Beech. I used to live at 916 Beech. Now it's a chiropractic office. The house on the left is where Deets and Walter lived with a lavender bathroom. "Ya gotta be careful in this neighborhood," Earl man says.

We pass Haag's Superette, now boarded up. I remember writing notes in cursive, signing my dad's name for a pack of L&M's.

"Careful of what?" I ask Earl man.

"Of the hoodlums," he says.

This is the city. There are hoodlums, prostitutes, and ministers. Not all people wear slim-fitting khakis; not everyone has a car born in the current decade.

Out of the eleven houses on the tour, three are category ones, meaning the structure is danger free. The others need serious maintenance. All are under $100,000 and within a two-mile radius of each other.

As we drive through the neighborhood, I think I see Don Hauser's mom hanging clothes in her back yard. I think I hear Trudell's car engine rumble and McKenna's dog howl. Once an East Sider, always an East Sider.

Back at 798 East Seventh, the Community Council Office, we end our tour an hour later. Inside, I grab free cookies and coffee. "We have to save our community," a young woman says. "We have to save these

Dayton's Bluff: Full of historic homes

houses, or builders will come in and tear them down. They'll build houses like those in the suburbs."

"What's wrong with the houses in the suburbs?" I ask.

"Well, have you ever been to the suburbs? All those houses are designed to keep people from getting to know one another."

I think about this and know what she means.

"You got to be careful of those neighborhoods. You could live there for decades and never know who lives next door to you," she says.

I get back in my car and drive past all eleven houses again. I recognize I've just experienced the wonderful housing opportunities in Dayton's Bluff, where the possibilities are endless, regardless of hoodlums or typos. Ya gotta be careful of this neighborhood, I think, not of hoodlums, but of memories.

▷ "After you've done a thing the same way for two years, look it over carefully. After five years, look at it with suspicion. And after ten years, throw it away and start all over." —Alfred E. Perlman, Saint Paul native and president of the New York Central and the Pennsylvania railroads

APRIL

S	M	T	W	T	F	S
28	29	30	31	1	2	3
4	5	6	7	8	9	10
11	12	13	14	15	16	17
18	19	20	21	22	23	24
25	26	27	28	29	30	1

26 Monday

27 Tuesday

28 Wednesday

29 Thursday

Saint Paul Chamber Orchestra

Festival of Nations

🏒 Alana Blahoski, Olympic ice hockey gold medal winner, was born today in 1974

April

Schmidt beer sign on the West Side

30 Friday Saint Paul Chamber Orchestra

Festival of Nations

1 Saturday Saint Paul Farmers' Market

May Day Saint Paul Chamber Orchestra

Festival of Nations

Como Memorial Japanese Garden opens

2 Sunday Saint Paul Farmers' Market

Festival of Nations

In 1848 William Finn, veteran of the Mexican-American war, becomes the first permanent settler in Highland Park.

Good Vibrations

Andrea Taylor Langworthy

My husband and I have a favorite restaurant, Pazzaluna, in downtown Saint Paul. The Italian eatery has happy-hour pizza and wine specials that keep us coming back. Even better, its energy is so good that a bad mood can be lifted just by walking in the door. Last week, I realized the source of the good vibes. As they say in real estate: location, location, location. Pazzaluna is located in the same place once occupied by Frank Murphy, a women's clothing store.

As many times as I have eaten at Pazzaluna, I hadn't made this connection until I finalized dinner plans with a friend last week. She wasn't sure where the restaurant is. "On the corner of St. Peter and Fifth," I said, "where Frank Murphy used to be." When the words popped out of my mouth, they surprised me. *Aha!* I thought. *Now I know why the restaurant has such great spirit.* Frank Murphy had been a favorite shopping place for the women in my family. So chic and up-to-date that it could have been in New York City. So lucky for us that it wasn't.

Just a few days after that conversation with my friend, an obituary caught my eye. Sadly, Frank Murphy's daughter had passed away. Once again, I remembered the many trips I took to that lovely specialty store. When I shopped there with my mother, this woman often helped us. When my teenage friends and I stopped in to look for dresses for dances, she never acted as if we were in the wrong place and should browse in the junior department of Dayton's instead.

Frank Murphy's give-away sales were world-famous. Held in the ballroom of the Saint Paul Hotel, just across the street, they received extensive news coverage. Because I couldn't bring myself to try on clothes in a giant room with no privacy and the possibility of television cameras, I never braved one of the sales. I'd seen the news reports, though: Hand-to-hand combat among crazed women ready to do battle over articles of clothing held no appeal for me. But my sisters, always stronger than I, were able to hold their own and bring home bargains galore.

Frank Murphy was the go-to spot for special occasions. When my daughter was a freshman at St. Thomas and lived on campus in a dorm, she called to tell me about a formal winter dance. Of course, she needed a new ensemble. She and I headed to Frank Murphy, the same store where we had found the fancy frock for her high school senior prom. "If you can't find the perfect party dress at Frank Murphy," I told her, "then the dress doesn't exist"—the same thing my mother had said to me.

Pazzaluna

In fact, years before, when my parents had divorced, my mother was down in the dumps. My year-younger sister and I knew just the pick-me-up she needed. We borrowed Mom's car and drove to Saint Paul, where we found three lovely outfits at Frank Murphy. Of course, being teenagers, we had no means to pay for Mom's gifts, so we put them on her charge account. And had them gift-wrapped.

When my husband and I meet our friends for pizza at Pazzaluna next week, I'll ask if they can feel the vitality and sparkle of the place. I'll tell them my stories about the building's previous tenant and propose a toast to the Murphy family, which made sure the women of my family were, as my mother would say, "Dressed to the nines."

Frank Murphy's dress shop in 1948

To that Old Lady

Katie Ka Vang

To that old lady
who had a river of sons.
drowned her luck in a piece of silver
to make a plantation of opium
and farm animals

To that old lady
who prospers as the empress of her table
guiding her sons in the Right direction
Left— Left—Left-right— Left,
pricking her teeth clean,
digging out the unnecessary
before decaying starts

To that old lady
queen of knives,
her sharpness surpasses
any sheath of a king.
Sharpened for survival

To that old lady, who carries
hundred pound struggles in her
heart, mind, bones, like a whisper
and pours it like fuel igniting life

To that old lady who
will dream in eternity
of crashing waves,
rippling mistakes
across the bodies of water
of her grandchildren

To that old lady who
was forced into marriage
and still set off sailing for
riches

To that old lady who
never learned to read, write,
type, ride a bike, or drive,
the movement is in your walk,
the pounding is out of your chest,
the writing is on your skin,
the reading is in your body

To that old lady who
will never have a mausoleum
for her offspring to bury her in,
You Will Rest Everywhere.

Irv Williams: A Life in Music

Pamela Espeland

In the spring of 2009, Irv Williams is playing a shiny new tenor saxophone. He has a young miniature schnauzer named Ditto who, in Irv's words, is "very exuberant about everything." He's writing new songs for his next CD, his fifth since 2004. He has two regular weekly gigs, one at the Dakota Jazz Club in Minneapolis and the other at Il Vesco Vino on West Seventh in Saint Paul. He's making plans to celebrate his birthday with parties at both the Artists' Quarter in Saint Paul and the Dakota.

On August 17, 2009, Williams—fans call him "Mr. Smooth"—turned ninety. He has lived in Saint Paul for forty-seven years, moving here in 1962 to be closer to his job at the Sherwood Supper Club, now long gone. Most of the clubs he has played over the years—Cassius's Bamboo Room, the Flame Bar, the Red Feather, Freddie's, the Crystal Coach, the Top of the Hilton, Suzette's—have shut their doors, been torn down or redeveloped.

Williams could have left town, hit the road with Duke Ellington, Count Basie, or Louis Armstrong, ended up in New York, and become a star. Instead, he chose to stay and become part of Saint Paul's history.

Along with playing at every jazz club in the Twin Cities since the 1940s, Williams has taught in the public schools, lectured at the University of Minnesota, and mentored many musicians. In 1984, he was the first jazz musician to be honored by the State of Minnesota with his own "Irv Williams Day." His picture appeared on the Celebrate Minnesota state map in 1990 (he appears on this year's *Almanac* cover; take a look).

Williams was named an Arts Midwest Jazz Master in 1995 and is a member of the Minnesota Jazz Hall of Fame. He plays a new sax because his old one is now in the "Minnesota's Greatest Generation" exhibit at the Minnesota History Center.

Acclaim is appreciated, but for Williams, it's all about the music. His first instrument was the violin, which he played as a cute little kid growing up in Cincinnati and Little Rock. The older he got, the more other kids teased him for playing a "sissy instrument." They also called him "Ir-vin-ee" because his name was Irvine, with an *e* at the end.

Williams dropped the violin and later the *e*. By the time he was eleven, he had switched to clarinet and then to tenor saxophone. He started playing professionally at fifteen. He attended college as a pre-med student, with plans to be a doctor like his father, but music's pull was too strong. Besides, there was plenty of work for young sax players during the Big Band era of the 1930s and early '40s. When World War II began, Williams joined

Irv Williams

the Navy and came to the Naval Air Station in Minneapolis with the U.S. Navy Band.

He had ample time to practice his horn and explore the Twin Cities. On his first weekend here, he met the great bassist Oscar Pettiford and his family. Pettiford introduced Williams to the local jazz scene and places like Buford's BBQ and the Elk's Rest. Williams remembers, "We walked into the Elk's Rest, I didn't have a horn, and a guy named Rail says, 'You can play my horn.' So I played it and their mouths dropped open. I always like that."

Two marriages and nine children followed. When money was tight, Williams worked two jobs: dry cleaner by day, jazz musician by night. Today he's free to spend as much time as he wants on his music. He walks and talks a bit slowly, and he admits to having problems with getting tired, but many people believe he has never sounded better.

After all these years as a musician—Williams started playing violin at age six, so he's had eighty-four years of playing and practicing, learning and trying to get better every day—does he still enjoy it? "I enjoy it more than ever now," he says. "I can't slack off. I have to put every ounce of myself into my music. That's what I do. It keeps me going—myself and my dog."

His tone is breathy and warm. Sometimes his playing is like a kiss on your cheek or a gentle hand on the back of your neck. He's a master of the love song. The next time you and your sweetheart are alone together, if you're old enough, forget the R&B and play a little Irv.

April

A Poem Called "Life"

Allison Rudolph

life
own my life
live for a reason
kind
reach my goal in life
respectful
let my soul fly like the wind
think
yelling, screaming
fun
free
smart
guide my own life
make hard decisions
have ideas
draw
parents
a home
wildlife
hunting
fishing
day
night
—life

This poem was written by my 9 (now 10)-year-old daughter. She is definitely a Saint Paul girl; we live and play in Saint Paul and wouldn't want to be anywhere else in the world. I just think this poem was really special and should be shared.

—Michelle Rudolph

May

Photo © Patricia Bour-Schilla

Hey! What a deal! Now it's May
And everyone's twenty, okay?
And slender and glamorous
And successfully amorous
And there's thirty-two hours in the day.

Garrison Keillor

May

S	M	T	W	T	F	S
25	26	27	28	29	30	1
2	3	4	5	6	7	8
9	10	11	12	13	14	15
16	17	18	19	20	21	22
23	24	25	26	27	28	29
30	31	1	2	3	4	5

⇨ Don Hudson was the first African American to become head football coach at a predominantly white college, Macalester College, 1971 to 1975.

3 Monday   *Saint Paul Almanac* Reading Series

World Press Freedom Day

4 Tuesday

5 Wednesday

Cinco de Mayo

🌼 Mai Neng Moua, Hmong writer and editor, was born today in 1974

6 Thursday

🌼 Judy Delton, prolific children's book author, was born today in 1931

May

Part of West Side mural

7 Friday

in Saint Paul,
a seed wants to have
already been placed
in warm soil for weeks,
preparing for the coming
of thunder, heat,
lightning
and growth.
Diego Vázquez, Jr.

Cinco de Mayo Festival

---

8 Saturday

Saint Paul Farmers' Market

Cinco de Mayo Festival

Saint Paul Chamber Orchestra

Minnesota Bonsai Society Bonsai Show

Summer Flower Show begins

---

9 Sunday

Mothers' Day

Saint Paul Farmers' Market

Minnesota Bonsai Society Bonsai Show

Saint Paul Civic Symphony Mothers' Day Celebration

May

May 9, 1884: George Wells becomes the first Saint Paul firefighter to die
in the line of duty after he develops tetanus from stepping on a nail.

The Great Escape

Louis DiSanto

Saint Paul's iconic Como Zoo has long been a charming, peaceful place to enjoy creatures great and small. But on the morning of May 13, 1994, the zoo was anything but peaceful when it became the scene of "The Great Escape."

I was working by the giraffes when a vendor came running toward me. Her words were a zookeeper's worst nightmare: "You better come quick. One of the gorillas is out!" My initial reaction was disbelief—until I saw 400-pound Casey roaming in the bushes above his yard. And the only thing between him and the rest of the world was a short fence.

I radioed the staff and within minutes we were evacuating the zoo. At first, some visitors barely moved, while a few others took pictures. Fortunately, Casey calmly watched the exodus. If he had gone into the crowd, there could have been a panic.

It was hard to fathom how Casey, whom I remembered giving horseyback rides when he was just a baby, got over a 15-foot wall. But he did, and our only concerns now were what he would do and how to contain him. An eerie quiet settled over the zoo as we watched and waited. But not for long. A huge hand emerged from the bushes and haltingly touched the fence, as if expecting to get a shock. And in a heartbeat, Casey was on the sidewalk and about to go where no gorilla had gone before.

Potential disaster loomed when Casey almost climbed into the kudu yard, which would have sent these skittish antelope into a frenzy. But he backed away and headed to the barn instead. Casey peered through the windows and pulled on the unlocked doors without success, much to the relief of the nervous visitors huddled inside, one of whom said it felt like being in a King Kong movie.

Perhaps realizing it was lunchtime, Casey ambled over to the concession stand and sat on a table. He looked around as if he wanted some service. Now what do you think a 400-pound gorilla would order? After a few minutes, Casey hopped off the table (he never did order anything) and began walking back to the gorilla yard, where keeper Steve Bridger was waiting with a tranquilizer rifle. He fired and the sting of the dart sent Casey bolting behind the primate building in high dudgeon.

But just when we feared he would get out of the zoo, Casey abruptly stopped. A man dressed in white was standing by the gate at the end of the driveway. Casey reared up as if he had seen a ghost—you could feel

Sculpture of Casey the gorilla at Como Zoo

the ground shake as he thundered back around the corner, vaulted the fence and went down the wall into his yard.

Well, Casey didn't see a ghost. The man in white was veterinarian Ralph Farnsworth, whom Casey undoubtedly associated with needles from when he had to be sedated for medical procedures. Hit with one dart already, the last person Casey wanted to see was Doc Farnsworth.

Considering all the bad things that could have happened, the improbable end to this surreal drama was truly miraculous. We later learned that the tranquilizer never injected, so if Casey hadn't encountered Doc, and if he had gotten loose in public, it might have been a much different story. As to how he escaped, a visitor told us Casey was perched on a rock in the side of the yard when he suddenly lunged to the top of the wall and pulled himself over, a testament to his strength and agility. A barrier was erected afterward to prevent further escapes.

Why did he do it? Maybe Casey just wanted his fifteen minutes of fame. And he certainly got that, making news around the world.

May

S	M	T	W	T	F	S
25	26	27	28	29	30	1
2	3	4	5	6	7	8
9	10	11	12	13	14	15
16	17	18	19	20	21	22
23	24	25	26	27	28	29
30	31	1	2	3	4	5

▷ The Harding-Johnson high school football rivalry, which began in 1932, is the oldest continuous competition in the Saint Paul City Conference.

10 Monday

11 Tuesday

🎵 "Whoopee John" Wilfahrt, polka musician, was born today in 1893

12 Wednesday

13 Thursday   Saint Paul Chamber Orchestra

🎵 Daniel A. Robertson, first U of M agriculture professor, was born today in 1813

May

Swede Hollow Cafe

14 Friday	Saint Paul Chamber Orchestra

15 Saturday	Saint Paul Farmers' Market
International Day of Families	Saint Paul Chamber Orchestra
	Bulb Sale, Marjorie McNeely Conservatory

16 Sunday	Saint Paul Farmers' Market
	Saint Paul Chamber Orchestra

The Old Muskego Church, built by Norwegian immigrants, moves from Wisconsin to the Luther Seminary campus in 1904.

Photo © Patricia Bour-Schilla

Why Beep Baseball for the Blind?

Dennis Stern

In 1975, a team of blind baseball players in Saint Paul competed against a team from Arizona in the first World Series. Our Minnesota team was called The Saint Paul Gorillas, and they won the game 15–10. Rules of the game changed from year to year, but the game had beeping "kitten balls" and buzzing bases, as it does today. In the late 1970s and '80s, the Twin Cities became a hotbed for the sport, with young Saint Paul jocks Tom Heinl, Chuck Huttle (both St. Agnes grads), Dennis Huberty, and Kevin Moldenhauer playing and competing at high levels—much like the sixteen to eighteen teams we have today in the United States.

But the game became too competitive in Saint Paul, with teams fighting over top players. The game fell on hard times and was not resurrected here until 2003, when the Saint Paul Midway Lions formed a team with Heinl and Moldenhauer as its nucleus. Many of the new players had physical and nervous system problems related to blindness, such as diabetes, pancreatic failure, and birth defects. One girl, age twenty-four, died after that first year after an unsuccessful pancreas transplant. Teammates mourned her death.

The team continued, however, its common threads a desire for fun comrades, exercise, laughter, and competition. The Midway Fighting Lions have played six seasons, and last year they had eighteen players on the roster. Our brand of beep ball is recreational, because it is played equally by men and women, and half the players are over fifty years old. Practices and games are played on Saturdays at Aldine Park in Saint Paul on Iglehart Avenue.

How can the blind play baseball? The beeping ball is pitched by a sighted coach, who pitches and calls out a four-count pitching motion and release. The pitcher aims at the spot where the batter always swings. The batter swings on the last count, and when the ball has been fairly hit, the batter runs outside of the first or third baseline to a buzzing four-foot rubber base 100 feet away. Meanwhile, six fielders (all wearing blindfolds) listen to a sighted spotter on the field for a number designating the direction of the ball. They then dive in front of the ball, knock it down, and pick it up. If they do this before the runner reaches the base, it is an out. If not, it is a run for the hitting team.

Here are some comments by two of our veteran players:

Beep ball is a fun way to get back in shape, exercise, and have fun. It is a healthy way to mix up the day. The nice thing about beep ball is it is a time for enjoyment and

Back row, L to R: coach John Teisberg, coach Kent Evans, Kevin Moldenhauer, Nikki Mattson, Jennifer Dubin, Matt McCoy, John Schmitz, Tom Heinl, coach Dennis Stern Front row, L to R: Joel Reinbold, Ricardo Maurao, Jerrry Lindau, Mike Hally, Nikki Schlender, Clarence and Nancy Schadegg

camaraderie among participants. All of us start someplace, and the only way any of us will know what we can or cannot do is to try.

—Clarence Schadegg, 55

One of the reasons I like beep ball is that I like to run, and there are very few areas where a totally blind person can run with total abandon. Speed and tactics are important in competition. I can certainly understand why people my age might be afraid to free fall, or even to run in some instances, but . . . we senior citizens need our exercise, too; we can all enjoy the wonderful game of beep ball together.

—Marilyn Highland, 70

The Fighting Lions team has many younger players just learning the sport, and, hopefully, some of them will play in the World Series in Rochester, Minnesota, in August 2010. In 2008, the Minnesota Twins sponsored a special night, when several players from the best fifteen teams in the country put on an exhibition. For more information on beep ball, see www.nbba.org.

May

⇨ St. Catherine University is named
for St. Catherine of Alexandria,
a fourth-century CE Egyptian
philosopher who was martyred
for her Christian faith.

S	M	T	W	T	F	S
25	26	27	28	29	30	1
2	3	4	5	6	7	8
9	10	11	12	13	14	15
16	17	18	19	20	21	22
23	24	25	26	27	28	29
30	31	1	2	3	4	5

17 Monday
Eid al-Adha

18 Tuesday

🐾 Harold G. Kurvers, Bataan death march survivor, was born today in 1918

19 Wednesday
Shavuot

20 Thursday

Visitor enjoying the Mississippi riverfront with downtown Saint Paul in the background

21 Friday

World Day for Cultural Diversity
for Dialogue and Development

🐾 Marice Lipschultz Halper, former president of the International Council
of Jewish Women, was born today in 1928

22 Saturday

Saint Paul Farmers' Market

Dog Stars

The asphalt wavers as we look skyward, follow clouds
that curtain the horizon, usher in night. Later

we build a fire, track sparks, watch them dart.
Amber and orange earthly constellations,

& we name them after lovers we've lost, ship sleeping
at the bottom of this sea,

23 Sunday

childhood dogs
that chased their tails,

circled like we do now. Our backs to the fire we say:
we are lost, we are lucky, drifting & drowning in a sea of stars.
Julia Klatt Singer

Saint Paul Farmers' Market

The Minnesota State Capitol is 434 feet long, 229 feet wide, and 223
feet high. The exterior of its dome is 89 feet in diameter.

My Nana is Rolling over in Her Grave

Andrea Taylor Langworthy

Every time I used to drive down Cretin Avenue, just as I got to Selby, and depending on which direction I was heading, I'd point to the left or right and say, "My father grew up at the end of the street. Down there." Whoever was with me would never look to the right or the left, but would answer, "I know. You always say that."

Alone one Sunday afternoon, with no one to share this nugget of family history, I made a split-second decision and turned to the right. I drove slowly down the block and parked in front of the house where Dad had lived with his two older sisters and their parents, my Nana and Papa. The house hadn't changed—it was the same cream color with chocolate brown trim that I remembered from childhood visits. I could see myself running up the front steps as I had so many Sundays, my little sister way ahead of me as usual. I watched as I scurried along the side to the narrow, long back yard where my siblings and I and our five cousins played tag, chasing each other toward the garage and alley—both off-limits and automatic outs. "Tag. You're it," I said to no one as I pictured the redwood picnic table where we'd eaten so many lunches together.

I could hear the slam of the back screen door as we scrambled up the stairs to the kitchen and through the dining room, each of us hoping to be first to reach the comfy stuffed chair next to the window in the sunroom. The pulsing of the foot massage machine Papa kept next to the chair, right where Dad had placed it one Christmas, sent a shudder up my back. With Papa's permission, we kids always took turns massaging our feet.

The window above the front door was where the spare bedroom had been. My older cousin Nancy stayed with Nana and Papa for a while and that had been her room. One night when we visited, Nana said Nancy was upstairs doing homework, and I should go up to say hello. Nana would have been dismayed to see that Nancy wasn't studying, but was listening to records on her record player and dancing in her stocking feet. "You know who Roy Orbison is, don't you?" she asked. Oh, sure, I nodded, even though we both knew it was a lie.

A knock on the window of my car brought me out of my reverie. A woman asked if I was looking for someone or needed directions. "Oh no," I said. "My grandparents owned this house. My dad grew up here."

She told me that two men had recently bought it. "They're not home now," she said. "I saw them leave a bit a go." She offered to give me their names and said she knew they'd let me go through the house. "You should see what they've done to it," she added, saying how beautiful it was. Did she say *red* living room? I wondered. I didn't dare ask. I could already see it. Ruby walls in Nana's living room. Oh, my. That meant the white lace curtains must be gone, too. Nana wouldn't like this at all, I thought. I thanked the woman and waved good-bye as I began to pull away from the curb. I could hear Nana cluck her tongue as she wondered what had possessed them to change the color of the neutral off-white walls. They probably ripped up the patterned carpeting she'd been so proud of, too. Oh, my.

▷ Hamline was designated as one of thirty-eight colleges to supply men for ambulance work during World War I. Twenty-six students were selected and served with the French army.

S	M	T	W	T	F	S
25	26	27	28	29	30	1
2	3	4	5	6	7	8
9	10	11	12	13	14	15
16	17	18	19	20	21	22
23	24	25	26	27	28	29
30	31	1	2	3	4	5

24 Monday

25 Tuesday

26 Wednesday

🐞 Norman B. Mears, businessman and inventor, was born today in 1904

27 Thursday

May

Blooming tulip in Como Park

28 Friday   Fourth Friday at the Movies

Alfred Nier, physicist and mass spectrometry pioneer, was born today in 1911

29 Saturday   Saint Paul Farmers' Market

Flint Hills International Children's Festival

30 Sunday   Saint Paul Farmers' Market

Flint Hills International Children's Festival

"Vision of Peace," the 60-ton, 38-foot onyx statue in the
City-County building, is unveiled on May 28, 1936.

The Strength of a Woman

New Foundations Writers

The strength of a woman is carrying the burden of family without
        expectation that someone will feel her pain or cry her tears.

The strength of a woman is the first one to wake up and
        the last to go to bed.

The strength of a woman is to pretty and doll up all the masks
        she has to wear in order to survive.

The strength of a woman is crying herself to sleep at night then
        embracing you in the morning with a hug and a smile.

The strength of a woman is my mother,
        a woman who says she's okay when you can tell she's in pain,
        a woman who smiles when the going gets tough and
        a woman who finds laughter after crying.

The strength of a woman is to raise a child she does not know.
The strength of a woman hears a child's cry and
        knows exactly what they want.

The strength of a woman is courage and independence.
The strength of a woman is doing whatever it takes to survive.
The strength of a woman is the backbone that holds everyone together
        . . . behind every strong man there is a strong woman.

The strength of a woman is her ability
        to hold her tongue when her significant other is wrong
        to stop her children from misbehaving with a look in her eye
        to pick herself up and dust herself off
        to make her family smile in the midst of a storm
        to multi-task and adapt to different situations
        to swallow her pride.

The strength of a woman is her unconditional love
  for her children and others.
The strength of a woman is to be a peacemaker.
The strength of a woman is to be able to feel things no one else can.
The strength of a woman is to be able.
The strength of a woman is having faith in God,
  for she knows God is the only one that has her back.
  Helping others when they are in need,
  always there to take the lead.
  Suffering hard times not for long,
  because her will is very strong.
  Makes you happy with lots of jokes,
  most importantly they are jokes of hope.
  Her colors are beautiful—scarlet red—
  lots of blessings upon her head.
  The strength of a woman we'll always know,
  because her strength will always show.

New Girl in Town

Elen Bahr

Each year, a small group of immigrants makes its way into Saint Paul from a foreign and misunderstood land. They may come for love, jobs, the promise of more house for the money. Willing to face great adversity, they pack their belongings and take a giant leap of faith across the mighty Mississippi.

These brave souls move their lives from Minneapolis to Saint Paul. I am one of them; this is my story.

In the spring of 2004, I crossed the Mississippi to begin my new life. I was scared beyond belief. Who knew what went on *over there?* I'd heard stories about a city where downtown was dark by 8 p.m., baseball included a pig, and the only water around was the river that meant to keep me away. My fiancé, Steve, a hometown boy, assured me I was doing the right thing. We had, in fact, found more house for our money, and to my delight, it had both electricity and indoor plumbing.

My west-metro friends promised to visit often. A few of them shied away from discussing the topic. (I did not hear from this group until the emergence of Facebook a few years later, when they could stay in touch without crossing the river.)

Soon after we moved in, friendly neighbors stopped by to introduce themselves. "Welcome to the neighborhood," they would say. "Where did you move from?"

"Minneapolis," I would answer, alongside Steve's reply, "the East Side." I would be met by a blank stare, while heads rapidly turned to engage Steve in a conversation about his past and what brought him to this neighborhood. Steve was among his people. Me, not so much.

By summer, I knew I had to claim my place as a Saint Paulite. I planned to prove myself with a trip to the Farmer's Market at 290 East Fifth Street. My Minneapolis brain told me to find the corner of Second Avenue and Fifth Street. Avenues would run north and south; streets would run east and west—just like in Minneapolis. So not true. I panicked when I realized that downtown Saint Paul had not been built on a grid; it had been built according to the curve of the Mississippi, the river that sought to break me. (If not for the kindness of a Saint Paul police officer who led me home, I might still be lost downtown.)

As the months passed, I was reminded that I did not belong in this town. I longed for a chain of lakes and a downtown I could navigate without a compass.

Image on a City of Saint Paul trash can

Yet this quirky town grew on me. I found myself trying to fit in.

By autumn, I started reading *The Villager*. I drank coffee at Nina's. When people asked me why I had moved all the way to Saint Paul, I told them I had fallen in love with someone for whom I would have crossed an even greater divide. When they asked me if I liked it here, I lied and said that I did.

When winter came, I did not know the rules for snow emergencies. (I fit right in with my neighbors, who did not know them, either.) I took my kids skating at Landmark Center during the Winter Carnival. I read the medallion clues but didn't know where to search.

By spring, I knew people meant the Saints when they said they were going to a ball game.

Five years have passed, and I've made great progress. I've traded Lake Calhoun for my friend, the Mississippi River. I let myself enjoy *A Prairie Home Companion*—in the privacy of my own home, with the windows closed. I have eaten at Mancini's, marched in the Fourth of July parade in St. Anthony Park, and cheered for marathoners on Summit.

When asked where I'm from, I proudly answer, "I've lived in other places, but Saint Paul is my home."

May

Police Work

An oral history excerpt with retired Officer Carolen Bailey as told to Kate Cavett of HAND in HAND Productions for the *Saint Paul Police Oral History Project*

Oral history is the spoken word in print. Oral histories are personal memories shared from the perspective of the narrator. By means of recorded interviews, oral history documents contain spoken memories and personal commentaries of historical significance. These interviews are transcribed verbatim and minimally edited for readability. The greatest appreciation is gained when one can read an oral history aloud.

—Kate Cavett, oral historian
HAND in HAND Productions

I graduated from the University of Minnesota, worked for Ramsey County Welfare Department, and then in 1961 I was hired as a Saint Paul police woman at what was basically a detective-level salary ($200-something a week). Police women were required to have a bachelor's degree. I began in the juvenile department, then Chief McAuliffe transferred me to the homicide unit.

Judge Bertrand Poritsky ordered that if police officers wanted to work undercover to arrest female prostitutes, they would also have to use women officers undercover to arrest male customers to avoid being discriminatory. So when that order came from the court, I went into Assistant Chief Bill McCutcheon's office and told him that I wanted to do this—that it was a great opportunity, and I believed in the equality of it.

Most of our prostitution problem at that time was on Selby and Western. Most of the girls working that area were twelve-, thirteen-, and four-teen-year-olds, very young girls. When I told McCutcheon that I should do this, he said, "Well, we'll try it, but I think you're too old." And I never let him forget it, because that first hour and five minutes, I had eleven arrests, and that first whole day, I had sixty.

Here is a picture signed in 1974 from the very first case I ever worked on. I had just pulled off my blond wig when Sgt. Paul Paulos pointed his camera at me, so I put the wig back on crooked, because I really didn't think he'd take the photo.

I wore colors that would remind anyone of a street light—bright red stop signs and yellow slow-down colors.

In the early years, when I was in Juvenile Division, most of the undercover work involved illegal after-hours clubs; it often was associated with drugs and, of course, sale of alcohol and prostitution, so a lot of

Carolen Bailey walking University Avenue
as a police decoy prostitute in 1974

crimes developed from those clubs. I went into a lot of them more than once. I just changed my appearance. In one case, José Flood—I raided him seven times, got in every single time, looking different—he'd say to me every time, "I'll know you next time."

There was a club called the Turtle Club that was infamous—there were so many problems about it, and nobody could ever get in. So I went over in Minneapolis and made connections with people who were going to go into the Turtle Club. I took a spit sample of the liquor I had while I was in there, and they came in and raided it.

It ended up in the newspaper. I went over to one of the detectives to talk to him when they raided the place, and a uniform patrol officer said, "Look lady, you're not leaving here." And the detective laughed and said, "Don't you know who this is?" And they explained who I was, and we all laughed, and that was the end of it.

The next morning I was called into the chief's office 'cause he was very alarmed that I had been mistreated. The newspaper quoted me as saying it was the most harrowing experience in my career to be arrested and hauled away. I told Chief Lester McAuliffe that that didn't happen, and he was reassured. He was very protective of me, and he used to say to the officers who were my backup, "If one hair on her head is damaged, mail your badges in, don't come in."

May

A Saint Paul garden: blooming is important

The Wisdom of the Urban Gardener

Connie Goldman

Much of her life, my friend Ruthy lived in Saint Paul. She's passed on now, yet every spring I think of her as the time for planting approaches. I know that when I get down close to the earth and feel the soil with my hands, there's a sense of connectedness to the living universe that opens my heart as nothing else can.

Many years ago when I resided in the Highland Park area I used to visit her garden. She was not only a master gardener but a wise woman. "A garden teaches you both patience and acceptance," my friend Ruthy sighed at one point in our conversation. "You put a seed in the ground one morning in the spring and then you wait for it to produce a bloom. Finally a bud comes out and you watch daily for it to open. Then, unexpectedly, overnight a squirrel eats it!" That was just one example of a life lesson in patience and acceptance learned in the garden.

Ruthy found that, no matter what the season, a garden teaches spontaneity and nonattachment. "You have to be able to respond to what's there and to the reality that nothing is permanent—a garden teaches you that you need to get rid of stuff that isn't right for you; it teaches you about birth and death and about what's important in between," she said.

Our conversation for that day was ending. As I waved goodbye and started to walk away, Ruthy had one more bit of garden wisdom to share.

"Blooming is important," she continued. "Coming to fruition is important." And a garden teaches us about audacity, Ruthy explained. "Seeds will blow in from who knows where and they'll shoot out of the ground and start to bloom. That's taught me to put my own two feet on the ground and grow into a flower that blooms—and to be audacious about it."

May

June

Life is too easy in June
In St. Paul so we howl at the moon
And we long for hailstorms,
Big romance, or swarms
Of mosquitoes and they come—rather soon.

Garrison Keillor

June

⇨ June 5, 1942: Captain Richard E.
Fleming of Saint Paul is killed during
the Battle of Midway while leading his
squadron in a mass dive-bombing
assault on an enemy battleship. He
is posthumously awarded the
Congressional Medal of Honor.

JUNE

S	M	T	W	T	F	S
30	31	1	2	3	4	5
6	7	8	9	10	11	12
13	14	15	16	17	18	19
20	21	22	23	24	25	26
27	28	29	30	1	2	3

31 Monday
Memorial Day

1 Tuesday

2 Wednesday

🌐 Dietrich Lange, naturalist, educator, and writer, was born today in 1863

3 Thursday   Music in Mears Park

June

Frederick McGhee and family at his home on 665 University Avenue in 1918

4 Friday

 Francisco Rangel, West Side activist, was born today in 1894

5 Saturday
World Environment Day

Saint Paul Farmers' Market
Saint Paul Chamber Orchestra

6 Sunday

Saint Paul Farmers' Market
Grand Old Day

 Walter Abel, movie actor, was born today in 1898

The Wildlife Rehabilitation Center is established in 1979 by a group of veterinary medicine students on the U of M's Saint Paul campus.

June

The RED Towboats
under the Old High Bridge

Captain Bob Deck

Robert E. Draine worked his whole life on the river. As a licensed steam and diesel engineer, he rode the old Blaske boats up and down the Upper Mississippi until he got the urge to be his own boss. He bought a little fleet of small towboats in 1971 from local riverman Old Man Harris and set up shop in Saint Paul.

Draine's initials are *RED*, so he painted his towboats red and white. Draine-O, as his crews affectionately nicknamed him, called his business Capitol Barge Service. He kept his new fleet of four harbor towboats moored to a small wharf-barge under the old Smith Avenue High Bridge.

Anyone walking across the old bridge between 1969 and 1987 could look over the Shepard Road side of the bridge and see the *Mike Harris, Harry Harris, Lois E,* or *Arlene* tied up to the wharf when towboats weren't busy pushing barges up through the locks at St. Anthony or up the Minnesota River to the grain facilities around Savage.

Draine could do any job on the boats himself. It wasn't unusual for him to get up in the middle of the night, jump into his jon boat, and locate one of the towboats pushing barges somewhere out on the river. He would pull up alongside and clamber aboard, tinker with something in the engine room, then head for the pilothouse to check on channel conditions with the pilot.

He was piloting the *Harry Harris* the day a kid jumped off the High Bridge in front of the office barge. Another deckhand jumped into the river and fished the limp body out, then dragged the jumper onto his boat, which was pushing loaded barges to Minneapolis. Draine-O touched up to the other boat with the *Harry Harris* and we took over the body. Once the boy was lying splayed out on the head deck, he whispered to me, "I wished I hadn't a-done that." Draine-O Grinned at me from the pilothouse. "Good. It means he's gonna make it."

I worked for Draine-O from 1977 until he sold the business in 1987. He hired me as a young deckhand, and after I gained some piloting experience, he took me on as one of his pilots. I was quite proud in 1982, when he allowed me to be the first pilot besides himself to drive the *Lois E*, named after his beloved mother.

Robert E. Draine, towboat operator on the Mississippi River

Working for the cranky old Scotsman was a unique experience. He could be extremely prickly about the smallest details. He chewed me out once for forgetting how to perform some minor task in the engine room of the *Mike Harris*. "I don't have time to retrain my utility men every year!" he growled.

But he could also be extremely patient, as he was once during a drought, when three days in a row I stubbed my tow of barges on a point bar below the 35W Minnesota River bridge. I expected to get a pound of my rump bitten off and handed back to me. Instead, Draine-O simply said, "Well, did you learn anything?"

Years later, he paid me his highest compliment: "Robert, I hope you work for me until they pat dirt on my face."

The barge business dropped off dramatically over the years, and Draine sold out to a big grain outfit from St. Louis the year before they tore down the old High Bridge in 1985. He stuck around for another year, trying to teach the new owners how to run towboats in Saint Paul, but the company went under a few years later. They just weren't able to run a business the same way here that they ran their operations downriver. There are no more men like Draine-O, who could wrench on the engines, turn the ropes loose, drive the boat, and then manage the finances. It's all pencil pushers and business majors now. The days of "towbiz" are gone, and with them a bit of Saint Paul's history.

June

➩ June 8, 1910: Stephen Theobald
is ordained and then appointed
pastor of Saint Peter Claver
Church. He focuses on the
African American community
and educating young people.

S	M	T	W	T	F	S
30	31	1	2	3	4	5
6	7	8	9	10	11	12
13	14	15	16	17	18	19
20	21	22	23	24	25	26
27	28	29	30	1	2	3

7 Monday

Saint Paul Almanac Reading Series

8 Tuesday

9 Wednesday

🕸 Gary Hiebert, newspaper columnist, was born today in 1921

10 Thursday

Music in Mears Park

June

Photo © Patricia Bour-Schilla

The Northern Warehouse Artists' Cooperative in Lowertown

---

11 Friday Saint Paul Chamber Orchestra

Picnicking on a wooden bench overlooking the river an eight-year-old reveals the importance of sword-swallowing French fries, leap-frogging boulders, snatching leftovers from his mother and torpedoing them into a flickering bin.
Nora Murphy

---

12 Saturday Saint Paul Farmers' Market

---

13 Sunday Saint Paul Farmers' Market

June

The golden statue atop the Minnesota State Capitol Building, created in 1906, is officially named *Quadriga: Progress of the State*.

Ta-coumba Aiken

Jennifer Holder

I first met Ta-coumba Aiken in the summer of 2000 at the Peanuts on Parade opening reception in Saint Paul. Aiken was one of seventy-five artists chosen to paint five-foot statues of Snoopy installed around the city to honor Saint Paul–born cartoonist Charles Schulz. Since then, about once a year our paths cross, and despite the lack of regularity, the bond between our artistic spirits—mine, a budding writer/photographer's, and his, a blooming artist/muralist's—has flourished.

One dark night in the fall of 1969, on his way from Evanston, Illinois, to Madison, Wisconsin, guided by the starry skies, sixteen-year-old Aiken missed his exit on the highway, and before long he was entering the state of Minnesota. A walk around the beautiful oak trees in Fair Oaks Park in Minneapolis the following morning turned the previous night's mishap into the beginning of many adventures ahead for him in the Twin Cities. He fell in love with the stillness of his surroundings, the warmth of the people, and their unique rhythm.

Aiken studied at the Minneapolis College of Art and Design, where he learned to harness and integrate his calling as a healer with his creative gifts and, like his mother, to use them sensibly. At the focal points of Aiken's works are mostly circles, which symbolize for him an endless quality. "I go through journeys," he says, some of which lead to his past, while others afford him the opportunity to grow. In his world, the motto that he lives each day is, "I create my art to heal the hearts and souls of people in the communities by evoking a positive spirit."

Aiken's images have been on display in Saint Paul's public spaces, including murals. His first mural was done in 1975 for the Hallie Q. Brown Community Center; a recent one, my favorite, is on the walls of the Jeremiah Project's housing for low-income single mothers and their children on Concordia Avenue. Each mural is created as a gift to the community, says Aiken, and he strives to create imagery that will give people hope.

A recipient of national awards, Aiken has also earned a Bush Foundation Artist's Fellowship for visual arts, as well as numerous Minnesota State Arts Board grants. In winter 2007–2008, Aiken was honored as the featured artist in the exhibit *Call and Response* at the Minneapolis Institute of Arts.

A twenty-five-year resident of Saint Paul, Aiken has been involved with various community organizations, leading workshops for children and serving on arts boards such as the Saint Paul Arts Collective. In 2007, he

Part of one of Ta-coumba Aiken's murals, at Jeremiah Project

was the recipient of the Rondo community's Kwanzaa People's Award for his dedication and ongoing commitment to the community.

Aiken is extremely proud of his role in helping to develop the thriving artists' community in Lowertown. One of the original residents of Lowertown Lofts Artists' Cooperative, the first working and living space for artists, Aiken pioneered with other innovative people to make things better for everybody.

From the window of his co-op, he sees the mighty Mississippi River, and in his soft voice he talks to the flowing waters and believes someone downstream in the deep South will hear his message. He shares his soul with the river, and it also lives in the swirls and lines of his murals. "Things are okay," the spirits whisper.

When Aiken's children were toddlers, he thought of moving to a single-family house so they would have a back yard to play in. "No need to do that," they said. "Saint Paul is our back yard." Forty years from the first time he saw the shadows of the city from the highway, Saint Paul is still the place where Aiken lives and plays.

"Here in Saint Paul, it's not unusual for people to run into each other and simply say 'hello' and not get in your business," Aiken has said of our sporadic, accidental meetings, "As long as we do things to build self-confidence and to give a real positive sense of space."

June

▷ June 17, 1882: Officer Daniel O'Connell, the first Saint Paul policeman to be killed, is shot while investigating two suspicious men with handguns on Dayton Avenue.

S	M	T	W	T	F	S
30	31	1	2	3	4	5
6	7	8	9	10	11	12
13	14	15	16	17	18	19
20	21	22	23	24	25	26
27	28	29	30	1	2	3

14 Monday

Flag Day

🐞 Moira Harris, writer and publisher, was born today in 1935

15 Tuesday

16 Wednesday

17 Thursday

Music in Mears Park

Twin Cities Jazz Festival

Music and Movies, *District Del Sol*

June

Padelford Packet Boat moored at its dock on Harriet Island

18 Friday	Twin Cities Jazz Festival
	Back to the '50s Car Show

🏵 Blanche Yurka, Bohemian-American theater and movie actress, was born today in 1887

19 Saturday	Saint Paul Farmers' Market
Juneteenth	Twin Cities Jazz Festival
	Back to the '50s Car Show

20 Sunday	Saint Paul Farmers' Market
Fathers' Day	Back to the '50s Car Show
World Refugee Day	

June 15, 1933: William Hamm, Jr.'s grandson is kidnapped at the corner of Minnehaha and Greenbrier, near the Hamm's brewery, as he walks home.

June

Used Bikes and Library Cards

James McKenzie

"When I ride my bike, I can go anywhere I want," the man said. "I can point my bike to the east and pedal off in that direction. I can turn around and go west. I can bike north or south; no one can stop me. When I get tired, I can lay down on the grass and look at the sky. It's so beautiful." That's about as basic and ordinary an expression of the joys of bicycling as one can imagine.

But this was also a statement about freedom and healing, for the speaker was a client of Saint Paul–based Center for Victims of Torture (CVT), established by Governor Perpich, which celebrates its twenty-fifth birthday in 2010. He was speaking to the center's storied "bicycle lady," Cynthia McArthur, who had just repaired and returned to him a bicycle she had previously scrounged, shaped up, and passed along to him.

"He was overjoyed," she remembers. "'If I had a home,' he said, 'I'd invite you in as if you were my sister.'" If this man is like most of the center's new clients, he will have had two family members killed or disappeared and three others besides himself imprisoned and tortured. Among the Center's 2008 clients, 36 percent of them had been detained/imprisoned two to three times, 11 percent four or more times. The average length of their longest detention/imprisonment was 294 days. This client, as it happens, had been imprisoned for twelve years—not hard to envision the joys he took from bicycling freely.

Cynthia gathers her bikes from a variety of sources, haunting the annual spring and fall neighborhood cleanups, securing donations from community members, even working out parts at cost—or swaps—from Sibley Bike Depot, Grand Performance, Boehm's, and other local bike businesses.

Like Cynthia's volunteering, much of CVT's work is invisible. No signs outside identify its two clinics. Thousands of people pass by these large, ordinary-looking, well-maintained Victorian homes every day without guessing that they are world-renowned centers that have treated thousands of Twin Cities' residents. Counting the center's several clinics in Africa, CVT has served more than 25,000 people, "putting the soul back in the body," as one client summed up her healing process.

I was recently reminded of the joyful expression of unlimited possibilities that the bicyclist experienced when I encountered another client who was stunned to learn that Saint Paul's libraries are free. "I stay here?" he said, a question at first. He had received his card and wanted to know

A bicycle in the city: a joyful conveyance

if he had to take the ride back home I was supposed to give him. When I realized he was asking permission to stay at the library instead, I said he could do what he wanted, knowing he could walk home on his own. "I stay here," he said, repeatedly, all the way to the library door, bidding me good-bye and thanking me again and again. "I stay here; I stay here; I stay here," a preference and a celebration of his new status, a holder of a Saint Paul library card.

So it is with simple possessions easily taken for granted: a used bicycle, a humble library card. They point to infinities of possibility. Rudy Perpich, Jr., home on break from law school a little more than twenty-five years ago, had some sense of those possibilities when, as a member of an Amnesty International chapter, he said to his dad, "You're the governor; you could do something about torture." The rest is history; possibilities are still multiplying.

June

S	M	T	W	T	F	S
30	31	1	2	3	4	5
6	7	8	9	10	11	12
13	14	15	16	17	18	19
20	21	22	23	24	25	26
27	28	29	30	1	2	3

▷ June 18, 1913: The Saint Paul Federation of Women Teachers, Local 23, is founded and affiliates itself with the American Federation of Labor.

21 Monday

Summer Solstice

22 Tuesday

🐞 Richard Drew, inventor of masking tape and Scotch Tape, was born today in 1899

23 Wednesday

24 Thursday

Music in Mears Park

Music and Movies, *District Del Sol*

June

Egret at the shore of the Mississippi River near the Pool and Yacht Club

---

25 Friday
Fourth Friday at the Movies

> There was a young poet on Laurel
> Whose writing turned vaguely immoral
> In June, Not obscene
> Not blue—but so green
> And the adjectives utterly floral.
> *Garrison Keillor*

---

26 Saturday
Saint Paul Farmers' Market

International Day Against Drug Abuse and Illicit Trafficking

International Day in Support of Victims of Torture

Nick Coleman, veteran journalist and columnist, was born today in 1950

---

27 Sunday
Saint Paul Farmers' Market

Patrick J. Towle, developer of Log Cabin Syrup, was born today in 1835

A June 23, 1962, hailstorm breaks 90 percent of the greenhouse glass on the U of M's Saint Paul Campus.

June

Fire on Pig's Eye Island

Matthew Van Tassell

Pig's Eye Island owes its name to a nineteenth-century trader, Pig's Eye Parrant, who sold liquor and guns along the Mississippi's watery highway. The nearby settlers took his name for their growing town until they decided the more mundane sobriquet Saint Paul might lend more dignity to a territory that was soon to become a state. Pig's Eye Island kept the rascal's name because no one gave a damn about a backwater stretch so swampy and prone to flooding. Only individuals too crazy to have any sense or too poor to afford decent land would ever settle there.

Divorced geographically from the growing settlement by a curve in the river's course and mentally from the attention of the town's more prosperous inhabitants, the island soon became almost forgotten by all but the poor and the crazy. Or by the unfortunate souls who might be both.

My brothers, sisters, and I were raised on Pig's Eye Island in the 1940s. Situated about three miles south and downstream from Saint Paul's sewage disposal plant, we were in an ideal position to retrieve any floating debris that might wash up on the island's shores during one of the annual floods. We were little pirates, constantly searching for hidden treasure in the flotsam that found its way to our private beach. There was all sorts of interesting booty: furniture, parts of buildings, lanterns, old river buoys, toys. We claimed them as our own.

Our house was a green tarpaper shack measuring about twenty by thirty feet. There was a kitchen, the only entrance or exit door, and a two-burner stove and icebox. Another item in the tiny room was a slop pail. We kids used this as a toilet during the winter, when it was too cold to make the frigid trek to the outhouse. Every morning my father would take the bucket and empty its contents into the two-holer some distance from our shack.

To the left of the kitchen, another room ran the length of the house. There four of my brothers and sisters slept, along with my mother and father. For some reason, possibly because I was first born, I was privileged to have not-quite-sole possession of the remaining room at the rear of the shack. I shared this space with the oldest of my sisters, Joy, who slept in a crib near one of the room's two windows.

We had no electricity, and for water we had a pump outside that we primed each time we used it. On its handle hung half a coconut shell, used as a family drinking cup. Kerosene lamps provided dim light at night. A battery-powered radio was the only concession to the twentieth century in our nineteenth-century lives. It brought the outside world into our consciousness. Shows like *Inner Sanctum, Grand Central Station, Jack Benny, Just Plain Bill, Fibber McGee and Molly, Stella Dallas,* and *The Shadow* fueled our imaginations. In our minds, we saw the scenes these shows thrust at us using only voices and sound effects. *Inner Sanctum,* with its creaking door and sinister voice "welcoming" us inside, could scare the bejeepers out of us.

One payday night, my father was entertaining himself at the Hook 'Em, Cow Bar. My mother and I were listening to *Lights Out,* a show designed to cause nightmares. That night the story was about an escaped homicidal maniac hiding in the woods in the dark of night. Since it was black as pitch outside and we were sitting in the middle of the island's thick woods, it was not hard for us to conjure the maniac's murderously hostile eyes peering at us through our lamplit window. My mother was as frightened as I was, which served to scare me even more. Until my father came home late that night, we were too petrified with fear to sleep.

This was the power the brown box could wield, and the writers who wrote the stories engendering those reactions certainly earned their pay. Without the crutch of television's moving images, our minds were free to manufacture their own, more frightening pictures. Mom said she didn't understand why they would broadcast something that might scare someone in their audience to death, yet the next time we heard that creaking door, there we were, glued to the box, albeit with our feet off the floor.

One spring in the late 1940s, my father helped Richie Dufor throw up a shack near our own. Dufor had just been paroled from prison, had nowhere to live, and my dad felt sorry for him. Living with Richie was a woman named Ciel and her son, Kenny. Richie scared the daylights out

Photo © Mathew Van Tassell

Matthew at the beach . . . actually his front yard during spring flooding of the Mississippi River in 1946

of us kids. Often when he was drunk, he would fly into rages. Sometimes we could hear Ciel crying, and several times my father went down to their place and threatened Richie to keep him from abusing her.

Late one night, while my father was gone celebrating payday, and after Richie and Ciel had been living near us for several months, my mother woke me. "Look out the window," she commanded in a whisper as she roused me from sleep. Her tone communicated urgency combined with fear, and I was instantly awake. I heard animal-like noises coming from outside, and my heart began to beat fast as I imagined all kinds of reasons for the horrific howling coming from the direction of Richie and Ciel's shack.

"Come here, quick." She was at the window now, and I could see an orange glow through the white curtain. I untangled myself from my blanket and hurried to her side. "Look at their house." I looked and saw flames roaring from the windows and door of the black tarpaper structure. Backlit by fire, the shack looked spooky. I crouched by the window, my mother close beside me, watching the terrible show. From somewhere I heard myself say, "Isn't that a shame," and felt, rather than saw, my mother look at me.

Outside, Richie screamed and laughed as he prowled the dark, away from the area lit by the fire. It was him I heard howling when I awakened. Sometimes his voice trailed off into soft, crooning cries of "Ciel, Ciel," her name drawn out long and mournfully, like the wail of the steam locomotives we heard in the night. Horrified, I wondered if Kenny and his mother might still be in the blazing shack.

My mother left my side and went to the door. Taking one of our kitchen chairs, she wedged it beneath the knob. Seconds later, we heard Richie at the front of our house.

"Phyllis. Hey, Phyllis." His voice had changed to a harsh whisper as he called through the door. We heard him on the wooden step outside as he shifted his weight. The nails creaked. "Hey, Phyllis. I got those canned tomatoes of yours."

My mother motioned me not to make a sound, but she needn't have bothered. My throat was paralyzed. I crept closer to her as she reached into the corner where Dad kept his rifle.

"That's all right, Richie," she called out. "I gave them to Ciel to keep." As she unwrapped the oily rag my dad kept around the weapon, she motioned for me to hand her the box of cartridges sitting on the cupboard top.

"No, Phyllis. Ciel said she wanted me to give them back to you. We won't be needing them. Come on. Open the door and I'll set them inside for you." His voice was calm and persuasive. I looked at my mother to make sure she wasn't falling for it.

She was loading the rifle.

*Mathew's early practice as a carpenter in front
of the family home on Pig's Eye Island*

"Thanks, Richie," she said through the door as she slid the rifle's bolt home. "You keep them. I think you'd better get away from the house now."

There was silence for several seconds on the other side of the door. The smooth metallic noise made by the gun's bolt seemed to serve as final punctuation to my mother and Richie's conversation. The step creaked as a weight was removed from it. We moved to the window and saw Richie's silhouette outlined in flames as he ran past the pyre that had been his home. We heard the grind of his car's starter, and then he roared past our house, heading up the road with his lights off.

My mother sat in a chair by the table with Dad's rifle across her lap. I looked out the window at what was left of the shack. The fire had nearly gone out, for there was almost nothing left to burn. Red-hot embers outlined its perimeter. Here and there, stubborn little flames worked on something that had not burned, but nothing remained above the height of the long grass in the yard.

We didn't sleep for the rest of the night, and at dawn all there was to show that we once had had neighbors was a pile of smoking ashes. When Dad came home, we told him what had happened and the way Richie had tried to get Mom to open the door. Dad unloaded the rifle and rewrapped it in the cloth. He told Mom even if she had never learned to drive, he was glad she had paid attention when he taught her about guns.

Later we learned that Ciel had taken Kenny and left after becoming fed up with Richie's abuse. Richie went berserk when he found them gone, and that was what had led to their house's cremation. That Richie was a dangerous man when crossed no one doubted. But until that night, none of the adults who knew him realized to what lengths he would go to prove just how crazy he really was.

In Something Called Urban Renewal

Ashanti Austin

According to the University of Minnesota website, the Central Corridor will link three of the greatest traffic generators in the region: downtown Minneapolis, the University of Minnesota, and downtown Saint Paul with an above-ground train (the LRT) running from downtown Saint Paul, past the Minnesota State Capitol, along University Avenue, through the university's Minneapolis campus, to the Hiawatha light rail line in downtown Minneapolis. In 2006, at the prompting of Mayor Christopher Coleman, the Central Corridor Planning Committee laid out its vision for the future of the corridor:

> The Central Corridor will build on its assets to become a place that has stronger businesses, more vibrant neighborhoods, and more beautiful urban places. Along University Avenue and in the downtown, the Corridor will invite residents, shoppers, employees and visitors to linger on safe, pedestrian-friendly, attractive, tree-lined boulevards; establish a home and sense of stable and diverse neighborhoods; and work and invest in an area that provides a range of employment and economic opportunities.

As the light rail approaches, many are concerned about the impact construction will have on businesses and communities on the Central Corridor route. For some, the light rail is reminiscent of the urban renewal projects of the 1960s, which resulted in the construction of Interstate 94 through the center of Saint Paul's independent and thriving Black community. This project had devastating effects, which, according to the Rondo Avenue Inc. website, "displaced thousands of African-Americans into a racially segregated city, and a discriminatory housing market, that we weren't ready for and that wasn't ready for us."

In Saint Paul, despite its relative poverty, the Rondo community was unique because a large number of its businesses were Black-owned. Rondo residents were well educated, safe to leave their doors unlocked, mutually supporting, and independent from outside communities. When I-94 was built, many Black-owned businesses and over 608 homes were destroyed. Only in the late 1980s were measures taken by the Summit-University Planning Council to account for the devastating impacts of I-94.

Similar urban renewal projects begun throughout the country in the 1950s–1970s disproportionately affected low-income minority and African-American communities by destroying huge sections of their neighborhoods.

The Hiawatha Line in Minneapolis

Unlike these ravaging governmental programs, which centered on "producing wealth through real estate developments," the current project, says leading specialist on LRT construction mitigation Bill Knowles, "is what you asked for."

But what exactly did we ask for? Moreover, will the result still amount to the dislocation of low-income residents? How does the construction of the LRT figure in the haunted debates about community growth, gentrification, and dislocation in a post-industrial city?

In response to Saint Paul's history with Rondo Avenue (later renamed Concordia Avenue), city and county officials have made an effort to disseminate information and listen to the concerns of the community. In this sense, University Avenue is not a repeat of I-94, when local residents were unable to participate to ensure the health of their community. Federal Environmental Justice Title VI law requires transportation projects not negatively impact communities of color and low-income communities as was common with earlier federal projects.

As late as mid-summer of 2009, however, concerns of the Saint Paul community are yet to be fully addressed in negotiations with the Metropolitan Council. Community organizations and the University Avenue Business Association (UABA) want support for small businesses throughout construction of the LRT to mitigate impending tax increases and loss of revenue. Community organizations and UABA interests include providing support for small businesses before, during, and after the construction of the LRT to mitigate impending tax increases and loss of revenue. The Aurora/St. Anthony Neighborhood Development Corporation has provided the strongest voice arguing that the project may not be focusing enough on the real needs and issues of the community. Executive Director Nieeta Prestley of ASANDC states, "If the underlying premise is to 'spur' economic development, then the building of the LRT must be done right from start to the finish."

The Central Corridor Planning Commission's vision statement warrants a response. Although countermeasures are in place to address anticipated problems, and although Bill Knowles argues that increased foot traffic will offset parking problems, gentrification is here to stay. This is not another Rondo. It is still Rondo. What does this mean?

The LRT along University will produce the same process of dislocations that started in the mid-1950s. Light rail is another signifier of the cultural shift that has already taken place in a district central to post-baby boomer business and other urban professionals. The Central Corridor is one response to this shift in our economic climate. If people had instead asked for more jobs, cleaner streets, a remedy to traffic congestion, less private sector and more service-centered economic growth, then they would have found out that urban renewal is not usually associated with an equitable assembly of interests. According to political scientist Clarence Stone, "Land values and economic growth are the key issues in community politics." Urban renewal is the struggle for that land.

University Avenue did not achieve the same community coherence following construction of I-94 that earlier transportation projects did. I-94 reversed many gains of the Rondo community, and those losses reflect a moment in history in which issues of race and class intersected with the national agenda, which continues to distort the importance of Black entrepreneurship, leadership, academic merit, fellowship, and values of African-American communities.

As for the LRT, it is still too early to make clear socioeconomic projections. As we pass through this precarious moment, however, how willing are we to look at Rondo's past in order to rebuild our commitment to a sustainable community, with all of its members represented? The good news is the involvement of the community, in all of its diversity, and those community efforts to raise awareness and consolidate community interests over those of commerce.

July

Photo © Tobechi Tobechukwu

Just one more day
A yellow daisy day
A too hot sidewalk, barefoot day
A last mosquito day
A sunset at the beach day
One scorcher day to hold midwinter
At bay

Marcie Rendon

143

JULY

S	M	T	W	T	F	S
27	28	29	30	1	2	3
4	5	6	7	8	9	10
11	12	13	14	15	16	17
18	19	20	21	22	23	24
25	26	27	28	29	30	31

⇨ "Life is beautiful . . . drink every last drop. Kindness manifests it's own majesty, and love is smiling at someone on the street that you don't know."
—John Wozniak, rock musician

28 Monday

29 Tuesday

A paradise night in July—
The stars—a backyard—you and I—
And I do believe—
Any more joie de vivre
We might actually rise up and fly
Garrison Keillor

🐞 Joan Davis, movie and television actress, was born today in 1907

30 Wednesday

1 Thursday

Music in Mears Park
Music and Movies, *District del Sol*
Boom Bap Village

July Fourth fireworks seen from the High Bridge in Saint Paul

---

2 Friday

Boom Bap Village

Taste of Minnesota

🐞 Gentile Yarusso, writer of local history, was born today in 1912

---

3 Saturday

Saint Paul Farmers' Market

Taste of Minnesota

Hmong International Sports Tournament
and Freedom Festival

---

4 Sunday

Independence Day

Saint Paul Farmers' Market

Taste of Minnesota

Hmong International Sports Tournament
and Freedom Festival

A cannon shot fired in Fountain Cave during a Fourth of July
celebration in 1831 nearly collapses the entry.

Carving out a Life in Saint Paul

Frank Brown

The year was 1995; I began working at Quarra Stone Company in Madison, Wisconsin, as a hand stone carver. Not knowing how the work that I created would be attached to monumental buildings across the U.S., I didn't realize the impact this job would have on my career. Many of the projects contracted by this company have become part of the fabric of American architecture on many historical buildings throughout the United States. While working there, I hand-carved much of the stone ornaments for such buildings as the John Hancock Center in Chicago, the Fourth Street Presbyterian Church in Chicago (one of the largest Presbyterian Churches in the country), and the exterior balusters on Minnesota's State Capitol.

It was not until the summer of 1997 that I arrived in Saint Paul and noticed my work at the State Capitol building in Minnesota; it was my first time visiting the state. My first home in Saint Paul was the Days Inn, I asked if I could have a room with a small kitchenette, because I would be staying at the hotel for some time. The clerk assigned me a top floor room. When I entered the room, I opened the curtains and was excited to see the State Capitol building. It was then that I remembered carving the balusters back in Madison two years earlier. I felt a strong sense of connection to the City of Saint Paul and the State of Minnesota.

A week later I went to the Capitol to see if it was possible for me to see the balusters up close. When I entered the building and approached the information booth, I explained who I was, and my interest in seeing the balusters. She said that there were no tours scheduled at this time and that it would be difficult to allow me to see the exterior of the building. I would have to come back for a scheduled tour. I was a little disappointed, but stated I would return. I had parked in front of the building and was a few feet from my car door when I heard someone call out my childhood name—Frankie. I had not heard my name called in this way for 20 years or more.

I turned around and faced an old childhood friend whom I had known since I was six years old. I had grown up around his family for seven years before my family relocated to another city. He was working at the Capitol in the security department. We were thrilled to see each other. He had heard over his radio that an artist named Frank Brown, who had carved many of the stone ornaments, was in the building and wanted to see the work up close. He called down to the information booth, and when he found out that I was leaving, ran down to the front and found me.

Photo © Patricia Bour-Schilla

Sculptor Frank Brown

He was nice enough to escort me out to see some of my work. This only made me feel more positive about moving to Minnesota, and I moved into the Lowertown Artists' Cooperative on November 1, 1997.

Just like the earliest pioneers, my experience in Minnesota has been challenging, but I have overcome these challenges and continued my career as a sculptor in Lowertown, and now own my own business at 180 East Fifth Street, Suite 220, called Colors of Art.

Since moving to Saint Paul, I have had many struggles trying to live as a full-time sculptor. In 2003, I founded the Lowertown Artist Association, and was director until 2005. In April 2008, I opened Colors of Art, where I work and also display both my own artwork and that of many other artists in the Twin Cities.

I have displayed artwork at various office lobbies in downtown Saint Paul, and helped other artists do likewise. These offices include Unity One Credit Union, PAK Properties Lowery Building, Pino's Pizzeria, Anderson Cleaners, Allegra Print and Imaging, Great River Dental, Saint Paul Neighborhood Network, Saint Paul Radiology's Fourth Street lobby, Heimie's Haberdashery, and The Bulldog restaurant in Lowertown.

I have helped many artists pursue their dream of making a living as artists in Minnesota, and I continue to look for support from local companies to display the work of local artists in their office spaces in downtown Saint Paul. My experience here has been challenging, but it is through my faith in God, and the support of friends I call my secret angels, that I have survived through the difficult times.

JULY

S	M	T	W	T	F	S
27	28	29	30	1	2	3
4	5	6	7	8	9	10
11	12	13	14	15	16	17
18	19	20	21	22	23	24
25	26	27	28	29	30	31

⇨ "You can't have an underworld without an overworld, if you know what I mean." —Nate Bomberg, 1930s Pioneer Press reporter

---

5 Monday

Saint Paul Almanac Reading Series

Independence Day observed

---

6 Tuesday

Nine Nights of Music Series, Minnesota History Center

🌐 James Griffin, Saint Paul's first African American police captain, was born today in 1917

---

7 Wednesday

---

8 Thursday

Music in Mears Park

Music and Movies, *District del Sol*

Photo © Tom Conlon

Connie's Creamy Cone on Dale

9 Friday

10 Saturday   Saint Paul Farmers' Market
                                          Dragon Festival and
                                          Dragon Boat Races

🎭 Roger Awsumb, local television's Casey Jones, was born today in 1928

11 Sunday   Saint Paul Farmers' Market
World Population Day   Dragon Festival and
Total Solar Eclipse   Dragon Boat Races

Anthony Yoerg opens Minnesota's first brewery below
what is now Saint Paul's River Centre on July 6, 1849.

Hidden Falls Staircase

Kim Kankiewicz

We met him on the bank of the Mississippi, near a swaybacked cottonwood with a ganglion of exposed roots. He was a spry, white-haired man of about seventy. My children and I were in search of the waterfall at Hidden Falls Park, and our new friend was eager to set us in the right direction.

"Make sure to look at the staircase," he said, as we tramped through the grass away from the river. "It was a WPA project. It's really something."

The man told us he'd worked at the Ford plant until retiring and would visit the falls on his lunch breaks. He said he lived nearby and took frequent walks along the river. Before I could reply, he pointed to a pavilion that had come into view. "Follow the trail through those trees just beyond the pavilion," he said. "The staircase is at the top of the falls."

As we stepped from the August sun onto the shaded trail, we could hear the waterfall. My son ran ahead to spy it first. When I caught up, I saw my son's disappointment before I spotted the trickle of water that perhaps explained why we were the sole party hunting for Hidden Falls that day.

"Maybe there's more water earlier in the summer," I said. "Why don't we go see the staircase?"

The staircase, in contrast to the falls, was a child's daydream made real. Its stone steps wound along a fairy-tale wall. At the top we found an overlook we'd passed on our drive down Mississippi River Boulevard to the park entrance. We could as easily have found a fire-breathing dragon or a sleeping princess. Halfway back down the staircase, I sat against the wall and let the kids play. They climbed and jumped and shouted as characters in another world. I wished I could thank the white-haired man for sending us to this place of man-made wonder amidst God-made beauty.

Months later, as public officials and media pundits compared our nation's economic crisis to the Great Depression and some suggested New Deal strategies to speed our recovery, I wished again that I could talk with that man. I wanted to know what allowed his parents' generation to confront the fear of Not Enough with a stone staircase that enraptured my children seventy years later. I wanted to stand upon inherited wisdom the way that swaybacked cottonwood, though it looked so precarious, stood upon a great expanse of tenacious roots burrowing deep into the earth.

A Saint Paul Storm

Ellie Thorsgaard

This is my favorite memory of Saint Paul. It is a scary one, but still, it's my favorite. It happened on Mother's Day 2004, when there was a big storm. Here is what happened to me.

I had a wonderful day at the Minnesota History Center with both sets of my grandparents, my mom, and my dad. I enjoyed all the exhibits, especially the weather one, though I was scared by the tornado room. Little did I know I was about to experience a real tornado.

When we got home, it was drizzling lightly. My dad and I decided to go on a bike ride, since the sky was mostly sunny and warm. And as my dad always says, "We aren't witches. Water doesn't make us melt."

I was too young to ride my own bike, so I rode on a tag-along, a bike attached to the back of my dad's bike.

After a few blocks, it started raining harder. My dad said we wouldn't go on our normal route: we would just circle Como Lake a few times. Suddenly the wind started blowing harder, and the air felt foggy and heavy. We kept biking. Then Dad stopped pedaling. The wind was blowing so hard that it nearly blew me off my bike. Dad yelled for me to go lie down in the ditch. I lay so close to the ground I could smell the grass. Now the rain was pelting down on me. I could barely hear cars, even though I was right next to a street. The trees were swinging side to side, and I could hear branches crashing to the ground all around me. I was so scared. I wished Dad would finish with the bikes and come down in the ditch with me. I looked up and saw that the sky was green! It looked just like the tornado room at the museum. My fears suddenly multiplied. This was a tornado!

Before I had time to become utterly terrified, a small white car pulled up. The door opened, and an old lady's head poked out. She called out to Dad, "Do you and your daughter need a ride?"

Dad hurried me out of the ditch and into the car. It was super-crowded, with an old woman, my dad, and me in the back. Two more old women sat in the front. The car smelled musty but felt oddly safe for a stranger's car. Shivers ran down my spine as I looked out my window. The sky had suddenly turned dark, making it look like night, and rain was falling so fast that it looked like fog.

I snapped back when I heard the radio DJ announce a tornado warning for Ramsey County. While I was listening, I realized we had pulled into our driveway. I leaped out of the car and ran into my house. I ran to my mom and hugged her. I was so happy to be home.

JULY

S	M	T	W	T	F	S
27	28	29	30	1	2	3
4	5	6	7	8	9	10
11	12	13	14	15	16	17
18	19	20	21	22	23	24
25	26	27	28	29	30	31

⇨ "We are more casual about qualifying the people we allow to act as advocates in the courtroom than we are about licensing electricians." –Warren Burger, Supreme Court justice

12 Monday

13 Tuesday

Nine Nights of Music Series, Minnesota History Center

David V. Taylor, African American historian and educator, was born today in 1945

14 Wednesday

15 Thursday

Music in Mears Park

Music and Movies, *District del Sol*

Ernest DuCharme, noted citrus plant pathologist, was born today in 1916

Photo © Heatherjo Gilbertson

Monarch caterpillar

16 Friday   Highland Fest

17 Saturday   Saint Paul Farmers' Market

Highland Fest

Rondo Days

⚾ Toni Stone, first Negro League woman baseball player, was born today in 1921

18 Sunday   Saint Paul Farmers' Market

Highland Fest

Edward Phelan, John Hays, and William Evans, former soldiers at Fort
Snelling, file claims for land in what later becomes Saint Paul, July 1838.

My First Month in the U.S.

Richard Shwe

I came to the U.S. from a refugee camp in Thailand on April 2, 2008, at 9:30 p.m. I flew to the Minneapolis airport. In the airport, I saw my friends, who came to pick me up.

When I saw Minnesota at night, it was very beautiful, but the weather was very cold. I saw a lot of snow. In my life I had never seen snow, this was the first time for me.

In the morning, I tried to get up, but I could not get up so I slept again, because I came by airplane for twenty-one hours. It was a long time. I flew all day and night and it was a long time for me. In Asia it was day and in the U.S. it was night.

Everything was new for me. In the first week, I went to church and came back to my friend's house, but could not go inside, because the door was locked. Inside, nobody was at home. I waited outside in the snow about thirty minutes.

Playing Red Wing

Marjorie (Weaver) Bednarek

My father, Sonny Weaver, knew the Mississippi River's currents and sandbars as well as he knew the streets of his West Side neighborhood. Born in the river flats in 1891, he learned to love and respect the river. Hence no one was surprised when he secured a job as a violinist aboard a river boat in the early 1900s. The boat cruised round trip on summer nights from Saint Paul to Hastings, offering dancing and libations along the way.

One evening, two passengers, a man and a woman, became particularly inebriated, calling out various musical requests to the band.

"Play 'Red Wing'!" The man shouted over the din of the crowd.

Some band members began to play the song, but since Dad was not familiar with the tune, he stood silent.

"Stop!" the inebriate demanded. "You!" he pointed at Dad. "You, with the fiddle—you play 'Red Wing'!"

The evening ended on a sour note with the inebriated couple staggering toward the exit in a vain attempt to remain upright, bumping and jostling anyone who hindered their path.

"That #@@#&^% fiddle player wouldn't play 'Red Wing'!" the man snarled as he swayed sideways and fell against his companion.

Sonny Weaver with his violin

Like a domino, the woman fell against Dad, who toppled over the side of the boat and into the river. Clutching his violin case, he kept himself afloat with his free arm, swimming with the current while trying to reach a sandbar near the shoreline.

He was nearly out of breath and considering releasing his grip on the violin case when his foot touched the sandbar. He climbed out of the water and walked the familiar neighborhood streets toward home.

Reluctant to disturb his sleeping parents, he climbed the stairs to his room and fell into bed, exhausted.

The next morning, his father's voice held more than a tinge of hysteria when he called up the stairs, "Sonnyyyyyyy, are you up there?"

A neighbor had come to the door with the morning newspaper. Its headline read MAN DROWNS IN THE MISSISSIPPI RIVER. Shortly thereafter, Dad learned to play the song "Red Wing," but not before the Saint Paul newspaper printed a retraction to let the world know he was still alive.

JULY

S	M	T	W	T	F	S
27	28	29	30	1	2	3
4	5	6	7	8	9	10
11	12	13	14	15	16	17
18	19	20	21	22	23	24
25	26	27	28	29	30	31

⇨ "The test of a first-rate intelligence is the ability to hold two opposed ideas in mind at the same time and still retain the ability to function."
—F. Scott Fitzgerald, writer

19 Monday

20 Tuesday

Nine Nights of Music Series,
Minnesota History Center

🌐 Larry Millett, architectural historian, journalist, and novelist, was born today in 1947

21 Wednesday

22 Thursday

Music in Mears Park
Music and Movies, *District del Sol*
Rice Street Festival

Lily pad in Como Lake

23 Friday Rice Street Festival

Matt Birk, professional football center, was born today in 1976

24 Saturday Saint Paul Farmers' Market

Rice Street Festival

25 Sunday Saint Paul Farmers' Market

"Law is order in liberty, and without order, liberty is social chaos." —Archbishop John Ireland

Reminiscences of the Old Farmers' Market

Donna Martin

Both my parents' French Canadian families were farmers in the Hugo-Centerville area, settling there in the 1880s after emigrating through Quebec. They were hardworking, industrious newcomers, striving to clear land in order to raise crops to support their families and livestock. Part of their farming operation was devoted to raising extra foodstuffs to be sold at the Saint Paul Farmers' Market.

My personal experiences were with my grandmother, Louise Marier; I helped her during the summer months in 1949 and 1950. It took many days just to get ready for a weekend stint at the stall she rented yearly in the old, expansive market with its row after row of canopied space. She grew extra vegetables for the market, as well as many flowers. She also sold dressed fryers, stewing hens, and geese at times. Her real claims to fame, however, were her watermelons. The sandy, loamy soil adjacent to Rondeau Lake near Centerville was the perfect medium for growing huge, succulent melons. I remember working at the market as a very tiring experience, with all the hustle and bustle, and her customers coming back week after week to her stall for a liberal dose of her broken English conversation and farm-fresh produce—much the same as the farmers' market is today!

My father, Ivan Bernier, was a wonderful storyteller, highlighting his reminiscences of life at the farmers' market so that we, his six children, could fully grasp his experiences growing up in the early 1900s.

His family always grew extra potatoes for sale in late fall or early winter at the market. One of my favorite stories was about the many sales he made of 100-pound sacks of potatoes destined for the wealthy families of Summit Hill. Hired help were sent to the market on the streetcar to make the purchases, but of course they had no way of getting their potatoes back to the homes, so Dad made his deliveries after his day at the market was done. He told us about the beautiful ornate homes he saw, their cellars full to the top with cases of delicacies. Pretty heady stuff for a young farm boy experiencing big city life firsthand. Once he saw a crate of the largest oranges he had ever seen, and temptation to taste the fruit was too great for his soul. He was thoroughly disappointed: it was very, very sour—and only years later did he find that the "orange" had actually been a grapefruit. So much for tasting of the forbidden fruit!

Photo © Charles P. Gibson

Old Farmers' Market at Jackson and Tenth streets in 1902

My favorite among my father's stories also involved one of those treks in the early 1900s, all of which were made by horse and wagon, way before tractors. The trip home was long and grueling, especially after a delivery to Summit Hill. Darkness came early in winter, and Dad felt he could get a little nap in on the way home, because the horses were used to the trip and could always find their way once they were headed north on Centerville Road. So Dad loosened up the reins, tied them on the post, and lay back in the loose hay that he had brought along for just this purpose.

This sounds so idyllic, but you can imagine his surprise and horror when he was suddenly jolted upright by the horses lurching forward. Awakening enough to see through the darkness what had startled the horses, he spied the caboose of a Soo Line train—he had just narrowly missed being hit by it. His fast-thinking horses saved his life and their own that day.

He didn't try to nap on later trips.

JULY

"If at any time I've ever had any doubt about what I'm doing, all I have to do is see a patient, and talk to her, and I realize it's the right thing."
—Dr. Jane Hodgson, pro-choice pioneer

S	M	T	W	T	F	S
27	28	29	30	1	2	3
4	5	6	7	8	9	10
11	12	13	14	15	16	17
18	19	20	21	22	23	24
25	26	27	28	29	30	31

26 Monday

27 Tuesday

Nine Nights of Music Series,
Minnesota History Center

28 Wednesday

29 Thursday

Music in Mears Park

Music and Movies, *District del Sol*

Leo Damiani, conductor and composer, was born today in 1912

Heron on the Mississippi River

Photo © Patricia Bour-Schilla

30 Friday	Fourth Friday at the Movies
31 Saturday	Saint Paul Farmers' Market
1 Sunday	Saint Paul Farmers' Market

1890: *The Farmer* magazine moves from North Dakota to Saint Paul to be near the University of Minnesota's Department of Agriculture.

Saint Paul All Stars Shine
on the Big Stage

Daniel Gabriel

On a glorious summer day in July 2008, major league baseball held its annual all-star game in Yankee Stadium. It was the stadium's final year, and the symbolism of bringing the finest players in the game together one more time in The House That Ruth Built wasn't lost on the participants. For once, not a single chosen all-star begged off. In fact, as plans for the opening ceremony developed, it became apparent that both fans and players were going to be in for a rare treat.

Given the nature of the setting—the last of 85 seasons in baseball's finest cathedral—it wasn't surprising that the opening ceremony would emphasize history. But it wasn't until the first of the announced guests began trotting out to old positions on the field that it became clear what was happening. The announcer's voice rose in excitement as he pointed out, "This is the biggest gathering of Hall of Famers ever on one field." Dozens of the game's greatest stood tall—or as tall as their aging backs would allow—in the spots they had once dominated: George Brett at the hot corner, "Little Joe" Morgan at second, an aged Willie Mays almost buried under the ovation as he made his way out toward center field.

Once the Hall of Famers were in position, the starting nine for the home team American League were sent out one by one to join them, a visible circle of continuity within the Grand Old Game.

It was when Joe Mauer emerged in his catcher's gear that it hit me: no fewer than three of these celebrated players were from Saint Paul. Besides young Joe (who would go on to win his second American League batting title at season's end), Dave Winfield stood out in right field, along with Paul Molitor, the sole designated hitter represented in the Hall of Fame. Three Saint Paulites, standing there among the all-time greatest. Three kids off our local playgrounds, from our local schools, veterans of our Little Leagues and American Legion teams, standing out there proud, wide, and handsome.

Baseball is a serious matter in Saint Paul, and in my mind's eye I could see those three young boys—like countless others who played alongside them, or followed in their trail—honing their skills on the double steal or learning to block the plate on the dusty base paths of a Saint Paul ball field.

Winfield (after attending Saint Paul Central) and Molitor (after Cretin) both starred at the U of M, and then finished their professional careers as two of about two dozen players ever to record over 3,000 hits. Think about that for a moment: what an achievement it is to play professionally at all, whether it's for the Twins, the Saint Paul Saints, or whom-ever. Think about the many, many thousands of minor leaguers who have ever played, then about the thousands of former major leaguers. Only a couple handful of players have had the longevity and quick, sharp stroke needed to lace those 3,000 hits. Two of them are ours.

Molitor, who spent most of his playing days with the Milwaukee Brew-ers, had a career arc beyond the age of thirty that was more remarkable than any player's in history, other than perhaps Dazzy Vance's. He went from being a solid but oft-injured infielder up until his thirtieth year to one of the finest late-career hitters in the league. From his record-setting five-hit game in the 1982 World Series to his 225 hit season in 1996 (with the Twins, at the age of thirty-nine), the man could stroke, not to mention hustle. And to think he might have just been known for ending Dennis Den-ning's career. (As a scampering fourth grader, he ploughed into Denning, who was coaching first base, during a St. Luke's playground game, thereby wrecking the young prospect's knee. Or so they tell me. But maybe Denning was simply destined to stay in that coaching box, so he could later lead the University of St. Thomas to a Division III national championship.)

Winfield's career at the U of M was the stuff of legend: his pitching not only led the baseball team to the College World Series; his rebounding helped bring the basketball team a rare Big Ten Championship. Winfield was so athletic that when he left college he was drafted by four teams in three professional sports. And then, in the one he chose, he switched from pitcher to outfielder! The conventional wisdom was that Winfield would never hit successfully in the big leagues because of the exaggerated hitch in his swing. Tell that to the Padres (eight seasons) or the Yankees (nine seasons), or even the Twins, where big Dave returned near the end of his career. Four hundred sixty-five homers and 1833 RBI later, the man was still crushing the ball to all corners of the field.

Mauer went straight from Cretin-Derham Hall onto the national stage, signing a $5 million-plus contract with the hometown Twins, as the number one overall pick in major league baseball's amateur draft. In all of baseball history, no catcher had ever won the American League bat-ting championship. The position is just too rugged, too demanding; the focus on defense and cajoling a pitching staff distracts too much from a hitter's stroke (not to mention the toll exerted on his legs by squatting). Yet Mauer has done it. Not once, but twice. And who knows how much more is yet to come?

The next time you happen past a ball field or a playground in Saint Paul—at Dunning, maybe, or Groveland, or over at Parkway or El Rio Vista—stop and check out the action. You never know who you might be watching.

Pig's Eye: A Journey through Time, Space, and Spirit

Robert Van Tassell

The Island: Innocence

Pig's Eye was the original settlement for the city of Saint Paul. The island was named after the French settler known as Pig's Eye Pete. Pete's malfunctioning eye squinted like the blank stare of an old sow looking through layers of dry crusted mud. Dry and crusted was not a way to describe the riverbanks and makeshift roads of the island. Rains and high water kept the island terrain a soupy mix.

Liquid, be it rain from the sky, river water, or bottled spirits, has a way of changing things. Towering vegetation shadowed the surface of the island.

Pig's Eye Pete Parrant, a scoundrel of history, had personality traits that seemed to align with my pop's. Fascination for those spirits from the bottle made them members of a group who got lost in their liquid logic, a place I call DDT—drama dysfunction time. Pop's DDT's always started with a fresh air outing.

With the spring floods and ever-changing swelling of the river came the swelling of Mom's belly. I had already discovered that as sure as spring comes, so did babies.

Pig's Eye Island is where your past and your present cross paths. It was the summer of 1946. I say summer, although who can remember that long entrance from the womb, let alone that proverbial slap on the rear end? I think back to that slap, and wonder how it is that the human race has not progressed enough that the first moment on earth should not be a hug, a kiss on the cheek, or merely some other reality check.

I think about all the alcohol some great writers have consumed in the pursuit of their art. Surprisingly, it's the words and the memories that are my drug. They intoxicate me.

Pop was working long days across the river at the South Saint Paul Union stockyards. The stockyards were like an urban oasis for farm boys and cowboys. Pop would rise at 6 a.m., row across the river, and work eight to twelve hours. Sometimes, the latter part of his workday would be spent at one of the corner saloons for a fresh air outing before returning to the island.

One of the fresh air outing days went extremely fast: destiny, along with a little help from Brother Ollie and Sister Melodye, reminded us once again that life is ever changing. Mom was saying, "Ollie and Melodye, go into the house and get lemonade out of the icebox."

One was to bring glasses, the other a pitcher of freshly squeezed juice. Who was to carry the most important item—in this case, the juice—immediately became an issue. Ollie spoke up. "I'm bigger, I will carry the juice, you get the glasses."

Melodye replied, "I want to carry the juice." We watched them cross Grandma's front yard, bickering back and forth all the way into the house, the screen door slamming behind them. Within minutes, they were both running from the house, screaming that the other had broken the beautiful lemonade pitcher. It was the lemonade pitcher just acquired a week earlier from the M & H gas station on the East Side of Saint Paul. The pitcher had cost an entire book of stamps to become part of our kitchen.

The rest of us kids were sure that Ollie and Melodye were in big trouble. We didn't realize how much trouble. As Mom was trying to bring harmony back to this group of little helpers, a strange odor disrupted our attention. We looked back across Grandma's front lawn and noticed smoke coming from the front door of the little four-room tar paper shack we called home. It seems the pitcher had broken on top of the kerosene stove, which somehow exploded. In minutes, black, smoky mushroom shapes billowed out of the windows against the blue sky. I had never seen my mom move so fast. She ran into the house, and before we knew it, books were flying out of every window. Mom was unable to stay in the house; the smoke was too overpowering. The old lumber and tarpaper made perfect fuel for the fire.

Photo courtesy Robert Van Tassell

Robert's mother Phyllis Elizabeth Bair Van Tassell
rowing her children across the Mississippi River to school

Downtown: Integration

I am sitting along the river's edge, just a couple of miles upriver from the island. It is a warm, peaceful day, and the sun is shining brightly. The river is the same now as it was forty-four years ago. The odor of the mud, the smell of the woods, all help me to journey back.

There really wasn't much preparation needed for the move from the island. We had not acquired many new possessions since the fire. Pop was worried—expenses on the island were few, and the move to the city meant a lot more responsibility. All of our minds were bursting with the idea of a new home. Would we have a yard? Would we have a garden? Would we still have to use a coffee can when it was too cold to sit in the outhouse? Our new home was called the Minnesota Hotel. I was sure that any place with such an important name would be a palace. At four years old, I knew that Minnesota was the name of the entire state.

We spent the next day loading the pickup truck with the few items acquired over the past couple of months. The books and the cookie jar were among them.

As we crossed the road that connected the island to the sewage plant near the south end of Saint Paul, I looked over my shoulder, not yet realizing that the love learned in our private paradise would prepare me for growth and sometimes an overwhelming flow that comes when the heart is open.

Mom was always the first to recognize any saving grace in a situation. In this case, the saving grace came in the form of the Saint Paul Public Library. This was the main library, and most buildings were not like it. My mouth dropped open when I first entered. The ceilings were higher than normal and the walls were made of stone. I had a special feeling when I was inside the building; it was a feeling of security and expansion at the same time. I am sure that my comfort in often asking why, what, and how came from my exposure to that library. My brothers, sisters, and I spent most of our days using the library as a private playground. My oldest brother, Matt, was especially happy with this new place. The library had everything—puppet shows, books, and a nice little old lady who knew each of us by name. Mom always told me that with the library, we could expand our world. The library did just that.

From childhood to adulthood, my journeys within and through books made the spirit of adventure a reality as I traveled around the world. In 1957, at age eleven, the imprint of my first solo trip to Gulfport, Mississippi, set the stage for my craving to see the world. From Pig's Eye Island, I've traveled to Paris, Germany, Mexico, even Tibet. I've learned that the unity of souls speaks loud in our time. The desire for peace and joy is truly a universal cry.

Spam Burgers

Anita Clingman

Ingredients:
1 can Spam
½ lb. Velveeta or American cheese
1–2 large slices of onion, cut up small
1 teaspoon mustard
3 tablespoons mayonnaise
3 tablespoons ketchup
1 package hamburger or hot dog buns

Directions:
Preheat oven to 350° F.

Grind Spam, cheese, and onion in a meat grinder using middle holes. Stir together mustard, mayonnaise, ketchup, and mix into Spam, cheese, onion mixture. Fill buns. Cover with foil: bake approximately 15 minutes at 350° F. until cheese melts. Makes about 12 servings. A favorite with kids.

From Knox Cooks, *published in 1985 by Knox Presbyterian Church, 1536 West Minnehaha, in honor of their 95th year.*

The O'Shaughnessy Theater

Annelia Anderson

When I decided to choose my favorite place in Saint Paul, I didn't give many other cool places any thought. The O'Shaughnessy at the University of St. Catherine struck me right away. For most who have seen a fantastic performance at The O'Shaughnessy, they would think of writing about it also. They would have memories of the grandness of the theater. They would remember the anxious feeling they had as they waited for the main curtains to open, the excitement in the air when the show was finally about to start, catching glimpses of actors in the wings, the melancholy feeling they would get when the curtains closed to end the show.

Of course, anyone who had that experience would decide to write about it, but my time at The O'Shaughnessy was even better: I got to be backstage! It was wonderful seeing all of the actors coming up the long staircase from the dressing room. They would go down as everyday people you would see on the street, and they would come back up in their costumes, makeup, and hair, looking magnificent. I loved talking to the youngest dancers, who were not yet in kindergarten.

When the show finally began, I sat in the green room to watch the beginning on a TV that showed the stage. The green room is where the actors wait before going onstage. The performance was great! I got butterflies in my stomach. That was because the show was the first real show I have ever been in.

Better yet, it was held at The O'Shaughnessy theater in Saint Paul.

Photo © Patricia Bour-Schilla

The O'Shaughnessy theater at the recently renamed University of St. Catherine

August

Photo © Patricia Bour-Schilla

State Fair 7:00 p.m.

Weary feet hanging from the gondolas
As we pass the grandstand a glimpse
Of the big hair rockers finishing their sound check.
They were as popular once
As the roasted corn stand
Where the sidewalk is yellow with butter stains,
Ankle deep in blackened husks
As we trudge toward the Midway lights.

Loren Niemi

AUGUST

S	M	T	W	T	F	S
1	2	3	4	5	6	7
8	9	10	11	12	13	14
15	16	17	18	19	20	21
22	23	24	25	26	27	28
29	30	31	1	2	3	4

↪ "Historically, books do okay in bad times. It depends on how bad the misery gets." —David Unowsky, former owner of The Hungry Mind bookstore

2 Monday

3 Tuesday

Nine Nights of Music Series, Minnesota History Center

🐞 Nina Clifford, infamous brothel-owning businesswoman, was born today in 1851

4 Wednesday

5 Thursday

Music in Mears Park

Music and Movies, *District del Sol*

🐞 Herb Brooks, hockey player and coach, was born today in 1937

Cracked earth on the Mississippi mud plain

6 Friday

When an author is signing your book,
STAND BACK AND SHUT UP—the poor schnook
Is likely to steal
What you think—how you feel—
And—the unkindest cut—HOW YOU LOOK!
Garrison Keillor

7 Saturday   Saint Paul Farmers' Market

8 Sunday   Saint Paul Farmers' Market

A Century Ago: Herbert Keller is elected Saint Paul's mayor and serves
for four years. Keller Lake and Keller Golf course are named after him.

I Miss My Refugee Camp

Chong Xiong

I grew up in Thailand in a refugee camp. I have four brothers and four sisters. My parents worked in the house. My house was near the garden. I went to school every day. My camp was named Ban Vinai. I miss it very much, because we had many things: pigs, a dog, a cat, birds, chickens, and turkeys. My parents planted vegetables, papaya trees, mango trees, and tamarind trees. Every night my family watered the plants and fed the animals.

After they closed the refugee camp, my family moved to Wat Tham Krabok, because they didn't want Hmong people to live in Ban Vinai. I liked my house there because I had many friends come to visit me. We ate together, sewed clothes, and talked to each other every day. My friends couldn't go to school because they helped their parents work at home. I went to school and studied every day. On the weekend I helped my parents sew clothes and visited my friends at their homes.

In 2004, I moved to the U.S., to Rhode Island. In my first two weeks, my child got sick. We took her to the hospital. I couldn't speak English. The doctor talked to me, I didn't understand what he said. We stayed in the hospital for one week. My child got better and we came home. We lived in Rhode Island for one year and five months. We moved to Minnesota, because few Hmong people lived in Rhode Island. They didn't have Hmong interpreters. I wanted to go to different places like downtown and clinic. But it was very difficult for me. I heard that in Minnesota there are many programs to help people from different countries. I moved to Minneapolis. I am trying to learn more English.

In the future, I hope I can speak English and have a good job, because I have to help my family. I hope my children grow up and have a good education for great ability and a good life.

Chong Xiong

The Hideaway

Kathryn Kysar

The purple tree was dust
in the moonlight, the bark purplish-
brown in its slow aged death,
the split in the branches low
enough to reach by standing
on a bike seat. Nestled into
the hollows of the wide branches,
we'd lean back and ponder
the shimmering stars in the
darkening late summer light,
leaves painted orange by sunset.

It was imminent—the start of school,
the change of season, our feet
outgrowing our beat up summer shoes,
the bombs falling on t.v.,
the girl running naked
through orange streets of fire.

The news was bad,
the body count climbing
my mother distraught,
my father taking his students
to peace marches, the men
in black cars parked outside
on our silent street, waiting.

That girl, running on
a flat dirt road, her naked child
body slick, smooth, and strong,
how could I share my favorite
bell bottoms and purple shirt,
ride her on my banana bike,
let her lean back into the arms
of the tree, the only flames
the sunset in the distance?

⊃"Ideas are powerful things, requiring not a studious contemplation but an action, even if it is only an inner action. . . . They demand to be stood for." —Midge Decter, journalist

S	M	T	W	T	F	S
1	2	3	4	5	6	7
8	9	10	11	12	13	14
15	16	17	18	19	20	21
22	23	24	25	26	27	28
29	30	31	1	2	3	4

August

9 Monday
International Day of the
World's Indigenous People

🏵 Edward D. Neill, pioneer minister, educator, and writer, was born today in 1831

10 Tuesday
Nine Nights of Music Series,
Minnesota History Center

11 Wednesday

🏵 Richard Moore, attorney and civic leader, was born today in 1915

12 Thursday
International Youth Day
Ramadan begins

Music in Mears Park

Photo © Steve Rouch

Como Lake Reflection

13 Friday   Irish Fair

14 Saturday   Saint Paul Farmers' Market
                                            Irish Fair

15 Sunday   Saint Paul Farmers' Market
                                            Irish Fair
                        Japanese Lantern Lighting Festival

"Beware of over-confidence; especially in matters
of structure." —Cass Gilbert, architect

I Write Because (Dotty's Diner, 1956)

Karen Karsten

People stampede in my head, kicking shoes, banging doors, punching holes in my sleep. "Let us out!" they shout, and we're all back in my mother's restaurant, Dotty's Diner, over fifty years ago, where the potatoes have been mashed since 11 a.m., when Uncle Maynard the milkman always does it. Fragrant beef and pork roasts are sliced, hamburgers pattied; all in the relative calm between coffee breaks and lunch rush.

It's summer, I'm not in school, I work mornings and afternoons, leaving before noon rush so I'm not in the way. Now lunch is in full swing at Dotty's, but I'm next door on Chestnut Street, in our pink house, right around the corner from Irvine Park in Saint Paul. Someone is banging on the door. It's George, our Wonder Bread delivery man, and he yells at me I better get on over there, Gracie didn't show up, and there's no one to bus dishes. So I get on over there. The crowd is thick, noisy, familiar, they've been coming in here for years. A cheer goes up as I push my way back to the kitchen to help Mama Rainelli, our dishwasher. I haul bins of dirty dishes back to Mama, who can't walk out front to do it herself—she's too big and has bad feet—but my mother knows Mama can't get a job anywhere else, so she keeps her. She's the best dishwasher in town, and she makes the authentic Italian spaghetti sauce every other Wednesday.

I ice water glasses, stack butter pats on plates that have one light and one dark slice of bread. Colleen is negotiating plates, cups, glasses through the dense crowd. She is short, plump, has curly dyed-red hair, long brown-penciled eyebrows, is already desperate for a smoke. She is our snotty waitress. Maureen is right behind her, tall, elegant, long dark hair pulled back. She is our snottiest waitress by actual vote. My sister Kathy's pony tail bobs furiously, huge blue eyes dance, this is her first summer waitressing, and she's determined to keep up, hopes to be voted snotty, too. They move gracefully, high speed ballet dancers in crisp blue-and-white-checked American Linen uniforms. They shout orders to my mother, who sweats over the grill and steam table. Dotty's never uses guest checks—too slow. My mother remembers every order called, and the waitress always just tells you how much your bill is.

"One with!" another burger slapped on the crowded grill, sprinkled with onions, "Special, special, roast beef special," my mother turns out plate after plate of steaming food, and they'd better be picked up before the food gets a minute cold and you'd better remember who it belongs to. Every so often, Mother would turn away from the grill, face the two small horseshoe counters and four booths to see who didn't have food yet. One hundred pounds of

Photo © Karen Karsten

Dotty in the diner on bread-baking day (the big bowl is where the bread would rise) in May of 1960.

dark-haired concentration, gray eyes that never missed a thing, and she never let up: "Hey Needlenose, what'd you order?"

"Fat friend, aren't you eating today, or were you so bad they won't take your order?" Or someone would make a mistake, order eggs at lunch. Mother would turn around fast, spatula in her and, "Who said that? You know we don't do eggs on my grill between eleven and one, grill's too hot."

Plate after plate of meat loaf, mashed potatoes, gravy. No butter for Mr. Zuba, extra gravy for Chuck the trucker, always a hot pork sandwich for Faraway. Hurry-up burgers for the press crew from National Checking next door, in and out lunches for the Saint Paul Milk Company folks—not the drivers, they're the very early rush at 6 a.m. Colleen, Maureen, and Kathy deal with the chaos, mostly with their mouths, "Ya, ya, I'm coming with more coffee." "Do you talk to your wife like that? You'll have to sit in the kitchen with Mama if you don't behave." And they mean it. I haul clean stacks of dishes from the kitchen, heavy platters, plates, coffee mugs, try to keep out of the way, contain my adolescent clumsiness, as everyone darts madly for coffee, water, plates.

At one o'clock, the last piece of pie is slapped on the counter, Colleen lights that first cigarette, the grill is scraped clean, flame lowered for the slower afternoon. Everyone relaxes, cleans up; my sister jumps into a light blue convertible full of her friends; semi-trucks pull away; people dash back to work. The trucks leaving signals Ron, the beatnik painter up the street, that the rush is over, his favorite stool by the window is available.

It is all gone now: my mother, my sister, our pink house, Dotty's, National Checking, Saint Paul Milk, Grandma Barbato's big apartment house on the corner across from Cossetta's grocery, all leveled by Housing and Urban Development, or erased by time. It's all gone, but still stampedes in my head, demands to get out, live again, become poetry.

S	M	T	W	T	F	S
1	2	3	4	5	6	7
8	9	10	11	12	13	14
15	16	17	18	19	20	21
22	23	24	25	26	27	28
29	30	31	1	2	3	4

➪ August 21, 1965: The Crusher defeats Mad Dog Vachon and becomes the National Wrestling Association champion at a match in Saint Paul.

August

16 Monday

17 Tuesday

Nine Nights of Music Series, Minnesota History Center

18 Wednesday

19 Thursday

Music in Mears Park

🐝 Arthur Fry, inventor of Post-It Notes, was born today in 1931

State Fair reflected in sunglasses

20 Friday

21 Saturday   St. Paul Farmers' Market

🎷 Irv Williams, legendary jazz saxophonist, was born today in 1920

22 Sunday   St. Paul Farmers' Market

The two oldest continuously run restaurants in the city are Yarusso's, started in 1933, and The Lexington, which opened two years later.

Thursday

Tina Dybvik

I met the god of thunder half a mile from the stop
as I limped along Kasota
in a sudden summer storm.

There was a fearsome clap,
and a rig appeared from nowhere.
Then the driver called out to offer me a ride.

Time ceased
while I crossed the busy street
and climbed a silver ladder of mythic height.

In the cab,
I recognized his reddish hair and hero thighs,
which were clad in fraying cut-offs
that seemed out of place.

"What's your name?" he boomed.
He was friendly for a god.

"Thanks for stopping," I said vaguely,
(it didn't matter what I was called)
and we laughed to the end of the truck route,
because riders were not allowed.

Then I waved and hurried onward;
the rain had cleared,
and my limp was gone.

Memento

Mary Kay Rummel

The day before I entered the convent
I wandered the state fair with my boyfriend
in a jagged dream where
bleachers, stands erupted at angles
from steaming concrete streets crowded
with teens nuzzling each other.
Those who were going to college,
those who worked at the phone company
pretzled together on the roller coaster.

I didn't understand what freedom was
or how easy it could be given away.
If I had understood then
I would have eaten
two more corn dogs,
spent more time circling
on the carousel,
and on that small boat
through Ye Olde Mill,
given more quick kisses
in the dark.

I wanted to not be ordinary,
already beyond the familiar,
my heart left and leaving.
I went forth the way loons swim
underwater like arrows, slowly arcing
toward what I thought was freedom.

That night my friend gave me a crucifix
wrapped in a blue bow. He held
it outward, until his arms made
an angled cross in the August heat.
The next day I carefully placed it
on a small dorm bed
surrounded by white curtains,
an unlikely memento on my pillow.
This I thought was happiness.
This I thought was love.

➪ August 23, 1934: Gangster
Homer Van Meter is shot to
death by Saint Paul police near
the corner of Marion Street
and University Avenue.

AUGUST

S	M	T	W	T	F	S
1	2	3	4	5	6	7
8	9	10	11	12	13	14
15	16	17	18	19	20	21
22	23	24	25	26	27	28
29	30	31	1	2	3	4

23 Monday

24 Tuesday

Nine Nights of Music Series,
Minnesota History Center

🌑 Stephen Paulus, composer of over 350 works of music, was born today in 1949

25 Wednesday

26 Thursday

Minnesota State Fair

Saint Paul's Great Minnesota Get-Together
Count me among those throngs of sweaty souls, trudging, ogling—
determined to see it all
Junk food in hand—determined to eat it all
Our State Fair: The last blast before the winter fast
Wouldn't miss it for the world!
Carol Hall

State Fair steer billboard on Como Avenue

27 Friday

Minnesota State Fair

Fourth Friday at the Movies

🐾 Mary Elizabeth Downey, composer and concert pianist, was born today in 1895

28 Saturday

Saint Paul Farmers' Market

Minnesota State Fair

29 Sunday

Saint Paul Farmers' Market

Minnesota State Fair

The first mayor of Saint Paul, elected in April 1854, was David Olmsted. At the time he represented 4,000 residents.

August Wilson's Early Days in Saint Paul

Daniel Gabriel

Tennessee Williams. Arthur Miller. August Wilson. When you list the playwrights of American theater whose work transcends all others, those three names stand at the top. Much of Wilson's defining ten-play saga of African American life in the twentieth century, a massive undertaking with a play for every decade, was written right here in Saint Paul. That includes the first to hit Broadway (*Ma Rainey's Black Bottom*) and the Pulitzer Prize winners *Fences* and *The Piano Lesson*.

Penumbra Theater is in the midst of reviving the entire ten-play cycle. Penumbra brought Wilson to Saint Paul, Penumbra staged his first play (*Black Bart and the Sacred Hills*), and Penumbra—in the persons of Lou Bellamy, Claude Purdy, and Marion McClinton, among many, many others—nurtured and defined much of his work.

But it was Saint Paul itself that provided the ground from which Wilson's panoramic vision emerged. Wilson was not a traveler. Aside from the travels forced upon him by productions of his work, he spent his life mostly in three locations: Pittsburgh, where he was born and raised (and which provided the setting for many of his famous plays); Saint Paul, where he found his theatrical voice and ascended to the heights of Broadway; and Seattle, where he completed the last pieces of his cycle and lived his final days.

When I first met August in 1979, he was still writing scripts for the Science Museum and looking for a place to jump. My wife, Judith, and his fiancée, Judy Oliver, had become fast friends and were convinced that their two blues-obsessed, baseball-loving men needed to pull their writings out of the suitcase and into the light of day. Our first hook-up was at a party. I remember walking up to August and saying, "I hear you're into Charlie Patton," and that was all it took. We started off down the Delta and veered over into Chicago blues and then the Pittsburgh Crawfords and Hank Aaron, and four hours later the only movement we'd made was to sit down on the floor and rest our backs. The guy was fascinating . . . and completely self-taught.

He'd dropped out of school at the age of fifteen because his teacher refused to believe he'd written a particular assignment. (This at a time when August was already writing his sister's college term papers for her.) "The man didn't ask the white kids if *they'd* written *their* papers," said August. "And he was Black."

*Randi Yoder, Daniel and Judith Gabriel, Judy Oliver
and August Wilson celebrate future success, 1981*

"So what'd you do?"

"Next day, instead of going to school I went to the court right outside his room and played basketball. But he never came out. He never acknowledged me. And I never went back."

What he did instead was haunt the library, reading widely and deeply and following his own instincts toward what he thought he needed to know. At times, it left him with curious gaps in his knowledge—items that every school kid was made to learn might be ones he never touched upon—but by chasing his own train, he rode a whole lot further than any formal learning could ever have taken him.

With August, I learned to just toss out a subject and see which hooks he took. Jorge Luis Borges . . . Romare Beardon . . . Bob Marley . . . the real story of the Johnstown flood . . . Jack Johnson and Joe Louis . . . the spot where the Yellow Dog crossed the Southern. It was all inside him, working around and seeping deep into his bones.

His poetry was already fully developed, a soaring melisma of sound and figurative speech that gained resonance when declaimed in the wee, wee hours. But his attention was already refocusing itself on the theater. The beginning of the '80s was a period of transition for him. In early plays like *Black Bart and the Sacred Hills* and *The Coldest Night of the Year,* he ennobled his characters' condition by filling their mouths with swooping poetic devices. As he said, "I hadn't yet learned that they had their own poetry already there in their everyday speech."

We were writing partners in those days, and gathered regularly in cafés to share each other's work, to critique and cajole and explore new side turnings. In some ways, it was hugely daunting. I remember telling my wife after one session, "What hope is there for *my* writing? This guy is incredible—and nobody's ever heard of him. Nobody even seems interested."

That was to change. But in the meantime, in those early '80s years before Lloyd Richards and Yale Rep turned up, August Wilson sat on neighborhood barstools and wobbly café chairs, smoking and brooding and, bit by bit, building stories inside him. He didn't drive, so he walked a lot, or took the bus. A solitary figure—always in a suit and tie, dressed like a 1930s itinerant bluesman—he'd tromp the streets of Saint Paul, arguing out character conflicts in his head.

Once, when he was new to town and riding the 21A, the man opposite squinted across and said, "You look like Latimer." *Who the heck is Latimer?* he thought. *A criminal? Someone on the lam?*

He shook his head quickly. "I'm not Latimer."

"Hell, I know you ain't Latimer. I said you *look* like him." Mayor Latimer would have been proud.

In time, he got a job as a cook for Little Brothers of the Poor, which not only got him out of the chair at the Science Theater but freed his word flow to serve the tunes he was beginning to hum. We played together on the Little Brothers softball team and August, of course, had his own unique theory on how to hit. He corkscrewed his hands tight, and then unwound them when he swung. It didn't always work, but when his timing was right, he generated amazing power. I can remember seeing him hit a ball over the backstop of the field *beyond* us, clearing both outfields and both infields.

My favorite moments when we met together came after he was done responding to my work. (He was always polite about his comments, though he wouldn't hesitate to cut through my pretensions and lazy imagery. Without him, I don't know that I would have ever found my way out of the thicket of words I tended to wind about myself.) That's when he'd talk about his latest work, maybe pull out a scene or two and read it aloud. He had a deep, often rough voice that hit every nuance and emphasis with the steady rhythm of the rails. Three moments in particular stand out:

The first was when he was honing *Ma Rainey's Black Bottom* and working the scene where Ma's nephew is supposed to introduce the song, but keeps stuttering. We got to laughing so hard that August's stuttering was real, and when he switched to Ma's voice, we only got worse.

With *Fences*, he was looking for a way for Troy to express his frustration over having been kept out of the Major Leagues because of the color

*August Wilson and his fiancée, Judy Oliver,
outside their Grand Avenue apartment, 1980*

line. August said something about how you could understand that you're not going to supplant Babe Ruth, but what about the guy who came after Ruth? Who was he?

"George Selkirk," I said. "And you talk about a tough act to follow. Selkirk never did live it down. Especially the year he hit .269."

"Selkirk, huh?" And then August launched off into an impromptu Troy Maxson diatribe—"Man hitting .269 playing right field for the Yankees! How is that right?"—that ended up almost verbatim in the script.

The third time I particularly remember was the day we got together, as usual, and he said, "I'm starting a new play. But all I got is the opening bit."

"Give it to me."

"Well, here's the thing. Man done a paint job for a grocery store, and the grocery man said how he's going to give him a ham. After he's done the job, man tries to give him a chicken . . ."

And then he dropped into character, and I listened to the whole scene develop, with August stopping only to wonder how long watermelons would keep. Would it be realistic to haul a load of them from the south up to Pittsburgh to sell? And away he went, setting Boy Willie in motion and creating the genesis of *The Piano Lesson.*

People like Lou Bellamy and Lloyd Richards and others were great helps to August Wilson in terms of structure and pace. But he never needed anybody to give him the language. That was all inside, like the voices of angels just waiting to sing.

Traditions

Steven M. Lukas

For thirty years, my wife, Dianne, and I had come to the State Fair. We always came on the first Thursday, early in the morning, before the grass became trampled, before it got too hot or too crowded. My mother had told me how her father got her and nine siblings out of bed by 4 a.m. so that chores could be done before everyone piled into the Buick for the ride to Lincoln to be first in line for the Nebraska State Fair. We brought that heritage with us when we moved to Minnesota in 1971. That first August, our friends in the other half of the duplex in Crystal introduced us to eighty acres of farm machinery and the Beer Garden. We introduced them to the importance of arriving early.

For each year thereafter, we came as our own family. We missed only once, in 1984, when Dianne was first diagnosed with breast cancer. Each year we pushed through the turnstiles, bright and optimistic. In 2001, the attendants held the side gate open for us as I helped Dianne through in her wheelchair for our last fair together. While we weren't as early that last year, we still came; Dianne wanted, as I did, to share again an important ritual of our life in Minnesota.

We abbreviated our normal route, rolling past the Clydesdales, through the sheep, past the Largest Boar. We still took time to see her beloved quilts and my Fine Arts Building, where only once had one of my photo entries made the cut to be exhibited in all its imagined artistic splendor. We rested in the concert shell where Dianne had dragged me each year to hear Michael Johnson. We shared a drink in the old Beer Garden, where it all started. We talked about how we had visited with Gwen Iffel of PBS under an elm tree one hot afternoon, all of us agreeing that Paul Wellstone was indeed an important voice on the national scene. We remembered how John Denver had helped us grieve the loss of the *Challenger* and its crew when he sang, "Flying for Me" on a sun-filled afternoon in the grandstand. We smiled as we remembered bringing our three sons in strollers and backpacks until they could walk erect alongside us and then graduated from All-You-Can-Drink Milk to the vices of the Midway. They came with us each year, even through college. We laughed about the times they had sat slumped over the mist-covered counters at Andy's Diner for our annual breakfasts, perhaps suffering from the demands of study, but more likely from too much fun the night before. But they came. We were all there, each year, each first Thursday.

Entrance to the Minnesota State Fair

This year, I will be there with my family again. The gate next to the turnstiles will swing open, no longer for a wheelchair but for the stroller carrying my granddaughter, Miranda Dianne. I will watch as everyone shuffles through early on the first Thursday morning, before the crowds, before the heat, and while the grass is still crisp. I will watch with pride as my sons and their families build their own State Fair traditions, like their mother and me before them, and our families before us.

Fair

Mary Kay Rummel

There was an old yellow streetcar.
There were so many chances before us.
There were three steps and a window seat.
There were waves of heat in the August air.

Chance was wide open.
The streetcar stopped at the gates.
Waves of heat rolled over us.
It was kids for free day at the fair.

We got off at Como and Snelling; the gates waited.
Coins in our pockets, a feast of booths before us.
We were full and forever and it was free this day.
Dreams were simple, a necklace strung bead by bead.

We walked the streets of the fair, our coins heavy.
Parents worried about polio, iron lungs, money, bombs.
Our dreams were beads fingered one by one.
The life we didn't know was the one we wanted.

Parents worried their fingers, polio and bombs.
What would we give now for the fair of innocence.
The life we didn't know was what we wanted.
Now what would we give for the smells of sweat and dust.

There were three iron steps and a window seat.
The life we didn't know was the one we wanted.
What wouldn't we give to see the yellow streetcar
Coming toward us through waves of August heat.

September

Photo © Patricia Bour-Schilla

The Gleaner

A sole red potato, a scarred zucchini,
a bruised apple, a skinny green bean,
a half-squished tomato, the odd onion . . .
A bent over old man with a brown bag
methodically crisscrosses the sheds
after all the growers have gone home,
bending down here and there to harvest
every single fruit and vegetable lost
and found at the farmers market.

Mike Hazard

▷ September 1, 1900: The first campus of what will become Rasmussen College opens its doors in Saint Paul with secretarial and accounting programs.

S	M	T	W	T	F	S
29	30	31	1	2	3	4
5	6	7	8	9	10	11
12	13	14	15	16	17	18
19	20	21	22	23	24	25
26	27	28	29	30	1	2

30 Monday — Minnesota State Fair

🏵 Roy Wilkins, writer and civil rights activist, was born today in 1901

31 Tuesday — Nine Nights of Music Series, Minnesota History Center

Minnesota State Fair

1 Wednesday — Minnesota State Fair

2 Thursday — Minnesota State Fair

🏵 Helen Hart, prominent plant pathologist, was born today in 1900

Trombone from the street band the Brass Messengers

3 Friday   Minnesota State Fair

4 Saturday   Saint Paul Farmers' Market
                                                Minnesota State Fair

5 Sunday   Saint Paul Farmers' Market
                                                Minnesota State Fair

"It is not to be expected that human nature will change in a
day." —Frank B. Kellogg, statesman

Tour de Farce

Margery Peterson

I was a guide at the Minnesota State Capitol in Saint Paul. I got to talk talk talk and tell stories and lead people around. It was the best job for me.

People come from all over the world to visit Minnesota's Capitol, known as one of the most beautiful. I often wondered how people from Mali or Togo or Madagascar even heard of Saint Paul. Many said it was through relatives who attended college here.

I led tours of German teenagers, priests-in-training, Russian businessmen, Hutterites, preschoolers, legislators, and Southerners who hadn't accepted the North winning the Civil War. I guided artists, historians, dirty construction workers, war enthusiasts, peace enthusiasts, brides craving photos on the roof by the golden horses even if it is just a rear view, and immigrant English classes speaking a dozen native languages. Plus my share of 25,000 or so sixth graders who swarm the place every spring and hundreds of Girl and Boy Scouts working on government badges.

All Capitol guides are well-trained in Minnesota history, government, art, and architecture, and make every effort to connect with tourists on some level—like showing Southerners the pink Tennessee marble on the second floor; or Brits the gold pineapples on the Senate wall, a Victorian symbol of hospitality. The French fleur-de-lis on the House ceiling is on all Boy Scout uniforms. It means peace *and* purity. (I never met a Boy Scout who knew that. One mother thought it was an ear of corn.)

Laws are rules for big people, we told tots. Find the *M*s and stars. Notice the Cinderella-like staircase, the zodiac symbols on the rotunda ceiling, the busts of Martin Luther King and Wabasha III, and plaques of outstanding suffragettes (which means to vote, not suffer, though they did that too for seventy-five years).

People wanted to see Jesse Ventura's portrait. And they often confused the State Legislature with the National Congress—even the well-educated did that. But everyone asked lots of questions in the court. People understand guilt, innocence, and punishment in any language.

In summer, aides from Bethesda Rehab Center behind the Capitol pushed their wheelchair-bound patients across the street to look at something new and stimulating. The patients were in various stages of disability, but we usually found something to interest them.

The Capitol Building in Saint Paul

One day, I guided two young men in laid-back wheelchairs. They couldn't sit up, hold their heads still, their mouths closed, or focus on anything, least of all my voice. (Sort of like my teenage son.) But I tried, pointing up to the expansive skyward thrust of the rotunda or the sparkly chandeliers in the governor's reception area. Nothing. Nada. No contact. No understanding that I could see.

Leaving the governor's office, I walked backward down the hallway—an odd skill guides develop—so these young men could see my mouth as I talked. Absorbed in getting their attention, I suddenly found my feet teetering on the edge of a downstairs stairway and yelped.

The young men laughed their heads off.

⇨ "Another very great nuisance with which we have been afflicted . . . is the myriads of mosquitoes with which the country abounds. . . . Their depredations at night are beyond description." —Horace Bigelow, *Saint Paul Pioneer*, September 10, 1854

S	M	T	W	T	F	S
29	30	31	1	2	3	4
5	6	7	8	9	10	11
12	13	14	15	16	17	18
19	20	21	22	23	24	25
26	27	28	29	30	1	2

September

6 Monday

Labor Day

Minnesota State Fair

7 Tuesday

🏵 Yang Dao, first Hmong to earn an academic doctorate, was born today in 1943

8 Wednesday

International Literacy Day

9 Thursday

Rosh Hashanah

🏵 Eva McDonald Valesh, labor journalist, was born today in 1866

*Police in riot gear at the September 2009
RNC Convention in downtown Saint Paul*

10 Friday

Eid-al-Fitr

🐱 Carl Weschcke, publisher of occult books, was born today in 1930

11 Saturday

Saint Paul Farmers' Market

Selby Avenue JazzFest

Payne-Arcade Business
Association (PABA) Festival

12 Sunday

Saint Paul Farmers' Market

Payne-Arcade Business
Association (PABA) Festival

John Hays, whose body is found in the Mississippi River near Carver's
cave in September 1839, is the first person murdered in Saint Paul.

Lovin' the Skin I'm in

Andreesa Wright

Lovin' the Skin I'm In is a movement for girls that explores societal standards of beauty, media influences on self-esteem, and identity, that was inspired by the phenomenal book by Sharon G. Flake, *The Skin I'm In* (Hyperion, 2000). Started by Robin P. Hickman and SoulTouch Productions, Lovin' has engaged groups of young people, adults, faith-based organizations—literally thousands of people from various communities and educational organizations. Over the past five years this movement has served as a catalyst for personal and community healing by nurturing and promoting the positive and powerful voices, images, and visions of our youth. Lovin' is committed to giving young women the spiritual, mental, and emotional support and tools to "love the skin they're in," so they will feel prepared to take their rightful place in the world and their communities. With the empowerment and support from various community organizations and individuals, Lovin' the Skin I'm In flourishes on their blessings.

I have been a part of Lovin' the Skin I'm In since I was twelve. I was one of the main persons in the core group who started this movement

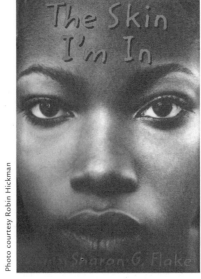

Photo courtesy Robin Hickman

Lovin' the Skin I'm in *by Sharon G. Flake*

and passed it on to many other people. Lovin' the Skin I'm In was like an extra class that I took after school at Dunning Recreation Center. I learned about issues in media that affect African American women. I gained knowledge of historic women leaders such as Sojourner Truth, Harriet Tubman, and Rosa Parks. I even learned how to create my own media to give women a better understanding of how they have been previously portrayed. As a group, we filmed skits and created film samples of magazines and short stories. My life without the Lovin' the Skin I'm In classes would be closed minded; I would only know the things that I learned from my textbooks in school. I now have a better understanding of my culture and other cultures.

Being a part of Lovin' the Skin I'm In has been a journey. There have been some ups and there have been some downs, but in the end it all worked out for the best. For me, Lovin' was a safe haven; if I had a bad day or a good day I wouldn't be the only one, but most of all I liked the fact that we could just come and talk. Some days it would be about how our day was going or how we were feeling, only because we hadn't made it through the agenda. And other days it would be about boys or just life in general. But when we did get down to business, we got serious. We would discuss problems in the media and the world, and how they affect each culture every day. We were trying to get this movement to grow throughout the Twin Cities, which it has in many ways. Lovin' the Skin I'm In was and is more than just a movement. It is life!

The Lovin' the Skin I'm In movement grows every day. This past school year, in partnership with EMID (East Metro Integration District), Lovin' groups included Ramsey Junior High School, White Bear Lake Middle School, Gordon Parks High School, South St. Paul High School, Capitol Hill, Mahtomedi Junior High School and Harding High School. The program also worked with Maxfield sixth graders and girls at the YWCA.

For more information about Lovin' the Skin I'm In, contact Robin P. Hickman, SoulTouch Productions, 651.291.9700, robinphickman@msn.com. For more information about Sharon G. Flake's book, check out her website, www.sharongflake.com.

⇨ September 13, 1893: Concordia
University, a Lutheran institution,
welcomes its first students to
its temporary quarters.

S	M	T	W	T	F	S
29	30	31	1	2	3	4
5	6	7	8	9	10	11
12	13	14	15	16	17	18
19	20	21	22	23	24	25
26	27	28	29	30	1	2

13 Monday

14 Tuesday

🕸 Sister Giovanni, founder of Guadalupe Area Project, was born today in 1914

15 Wednesday

16 Thursday   Saint Paul Almanac Book Release Party

*Republican National Convention (RNC) protestors
in September 2009 on Kellogg Boulevard at the Wabasha Bridge*

17 Friday Annual Twin Cities Black Film Festival

18 Saturday Saint Paul Farmers' Market

Yom Kippur Annual Twin Cities Black Film Festival

19 Sunday Saint Paul Farmers' Market

Annual Twin Cities Black Film Festival

Georgia Ray, writer and biographer, was born today in 1926

Telephone communication is established between Saint Paul
and Minneapolis in 1880.

Putting a SPNN on Saint Paul

Rick Mantley

I recall being among that first group of eager and apprehensive citizen-journalists who gathered together inside one of the Saint Paul Neighborhood Network (SPNN) studios on Jackson Street in downtown Saint Paul on a gray day in November 2007. Everyone present had been accepted to participate in the initial launch of the Saint Paul News Desk Project. We also became temporary members of SPNN by virtue of our participation, and Sherine Crooms, the project producer, not only made us feel at home, she even thanked us for signing up for the opportunity. We were told at the first meeting that we had the green light to make at least four video segments of approximately three to four minutes in length. The segments could be about any subject we chose—as long as it pertained to Saint Paul. I learned that more than a few of those on hand already had extensive experience as television producers and/or videographers. For complete novices like me, SPNN planned to offer crash courses in video camera operation, lighting, and editing. The classes were quick but comprehensive, and gave me enough confidence to take the plunge into shooting my first video. I submitted my proposal for the project and felt ready to check out the necessary equipment and start filming.

My subject was Tom Fletcher, co-owner and operator of The Essence of Nonsense, a marvelous toy store on St. Clair Avenue, which has been in business since 1996. What's unique about Tom is that for the past twenty years, he has sponsored the St. Paul Annual Marble Tournament. The tournament is held annually in the store's back lot. Players are sorted into divisions by age. Men and women as well as boys and girls are welcome. The name of the game is St. Paul Ringer, and at least two people are needed to play. First, the players agree upon the size of the circle, which can be created with a string or drawn in the dirt. A coin flip decides who goes first. The rules state that players must "knuckle down" with at least one knuckle touching the playing field when shooting, and may not lift (heist) or slide (hunch) at risk of losing a turn.

Each person puts five small target marbles inside the circle and then agrees,

Photo courtesy Rick Mantley

St. Paul Marble Tournament poster

"Game set." Taking turns, the players use a larger shooter to try to knock one or more of the smaller target marbles out of the circle. Knuckling, flicking, and popping are all acceptable shooting styles.

If the shooter knocks a target out of the circle but remains inside it, the player gets another turn. The first player to knock six marbles out is the winner. Play can be "for keeps" or "for faith," the latter meaning that each player's marbles are returned.

Rick Mantley

Tom collects marbles from all over the world in a fabulous array of color, design, and sizes. The basic sizes are peewees, shooters, and boulders. Peewees are the smallest; they are the marbles that are contested for in a game. Shooters are used to knock the peewees out of the circle, and boulders are the largest marbles, which are usually given to the winner as a prize. Steelies are marbles that were originally ball bearings. Tom showed me some large (25, 35, and 50 millimeter), particularly colorful, handcrafted marbles awarded as prizes to the winners. Included in his collection are marbles made by Tom Reddy, a renowned Saint Paul glassmaker, who makes no two marbles alike.

Making a three-to-four-minute video is exciting but arduous. I did not have a car at the time. Lugging around the video camera and lights on the bus or in a taxi was a challenge. After arriving at the location, I immediately began setting up the equipment so I could shoot. One thing you get is plenty of what is referred to as B-roll: extra footage that invariably comes in handy when you begin editing. After my first shoot inside The Essence of Nonsense, I returned to get some B-roll footage of the exterior and interior of this Saint Paul landmark. Editing, I discovered, is the most time-consuming and labor-intensive part of making a video. I spent hours and hours in the editing suite, assembling and perfecting the final product. Once I saw the fruits of my labor on both television and the Internet, I knew it had not only been worthwhile, it was also extremely gratifying and exhilarating. My segment, "For All the Marbles," was one of twelve featured on the *News Desk,* channels 15 and 16 of SPNN, from June through August 2008. It can still be seen on YouTube.

⇨ "My countrymen respond to poetry.
. . . By reviving memories and traditions
dear to all Armenians, . . . I try to spread
the gospel of Americanism." —Krikor
Keljik, Armenian-born Saint Paul poet

S	M	T	W	T	F	S
29	30	31	1	2	3	4
5	6	7	8	9	10	11
12	13	14	15	16	17	18
19	20	21	22	23	24	25
26	27	28	29	30	1	2

20 Monday

21 Tuesday

International Day of Peace

22 Wednesday

Fall Equinox

23 Thursday

Dusk on Como Lake

24 Friday   Fourth Friday at the Movies

🏵 F. Scott Fitzgerald, novelist and screenwriter, was born today in 1896

25 Saturday   Saint Paul Farmers' Market

26 Sunday   Saint Paul Farmers' Market

I'm sorry to say I forgot
Who you are (and who you are not)
I thought I'd remember
You in September
And I don't. But I like you. A lot.
Garrison Keillor

In 1887, Saint Paul has twelve breweries.

My Unforgettable Lesson of the RNC

Ed Howell

It was Tuesday in Mears Park, the second day of the Republican National Convention (RNC). We had already marched on Monday as part of the crowd of 10,000 protesting everything from the war in Iraq to the presence of Ethiopian troops in Mogadishu. Being part of a large group like that, you tend to only see and hear those things in your immediate area. But someone mentioned that they heard a cop say there had already been tear gas used farther downtown. Immediately, rumors and opinions began circulating about police violence and innocent protestors being beaten up. It was only later that we would learn of smashed windows, vandalized police cars, bags of feces, and all the mayhem that goes with unchecked street violence hiding behind legitimate political protest. Whether you believed it was the fault of a few rowdies or the end result of a stifling police presence, it was clear by Monday night that we had trouble right here in River City.

Tuesday promised another march, this time focusing on domestic needs such as hunger, homelessness, and education. Everybody, and I mean everybody, expected more problems similar to the ones we had seen on Monday. My wife and I sat on one of the small hills overlooking the Mears Park pavilion, watching the crowd grow, and just generally checking out the scene. Then I saw them.

"This can't be good," I said.

A few feet off to our left, we spotted three young people, girls, each one wearing the stereotypical "uniform" of the anarchist troublemaker: dark clothes, baseball caps, bandanas around their necks easily pulled up to cover their faces, eye goggles at the ready to protect them from Mace and tear gas. And finally, each one had a sinister-looking rucksack, which I was sure was full of stones and debris for the coming battle. They were all unsmiling and clearly on edge. If ever there was a central casting image of a troublemaker, this was it.

After a while of people just milling about, my wife noticed a growing commotion at the corner of Wacouta and Fifth streets. We joined the crowd and headed that way. In the middle of the intersection, the police, fully clad in riot gear, were attempting to move people from the street back to the sidewalk. I was struck by the fact that there weren't that many police and they were quickly surrounded on all four sides by people. Most folks left the intersection, but one man refused. I should say he moved, but in a clearly unwilling, surly, and defiant way. Not to

Police and protestors at Mears Park

mention he moved toward the center of the intersection, not away from it. Finally, after the guy bumped into a police horse, the cops had had enough. He was pushed to the ground, put on his stomach and cuffed with a pair of flexi-cuffs. Naturally, the crowd began a chorus of boos and chants: "The whole world is watching," "Stop beating that man," "He didn't do anything," and so on. The crowd began to press in until one cop raised a high-powered tear gas sprayer and another brought a bean-bag gun to his shoulder.

Then I saw the three girls I had seen earlier in the park. They pulled their eye goggles up and raised the kerchiefs around their mouths. "Okay, here we go," I thought. They each put on pairs of sterile latex gloves. "Well, that's different, but probably something to do with finger prints," I surmised. Then they reached into the suspicious rucksacks they carried—and pulled out bottles of water. It dawned on me like the proverbial light bulb: They weren't the troublemakers I supposed. They were there to give first aid to anyone hit with the tear gas. The water would soothe the pain and clear the eyes. The latex gloves were simple precautions in a world full of potential dangers from human fluids. They were prepared to put themselves at risk in order to help others.

But my attention was soon drawn away to a few feet farther up the sidewalk. People were yelling, and I could see a body lying in the gutter. The police, although looking menacing and no doubt ready for whatever action they needed to take, had done nothing more than hold their ground. By the time my wife and I got to the spot, we saw more volunteer medics in a semicircle, holding hands and keeping the crowd back, while other medics tended to the man in the gutter. There was considerable blood around his head.

"What happened?" I quickly asked. One of the volunteers replied, "A man standing by the truck had a seizure and hit his head on the curb when he fell. There's an ambulance on the way."

I tried to ask her who she was and who organized this medical aid. But the crush of people made talking impossible.

So this was my unforgettable lesson: "If it looks like a duck, and it walks like a duck, and it quacks like a duck—there's a good chance you have it all wrong."

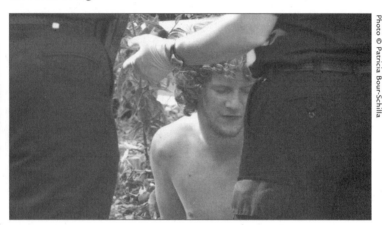

Medics assisting an injured person during the RNC protests

Saint Paul Whipping Club

Barbara Cox

We were looking for the peace picnic when we saw them. Our friends, home from their out-of-state master's program in Peace Studies, had invited friends and family to a get-together at Hidden Falls Picnic Pavilion. So there we were, salad bowl in hand, when we encountered not a gathering of peace-minded potluckers but a group of ten or so people, whipping.

Bullwhips. The men, and one lone woman whipper, were gathered around one of the beautiful old-growth trees in the park, where they had hung a three-foot, plush fake rabbit by its neck. One by one, they demonstrated their prowess with the long leather strap, alternately thrashing the bunny and stepping aside from the group for some freelance flourishes. Startled as we were, our curiosity won out over our fear.

"What is this?" my husband asked the whipper closest to us.

"The Saint Paul Whipping Club," he replied, as if such a thing were as common as curling clubs in Eveleth.

We didn't engage any further. We sat down to join the picnic, assembled adjacent to the whipping, and attempted to eat as the rabbit swung back and forth, slowly torn to pieces by the whips.

An unusual pastime at Hidden Falls Park

Illustration © Andy Singer

Peanuts in Saint Paul

Moira F. Harris

As you wander around Saint Paul, perhaps you have seen a figure of Lucy Van Pelt standing on a sidewalk, or a blanket-holding Linus in front of a sewing shop, or Charlie Brown welcoming guests to a Mexican restaurant, or a hockey-playing Snoopy in a hockey arena, or even Snoopy on top of his doghouse in a patio. Did you wonder when or how Charles Schulz's Peanuts gang marched into the city? The answer is easy. They began arriving ten years ago, just after the famed cartoonist from Saint Paul died.

Charles Schulz was born in Minneapolis in 1922, but grew up in Saint Paul. His father had a barbershop near Snelling and Selby, and the family lived nearby. Today, O'Gara's restaurant, proud owner of several of the *Peanuts* statues (including Snoopy as the knight Sir Lunchalot, who carries his dog dish on the tip of his lance), occupies the corner of the block.

Schulz showed an early aptitude for drawing, and hoped, he once said, to be another Andrew Wyeth. Instead, he created one of the most famous American comic strips ever drawn. By 1965, *Peanuts* was appearing in 700 American newspapers and over seventy-one others worldwide.

Schulz learned aspects of his trade by mail from the Art Instruction Schools of Minneapolis (then called Federal Schools), where he later taught. His first comic strip, L'il Folks, ran in the *Saint Paul Pioneer Press* from 1947 to 1949. When United Features Syndicate accepted the strip in 1950, they changed the title to *Peanuts,* because they felt that *L'il Folks* sounded too similar to Al Capp's popular *L'il Abner.* Schultz never liked the new name. After syndication, the *Peanuts* strip appeared in the *Minneapolis Star* (later the *Star Tribune).* Schulz moved to California in 1958, settling first in Sebastopol and later in Santa Rosa.

While successful comic strips often live on through the work of other artists once their creator dies, Schulz had long made it clear that he alone would draw and letter his strips. When he retired, *Peanuts* would end. The artist was diagnosed with colon cancer in the fall of 1999, and soon after, he announced that his last *Peanuts* strip would appear on February 12, 2000; he died the day before that Sunday's papers were delivered.

Newspapers and magazines across the country mourned his passing, sometimes using a portrait of a grieving Snoopy and the words "So long, Sparky" (Schulz's nickname). In Saint Paul, a family friend, Randi Johnson of TivoliToo Design, thought that the city should honor Schulz with

Lucy and Snoopy, his doghouse, and Woodstock in front of Candyland

bronze statues of his unforgettable characters, and the way to raise the funds to do that was through Animals on Parade, a project first conceived in 1998 in Zurich, Switzerland, that featured fiberglass cow sculptures placed around the downtown area to attract visitors; the "parade" was sponsored by local businesses. The success of the Zurich cow parade was copied in New York and Chicago, and soon throughout the world. Sharks, moose, hearts, pigs, even bridges (in Duluth), were among the sculptures chosen by different cities.

Snoopy began the series in the spring of 2000, which was launched with a giant paint-off in RiverCentre on June 10 and 11. Each Snoopy stood in front of his sponsor's business that summer, and a map was provided, along with newspaper features explaining each artist's concept. In September, all of the Snoopys were moved to the Mall of America (which then housed the Camp Snoopy theme park) for an auction.

In 2001, it was time for Charlie Brown, the character that Schulz said was the most autobiographical of all of the *Peanuts* gang. Fussbudget Lucy was the subject of 2002's parade. The following year brought Linus, with his security blanket draped over his shoulder.

Over the years, members of the Schulz family came to view the paint-offs, and in 2003, Schulz's friend Linus Maurer painted his own Linus figure. Usually, some of the *Peanuts* figures were moved to the State Fair, where they greeted fairgoers and posed for photographs in front of the Grandstand. Others were designated as traveling statues, delivered by truck to temporary locations. *Peanuts* statues also made appearances at Taste of Minnesota and Grand Old Days. Some of the *Peanuts* figures were later available to collectors as miniatures.

Photo © Patricia Bour-Schilla

Charlie Brown

The Rice Park party in September 2003 included the dedications of the bronze statues of the *Peanuts* characters. Designed by Randi Johnson's TivoliToo artists and cast in Howard Lake, Minnesota, by a firm called Casting Creations, the statues were placed downtown, in Rice Park across from the Saint Paul Hotel, and in what is now called Schulz Park east of Landmark Center. There, visitors can see Charlie Brown and Snoopy sitting under a tree, Schroeder playing his piano while Lucy listens, and Linus and his sister, Sally, looking over a wall. Peppermint Patty sits on a bench in Rice Park with Marcie playing nearby, not far from a statue of another famous Saint Paulite, author F. Scott Fitzgerald.

The last of the five *Peanuts* parades was The Doghouse Days of Summer in 2004, featuring Snoopy, his doghouse, and his tiny bird friend, Woodstock. At the event-ending picnic that year, a very popular activity allowed anyone to paint a tiny replica of the sculpture. The line for painting doghouses that afternoon was always long.

Another figure appeared in 2002, though it was not one of the regular Charlie Brown statues issued that year. This Charlie Brown wears a coat of bronze-colored paint, a brimmed hat, and a patched jacket; he carries a concertina, and at his feet are a suitcase and the bird Woodstock. Charlie Andiamo Americano, who stands at Eagle Parkway and Ryan Avenue, was donated to honor the Italian immigrants who settled on the Saint Paul levee.

October

The Fish Hatchery

The bluffs near Shepherd Road were steep, nearly
Worn away, over time, by the flooded
Sweep of the river. Minnow pools survived
Those years, there by the edge of the city
Near the cliffs. My dad took us to see
This odd place on Saturdays, this fish-filled
World where quick scales flashed in shallow-sided
Ponds, where slip gills and gray fins were simply
Too small to count. But we loved the bodies
Of the fish beyond what could love us, their
Small silver lives moving in slight rises
Beneath the water. And we mattered, there
Above the hatching lights, my dad's dark eyes
So full, so watchful along the river.

Mary Legato Brownell

S	M	T	W	T	F	S
26	27	28	29	30	1	2
3	4	5	6	7	8	9
10	11	12	13	14	15	16
17	18	19	20	21	22	23
24	25	26	27	28	29	30
31	1	2	3	4	5	6

⇨ September 28, 1976: Lou Bellamy founds Saint Paul's Penumbra Theatre Company, a forum for African American theater in the Twin Cities.

27 Monday

28 Tuesday

🕷 Mike Sanchelli, East Side writer, was born today in 1915

29 Wednesday

30 Thursday

🕷 George Morrison, Ojibwe artist and sculptor, was born today in 1919

October

Demolition of Xcel Energy's coal-burning plant below the High Bridge

1 Friday
International Day for Older Persons

🎲 David Arneson, co-creator of Dungeons and Dragons, was born today in 1947

2 Saturday   Saint Paul Farmers' Market

3 Sunday   Saint Paul Farmers' Market

October 1, 1911: St. John's Hospital on the East Side receives
its first patient, who is treated for typhoid.

Coming to Saint Paul

Lily Kaliea Yang

When I was in California, my mom and dad were getting ready to move out of our apartment. My mom was cleaning the house, and my dad was carrying the heavy items. When everything was put away in the U-Haul and our Mercedes, we went off to sleep over at my cousins' house. In the morning, we said "Good-bye!"

My dad was driving the U-Haul, and my mom was driving the Mercedes. After three days of sleeping in hotels, we finally arrived in Minnesota. First, past Mall of America, then Minneapolis, and last, to Saint Paul.

We were moving in with our auntie. As soon as we found our auntie's house, my mom called her. Our auntie came out, and she had a big smile on her face, and she said "Hi!" Our auntie called the whole family to come and help us.

Everyone was happy to see us all, and we were all happy to see them too. All of our aunties came to us and gave us kisses everywhere. My favorite uncle came to me and said, "Lily, the girls are at school, so when they're done, do you want to see them?"

And I said "Yes!" in happiness.

It was dusk, and I got to see my best cousins in the world. I was very happy to see them. When everything was put away in my auntie's garage, everybody said "Good-bye!" to us.

I didn't like the way I had to share a room with my brothers. I got used to it all, though.

Minnesota is an interesting place!

Fall Linens

Kathleen Vellenga

You resist when I take you down, refusing
to end your dance with the October breeze.
Flapping, twirling in your many threaded cotton
gowns, which contain the smells of maple, grass
and the geese sound, which blew in
and won't release.
Stiff, still filled with crisp air, you
bounce from my arms into the pile in
my basket, protesting. And lie
sulking and cold, in denial of
your identity, all the while
believing that bedding has
no worthy purpose. "We're Linens."
Until at last, I wrestle you onto the board,
Still heavy and redolent of summer's
mint leaves, roses, bee's repast.
A soothing massage, you yield
to the heat. My hand slides the warm
metal. No plastic, no copper, but iron,
wielding it back and forth, as regrettable
rough edges yield like petals.
I fold you over and over, and
with the iron's slap, slap, your
myriad of wrinkles hover on
the corners and the flap,
flap, mimics your dance under
clothespin's snap.
Scent and sounds don't leave,
when I crawl between you,
but evoke your autumn dance.
If I slept alone, you'd hope
to bring me to your dance,
a nighttime fling of dreams
your substitute for romance.
But I don't, so take
the strain upon your seams,
and relish in the dance which
autumn brings.

October

OCTOBER

S	M	T	W	T	F	S
26	27	28	29	30	1	2
3	4	5	6	7	8	9
10	11	12	13	14	15	16
17	18	19	20	21	22	23
24	25	26	27	28	29	30
31	1	2	3	4	5	6

⇨ "The fact that I am a professional musician has helped me greatly in becoming a writer. . . . In both disciplines, inexplicable and magical moments occur . . ." —Evelina Chao, Saint Paul musician and writer

October

4 Monday *Saint Paul Almanac* Reading Series

5 Tuesday
World Teacher's Day

 Virginia Brainard Kunz, historian of Saint Paul, was born today in 1921

6 Wednesday

7 Thursday

🐞 Tony Glover, blues harmonica player and author, was born today in 1939

View of First National Bank Building

8 Friday   Saint Paul Art Crawl

As dramatic as Tolstoy or Flaubert
Are the mighty campaigns of October
Til November the 4th—
JUBILEE IN THE NORTH—
Until then we stay steady and sober.
Garrison Keillor

9 Saturday   Saint Paul Farmers' Market

Saint Paul Art Crawl

Saint Paul Oktoberfest

Fall Flower Show begins

10 Sunday   Saint Paul Farmers' Market

Saint Paul Art Crawl

Saint Paul Oktoberfest

October 6, 1962: President John F. Kennedy comes to Saint Paul
for a bean feed and speech at the Hippodrome Arena.

From Lefse to FuFu:
A World of Camaraderie
in the Kitchen at Lyngblomsten

Penny Ueltschi and Annie Wilder

Vladimir from the Ukraine had a big heart and would help the girls from the dish room take the garbage out. Eleanor, who worked until she was eighty-five years old, was the baker and backup kitchen supervisor who would treat everyone on the tray line to a dinner roll, dessert bar, or piece of cake. Sandy from Liberia was the comic relief in the kitchen. Away at college now, Sandy started in the dish room and eventually worked his way up to being jack-of-all-trades and every-other-weekend supervisor. And Miss Henry was a dedicated boss who came in every single day, including half days on Sundays. Miss Henry had high standards and a strong work ethic, and if she heard people talking while working on the tray line, she'd remind them in a stern voice, "This is not a coffee klatch!"

From 1978 to 2003, my mom's cousin Penny worked in the food service department at Lyngblomsten Care Center in Midway, by the state fairgrounds. Founded by eleven Norwegian women in 1906 and opened in 1912, Lyngblomsten was named after the purple mountain heather that is Norway's national flower. Over the last quarter century, the kitchen staff has had an interesting mix of young and old employees, long-term staff and part-time student workers, and people from a variety of countries, including Nigeria, Liberia, Burma, Cambodia, China, and the Ukraine.

Penny, who is retired but still volunteers at Lyngblomsten each week with her husband, Jim, gives me an informal tour of the place that she says feels like home. As we make our way from the administrator's office to the kitchen to the chapel, with pleasant introductions all along the way, Penny adds, "The best thing about working here was the friendships and knowing different people. You get to visit with people."

Sue, the friendly and low-key food production manager, has worked at Lyngblomsten for twenty-four years. She tells me they like to have fun, and the fun usually involves food. "We're kind of known for our international potlucks," she notes, adding that the staff are invited to dress in traditional costume and share food and stories from their country of origin. She lists some of the favorite dishes from past parties: *fufu*, meat

Lyngblomsten near the State Fair grounds

pies, egg rolls, and *falouda*, a fruity dessert the kitchen staff have nicknamed "the pink stuff."

Kitchen work in any setting is labor intensive and not glamorous. And most of the people at Lyngblomsten work evening, weekend, and holiday shifts. To express appreciation and keep the vibe positive, the kitchen staff are always cooking up a friendly competition of some sort, like chili or wing cookoffs, pumpkin-carving contests, and informal holiday costume contests. They also host themed parties—one year, they turned the kitchen into a Santa's workshop of bakery treats and goodies—and invite all the residents and their families to come.

As I look at Lyngblomsten's gallery of vintage photographs, I think about how much has changed since the days when the staff and residents were all people of Norwegian descent, with a common heritage, religion, and customs. What hasn't changed at Lyngblomsten is the spirit of creating a place that feels like home. I think the original founders would be amazed, but pleased, if they could see what has become of their Norwegian eldercare home. Meanwhile, back in the kitchen, the staff are working hard but having a good time, building a sense of camaraderie and teamwork, one Russian teacake or *Julekage* at a time.

↪ "The machinery of government has been commandeered by a little clique whose blind obedience to Wall Street is responsible for the stupid, selfish and short-sighted policy that is retarding our prosperity . . ."
—Oscar Keller, Saint Paul congressman

S	M	T	W	T	F	S
26	27	28	29	30	1	2
3	4	5	6	7	8	9
10	11	12	13	14	15	16
17	18	19	20	21	22	23
24	25	26	27	28	29	30
31	1	2	3	4	5	6

11 Monday
Indigenous People's Day

12 Tuesday

🏵 Juanita Rangel, accordion player with the Rangel Sisters, was born today in 1921

13 Wednesday

14 Thursday

🏵 Judy Mahle Lutter, health researcher, founder of Melpomene Institute, was born today in 1939

Top of the Blair Arcade Building on Selby

15 Friday

---

16 Saturday   Saint Paul Farmers' Market

World Food Day   Zoo Boo

---

17 Sunday   Saint Paul Farmers' Market

International Day for the   Zoo Boo
Eradication of Poverty

🏵 Mary McGough, early teachers' union leader, was born today in 1885

Saint Paulite Howie Schultz plays for both the Brooklyn
Dodgers and the Minneapolis Lakers in the 1940s.

Photo © Patricia Bour-Schilla

A Kilometer of Cheese

Janaly Farias

I will never forget the first time I entered a Mexican store as an eight-year-old and tried to buy something. It was after I had emigrated from the United States to Mexico. I had trouble with ordinary words, like asking to use the bathroom. I had to tell one of my older sisters to do it for me, because they knew more Spanish than I did.

One day, my dad sent me to the store to buy *leche* (milk). I had a very puzzled expression, so my sister slapped me across the head and said, "It's milk, you retard."

"Well, sorry, miss know-it-all!" I answered her back while rubbing my head.

As it turned out, my sister went for the milk.

A few months later, my grandma needed some stuff from the store. It seemed like she trusted my Spanish, because she didn't send my sister.

"Bring me one pound of cheese and one liter of milk. Don't forget," she told me with this look on her face that said, Am I really sending her?

I started on my way to the store, repeating it in my head over and over: "One liter of milk and one pound of cheese . . ."

When I got to the store, though, I asked the lady at the counter, "Can I please have a kilometer of cheese and a pound of milk?"

She turned red, grabbed her stomach, and fell to the ground. I got really scared. I thought I had done or said something wrong, so I left.

When I got home, my mom said, "Where's the stuff that we sent you for?" She sounded upset.

"I asked her for the stuff, and she turned red and fell to the ground. I got scared, so I left."

"What did you ask for?' she said in a curious way.

"For a kilometer of cheese and a pound of milk."

"Ha, ha, ha! Don't you think that's enough cheese, kid? No one could find that much cheese in a store," my uncle said.

Ten years have passed, and I am back in the United States. Whenever I call my grandma or uncle, they always ask me, "Are you done with that cheese you asked for?" I just laugh.

Now I know how Hispanics struggle when they come to the United States.

Saint Paul Skyways = Freedom

John Lee Clark

I'm sure there are many who say they love Saint Paul more than any other place on earth, but for me to say that would be an understatement. That's because living anywhere outside of downtown Saint Paul would be like being in jail. I live in the heart of the skyway system in downtown, and for me it is freedom. You see, I am both deaf and blind.

Many deaf-blind Americans live within invisible prison walls. No, it's not because of deaf-blindness itself, but because many places don't have the transportation, services, and access that would make it possible to be independent without hearing and sight. So, in many places, deaf-blind people feel stuck, just as anyone without legs would feel stuck if there's no wheelchair and there are no sidewalks outside. But Saint Paul isn't one of those bad places for people with slightly different bodies. Minnesota has some of the nation's very best transportation services and other accommodations for accessibility.

The skyway system, though, is the frosting on the cake. It is so much easier to get around through skyways instead of crossing streets outside. It is not safe for me to cross a street on my own, so to do that, I hold up a card and hope someone will come along soon, see it, read it, and then offer to help me across. That works, and I do that if I am traveling beyond the skyways. But it's so wonderful when I don't need to hold up that card and wait in the cold.

Thanks to the skyways, I can experience the same ease that most people do. Most things out there are designed for people's convenience, but they're for hearing and sighted people. If you feel like coffee, you can drive to the nearest coffee shop. And that's going to be very near you from anywhere you may be coming. But many of my fellow deaf-blind citizens don't have that privilege. They have to call paratransit to book a ride three days later—imagine how bad their hankering for that mocha latte must be by then! But I, I can just up and go. Just elevator down to the skyway level and then tap the tip of my white cane on the variously textured surfaces through different buildings.

After living here for five years, I know downtown Saint Paul like the back of my hand. But the landscape in my mind is very different from what you might see and store in your mind. I wouldn't be surprised that there are many ugly sights, such as all those bland logos of fast food chains. Perhaps the skyways feel claustrophobic to some, and to others they may be just another gray patch of corporate America. But for me, they're more than pure beauty. They're freedom.

➭ "I had found my spot on the roof of a red woodshed in the back yard. . . . An inveterate reader, . . . I could remain concealed, safely ignoring any voice calling me from below." —Blanche Yurka, Saint Paul–raised actress

S	M	T	W	T	F	S
26	27	28	29	30	1	2
3	4	5	6	7	8	9
10	11	12	13	14	15	16
17	18	19	20	21	22	23
24	25	26	27	28	29	30
31	1	2	3	4	5	6

18 Monday

19 Tuesday

20 Wednesday

21 Thursday

❀ Father John C. Gruden, long-time St. Agnes priest, was born today in 1884

October

Nighttime in downtown Saint Paul

22 Friday   Zoo Boo

23 Saturday   Saint Paul Farmers' Market
                                                  Zoo Boo

24 Sunday   Saint Paul Farmers' Market
United Nations Day   Zoo Boo

Saint Paul Central High School's undefeated football team wins
the City Conference Championship in 1941.

Photo © Patricia Bour-Schilla

Running, Living, and Dying in Saint Paul

Deborah A. Torraine

Saint Paul is a provincial town, a green place of bluffs and rolling hills made up of culture swatches—Old Timers and Newcomers—that sometimes clash and bump up against each other. But eventually, with a little nip and tuck here and a stitch or two there, we settle into a quilted work that is strong and wide enough to cover us all. Saint Paul is a haven for the creative and the faint of heart; those of us who long for a little less struggle and a lot more quality. So, I ran. Yes, I ran away, away!

I came to Minnesota back in the earliest of the 1990s when the floods washed out levees and flooded barns. It seemed as if it rained for two months; maybe it was just four weeks. I'd been on the road doing a vision quest, which means I didn't know where I was going or where I would wind up. Minneapolis gave me a place to lay my head and offered to fill my belly. But it would be Saint Paul that I would eventually call home; it was quieter, smaller, cleaner; and I still believe it loves me.

But that didn't stop me from running away from Minnesota twice; I was afraid of getting stuck in a winter wonderland. I ran to Oklahoma (I grew in Oklahoma). I ran to Colorado (I loved Colorado but it broke my heart). I even returned to my hometown of Washington, D.C. (My father died). I ran and ran until I answered a call from my Saint Paul friends. They asked why I would run away from people who loved me.

When I returned later that year, the city saw me first. Saint Paul seemed to exhale and whisper to me that I was forgiven for abandoning the garden. The trees waved red-rust autumn leaves as I walked through Frogtown. The sunlight shimmered through the breeze. People actually said "Excuse me" when I bumped into them! I effortlessly found a job as a coffee barista at Kapernicus on Prince Street years before it would become the Black Dog—one of the best jobs I ever had. There I became "Queen of the Coffee Bean." We had Spoken Word nights. Teens felt safe enough to hang out, and we would sometimes give them coffee. They were our kids, too, weren't they? They didn't need to run away; we would love them just as they were. Eventually I would move into the Northern Warehouse Lofts above the new café.

Welcome to an old-school artists' community! I had found a community that reminded me of the old days in San Francisco. The Rossmore was like San Francisco's Project Artaud, an artists' co-op in a renovated ware-

The Rossmor Building on Robert Street

house. At the Rossmore, on Robert Street, artists, musicians, craft people, veterans, and some losers coexisted over shops, restaurants, gay bars, and an employment office. It was a jacked building; we were not supposed to be living there, but we were—surviving and thriving, like hippies from the '70s. These were my friends, my new family now.

Depending on how one counted time, Saint Paul seemed at least ten to twenty years behind the curve, and that was just fine with me. Time slowed down enough for me to catch up. I have found my way to a new life and to new folks to love back. With myself in tow, I've just resigned myself to living and maybe dying in Saint Paul. It's not been such a bad place to live. The sky is wide and quiet, and there are lots of babies here. White babies, Black babies, brown, tan, mauve . . . all of them are new babies. That's the thing about babies—they are all newcomers; little swatches of newcomers! Might not be such a bad place to die. Simply lay my body upon a quilt made of many swatches and light the fire high.

October

⇨ "The death penalty experiment has failed. . . . No combination of procedural rules or substantive regulations ever can save the death penalty from its inherent constitutional deficiencies." —Harry Blackmun, late associate justice, U.S. Supreme Court

S	M	T	W	T	F	S
26	27	28	29	30	1	2
3	4	5	6	7	8	9
10	11	12	13	14	15	16
17	18	19	20	21	22	23
24	25	26	27	28	29	30
31	1	2	3	4	5	6

25 Monday

🕸 Chad Smith, Red Hot Chili Peppers drummer, was born today in 1961

26 Tuesday

27 Wednesday

October Swede Hollow
Leaves release the branches.
Dark comes too soon,
Season of plenty is over,
Frost covers the last tomatoes,
Wing beats of departure turn toward
The Southern horizon as I stack wood.
Loren Niemi

28 Thursday

🕸 Frederick L. McGhee, African American lawyer and civil rights activist, was born today in 1861

October

BareBones Productions performers at Hidden Falls Park on Halloween

29 Friday   Fourth Friday at the Movies

30 Saturday   Saint Paul Farmers' Market

Dia de los Muertos Family Fiesta

October

31 Sunday   Saint Paul Farmers' Market

Halloween   Great Pumpkin Festival

Approximately 2,600 families are evacuated from the Mississippi River flats in 1951 because of record flooding.

In a City Classroom

Linda Kantner
with memory support from Jane Sevald

I learned how to be a Saint Paul therapist from movies like *Ordinary People* and *Sybil*. Being painfully shy, I hoped I could keep my conversation to "Hmmm," and "How do you feel about that?" I imagined a Summit Hill female clientele who struggled with color schemes and what to wear to University Club banquets.

Instead, my days were often spent on the floor at Expo Elementary, smashing trucks into walls and filing child abuse reports. After years of this, I quit and tried to be a writer. In September of 2001, I won a one-month retreat at Norcroft, a feminist writer's retreat in northern Minnesota. At Norcroft there were no televisions, radios, newspapers, or telephones. I learned a few sparse details about the tragedy of September 11 at Lutsen's Bar on Lake Superior. I waited in the lounge for my turn to use the pay phone and watched as the television silently showed strangers holding hands and jumping from the burning towers.

On my return to Saint Paul, I saw flags and yellow ribbons and signs saying, "Peanut Buster Parfait, USA All the Way." As the days passed, I had the strongest desire to gather people on the street and have a group hug. I wanted desperately to rise to the occasion, but I didn't know how. I felt like I was returning to a changed world.

My friend Jane Sevald was also entering a whole new world. At age forty-five, she was taking on her high school classroom teaching English and writing at Como High School to students from Ethiopia, Somalia, Laos and Iraq. She likes a challenge and takes to it like Lance Armstrong approaching a hill, but when we spoke on the phone about meeting for coffee, I heard something in her voice—something scared. It was the sound of riding injured.

Jane is a big woman, and I am kind of scrawny. She is loud, and I tend to mumble. She covers her shyness with grand gestures and a whopping presence. She is brilliant, in a far-flung fashion. She speaks Russian and knows what countries were named before they were what they are now, and she can find them on a map. She watches gory detective shows and reads ten mysteries a week for distraction. I have my own brand of intelligence gathered from the streets of Frogtown, downtown, Highland, and Hamline, where I have been riding my blue mountain bike for twenty-two years. Jane can talk to people about anything, and I can listen to people talk about anything.

Jane Sevald and Linda Kantner

When I returned from Norcroft, we met at the old Black Bear Crossings Cafe by the railroad tracks. It was a cozy place decorated with dream catchers, woodsy colors, and a stone fireplace. Jane was draped across the coffee shop couch, her big voice roaring with pain. "I'm a mess. I have never been so tired in my life, and I only work half-time. Whatever made me think I could teach high school? It's a disaster—you should come and see."

I choked on my skinny latte. "Why would I want to come and see a disaster?" In the space of that sentence, half of me was speeding down Lexington to her class and the other half was headed back to the woods. Like many social workers, I am a junkie for a good disaster.

"You could help me figure them out." Jane looked excited, as though she were having a good idea at that very moment, and didn't I want to get excited too?

"I hate meeting new people—it scares me. I don't know anything about kids from other countries. I've never met a Muslim before. I don't even know anyone who's visited Africa. It's a whole new language for me 'refugee,' 'foreign national,' 'despot.' My second language is street slang done poorly."

"I knew you'd want to come." Jane ignored my rush of concerns.

"I didn't say I wanted to come. I do wonder why so many people want to immigrate here if they hate Americans. But I can wonder from home."

"You should have seen us on September 11. I could have used you that day." The layers of complication and pain in Jane's voice drew me in.

I couldn't help myself, "What was it like?"

Photo courtesy Linda Kantner and Jane Sevald

She didn't answer right away. Her pale features turned sickly and she held herself very still. She shut her eyes, and with each word, her sorrow rose like a tired man climbing a steep ladder. "I put on CNN so the pictures could speak for themselves. I tried to interpret what they were seeing. I stared at the television and remained calm like the president asked. The students stopped talking. The look on my face must have scared them half to death.

"'Class, it is important that you listen,' but they were listening, they were waiting for an explanation. I tried to explain using the small words they knew. When I stopped, they waited for the rest, waited for the happy ending. All of the students had come to the United States for a happy ending."

"'America is a safe country, Ms. Sevald,' Shumi tried to comfort me, 'That's why we came here.'

"'That's true, it is not like Somalia,' Zamu was certain.

"But then Ali sat up in his seat. He looked me in the eye and asked, 'Will they kill us all?'"

The next Monday I slid into Jane's classroom, hoping to be unobtrusive. There was noise, like an international market on trading day. Holding my breath, I slipped toward the back. I was stopped by a beautiful young woman who held out her hand. "Hi, I'm Shumi from Oromia. Who are you?"

"I'm Linda, a friend of Jane's. She invited me to visit for a day. I don't even know where Oromia is."

Shumi continued holding my hand a little longer than an American would. "No one knows where Oromia is. You've heard of Ethiopia, right?"

Shumi spoke so fast it was like trying to catch words in a wind tunnel. I worked up a sweat just listening, and when she paused for a breath, I was ready to head to Sweeny's, my neighborhood bar.

"Listen up, people. This is my friend Linda, a real writer." Jane shook her head at the wonder of it. "She has published stories in books and magazines. She won the Minnesota Monthly Tamarack Award. Let's give her a big hand."

I was horrified. Was Jane the school bully? I gave a little wave and tried to sit down, but they kept clapping and hooting. Damn Jane, damn her.

I opened my mouth, "Ah." My tongue felt like a wad of paper mâché. "I have ideas and questions and worries about the world. I try to understand things by writing about them. I believe that stories can change how people think. Maybe if you tell me a story about yourself, I will know you a little bit better and I won't be afraid of you. The world will be a better place."

I found the courage to say a little more. "You have ideas too. You have stories people need to hear, stories I need to hear. You can be real writers too. You can do that." My heart had reached its limit; it was pounding so hard I could feel it in my ears. "Ah, well . . . That's all." I dropped in my seat.

"You should write a story about me."

"In Ethiopia they beat us if we write in our own language, so our stories never get written down."

The man who had asked, "Will they kill us all?" stirred from where he sat slumped in a corner. The room quieted, and the kids looked to him. "I'm Ali. I want to tell my story."

When the bell rang, Jane and I raced out the door along with the kids. We headed back to the Black Bear Crossings Cafe. Jane let loose a long and weary sigh, as though she had been holding her breath all morning. "So what do you think?"

The question was so inadequate to the force of the morning. We started laughing and laughed until we couldn't any more. In between gasps, I tried to explain.

"It was nice," I said, and we laughed harder.

"Good," I tried again. But it was neither of those. It was loud and chaotic. It was confusing and fascinating. It was intriguing and daunting and mysterious. I didn't know what it was.

"They talk a lot," I said.

"They talk all the time unless they are sleeping," Jane agreed. "When are you coming back again?"

"Why would I come back?" I felt myself shrink at the thought. I am not the type to get involved.

"Teach them to write, obviously," Jane's voice bounced off the walls. "They like you—they listened. Ali said he wanted to tell his story."

"I'd like to hear it."

"How am I going to have time to help him with the other thirteen bouncing off the wall?"

I wondered the same thing. Ali had left a haunting impression, and Shumi, the sparkling girl from Oromia. Maybe I could get out of bed for this, an hour, once a week, or maybe twice.

"Can they write?"

Jane pulled papers from her bag. "Last week, I asked them to describe themselves." She paused, reading the first paper to herself. "We might want a refill before we look at these."

I Am

Keng Lee

I am a Hmong boy who lives to eat rice.
I wonder how much rice can feed the world.
I hear the sound of Mama packing the rice from the "vab"
I see the steam from the freshly cooked rice that makes my mouth
    water.
I want to help mother in the rice fields in mid-November
I am a Hmong boy who loves to eat rice.

I pretend to be the snake found in the rice patties.
I touch the grains of rice as they fall from Mother's hands.
I cry when Mother is working so hard.
I am a Hmong boy who loves to eat rice.

I understand that working is painful labor
I say everyone should eat rice.
I dream about eating rice with a steak on a hot summer day.
I try to be the best Hmong boy.
I hope someday to see a sumo wrestler in Japan.
I am a Hmong boy who loves to eat rice.

Trouble in School

Abenet Amare

I love my mom because she does good things for me and tells me a lot of things. I am not doing what she tells me to do. She wants me to be smart, but I am not. I try to be smart, but I can't.

When I think about what I want to be, that is too hard for me, because now I am not good at anything. My life is messed up. I don't know what to do. I can't study. If I can't study, I can't get good grades. I don't want to let my family down. I want to disappear, because my family tells me to study, and they tell me they will take me to another state or to Disney World, and I still can't do it. I try my best in class, but I don't think the teachers can see that, and it makes me feel very bad. Nobody is happy with the grades I am getting.

I know that someday I am going to be good at something. That has to be right, because if I am not good in school, there has to be something outside of school that I'm good at. I will find something I am good at.

My Day with the Animals and the Martian

Alcides Andreas Xiong

It was September 5, 2000, 11:35 a.m., and the bell rang. It was my first time there for lunch—time to face the real world inside the school cafeteria. It was like a zoo inside: there were many kinds of animals—monkeys, lions, wild dogs, and some cougars too. I walked down a corridor between Martians. It was so different for me to talk with them.

I could smell the food, but the food did not smell like food in my homeland. I could not taste the same tastes I tasted in my home; the smells did not smell like my former real place. When I came in, I took a chicken sandwich with potatoes and chocolate milk, and I paid $1.50. The line was so long that I almost did not have time to eat—we had only fifteen minutes. For me, fifteen minutes was too short, and that day, I was the last to leave.

When I was in the real world, I did not know where to sit. I was afraid of the animals like monkeys, but I was not afraid of the blond girl who was there. I took a seat next to the cashier, and I sat there for all my first year in Como Park. It was difficult for me to meet someone like the blond girl because I did not speak English.

Now I feel like a person living in the jungle. Now I inhabit places I've learned how to survive in, this world of animals. Now I can feel as if everything has come back to normal. It was my life to adjust to this jungle. Now I feel like an American person.

Dribble

Evan Hall

Dribble dribble dribble shot!
Blackboard rebound bounce caught
Try again, I'll take a lot
Juke juke juke juke
G o n e.

Over the fence hits smack on the grumpy guy's door
hey, someone get the ball, unlucky one is me,
I gotta get the basketball,
Others start to run,
hey, the grumpy guy isn't home
I'm just gonna have some fun.

My Life in Saint Paul

Shalaya Avant

Do you have a special place where you like to go? Well, I do. My special place is a tunnel, and I think it's an important part of Saint Paul.

The tunnel is close to my cousin's house. Every time I go down there, I fall under a spell. It's like the blazing grass is waiting for me. As I walk on the path, it looks almost as if the trees are dancing or waving for me to come closer. Two ponds connect, with glazed fish swimming in and out, in and out. Then the path just ends.

Even when it does, I keep walking, hoping I will find something grand. I never do, but one day I will.

Even though I only went there once, I keep visiting this place in my dreams. When I go back there, it's always midnight. The fish are swimming, but not as fast as before. In my dream, there's a person waiting for me, a Native American. We walk down the path. Far off is an Indian village.

Then I always wake up.

I wish my dreams could come true. But that's as far as I get to go every night in my dreams. I want to visit the tunnel again so I can see if the village is really there, far down. Every day I think of that place. What if it was my home—how would I live? If I just had one full day to go there, I would figure out how the animals live and if there's a village. I hope there is. And if there is, I wonder if the people there get mad because we stole their land.

I hope they see the love and peace in my inner self.

November

I raise my baton,
a rake, a half-chewed stick:
dry leaves crackle, snap
tympani for the horn toot
of geese flying south.
Paired wings overhead
wind instruments
playing a downbeat of air,
I listen to the hushed prayer.

Diane Wilson

November

239

⇨ "I was a Depression baby. The year
I was born, my mother was fond
of telling me, enough material
for a dress cost only a nickel,
but no one had a nickel."—Judy
Delton, children's book writer

S	M	T	W	T	F	S
31	1	2	3	4	5	6
7	8	9	10	11	12	13
14	15	16	17	18	19	20
21	22	23	24	25	26	27
28	29	30	1	2	3	4

1 Monday
Saint Paul Almanac Reading Series

All Saints' Day

Dia de los Muertes / Day of the Dead

🐞 Gunther Plaut, rabbi and scholar, was born today in 1912

2 Tuesday

Election Day

3 Wednesday

🐞 Carl Bohnen, portrait artist, was born today in 1872

4 Thursday

🐞 Kenneth Tilsen, activist attorney, was born today in 1927

Grandview Theatre at 1830 Grand showing
"Ghost of Girlfriends Past" and "State of Play"

5 Friday

6 Saturday   Saint Paul Farmers' Market

7 Sunday   Saint Paul Farmers' Market
Daylight Saving Time ends

Saint Paul Jaycees bring Christmas lights to downtown in 1955.

S.O.S. Saint Paul to Buenos Aires
Juan Pablo, are You Listening?

Molly Culligan

Funny how two people
can get the feel of each other in two bars
two bars of a tango
a woman from the top of the world
a man from the bottom of the world
in the middle of a circus
in the middle of an industrial zone en el Rio Plata
in the middle of Buenos Aires.
Funny how they can take each other's measure
and throw it away
to course into a Piazzola tango, torso to torso
transmitting questions and answers
two birds mating in the sky wings akimbo
dancing the dance of love
Cuidado! Losing altitude! Hitch'er up!
Oooooooooooooooooooooo song's ending
even birds mating in the sky are finite
sink her over and atop your body
head cradled like a baby

Illustration © Kirk Anderson

Russia

Norita Dittberner-Jax

Dr. Sobkoviak of Frogtown, our dentist, stood looking out the window of his office at Western and University and saw Russia. As he changed the point of the drill, looking straight through Old Home Dairy across the street into the Kremlin, he warned me about Nikita Krushchev.

He was slow and thorough, stopping to polish his glasses in front of that window. In his starched white tunic, he was a true professional. He did me, a school girl, the honor of thinking out loud about the world, not with the passion of my father at the dinner table, but with the cool reason of fine instruments arranged on a tray. He was the first polite society I knew. The crease in his trousers was enough to break my heart.

The dentist chair itself faced the large front window. The corner was cut away as if to make a stage of the world beyond. To the right, sat a large glass box in which were stacked hundreds of white filters, a few of which he delicately inserted in my mouth. False teeth set in a deathly grimace warned me of what lay ahead, if I was not careful—what my mother was holding off with these punctual visits.

There was no receptionist. When the telephone rang, Dr. Sobkoviak left his work to answer: "Sobkoviak speaking." When he returned, he took up the pick and continued his political ruminations. These were not conversations. I never got a turn. As soon as I wanted to say something, he unhooked the drill, and I lay back with the pearly orange light in my eyes and thought of Russia. I never knew there was such a thing as Novocain until I left home. He never offered it. We took pain straight in Frogtown.

Previously published in Sidewalks *literary magazine.*

November

⇨ November 14, 2008: Heidemarie Stefanyshyn-Piper, a Saint Paul native and Cretin High School graduate, blasts off and becomes the first female lead spacewalker.

NOVEMBER

S	M	T	W	T	F	S
31	1	2	3	4	5	6
7	8	9	10	11	12	13
14	15	16	17	18	19	20
21	22	23	24	25	26	27
28	29	30	1	2	3	4

---

8 Monday

🐞 Bill Mahre, Saint Paul Ski Club Hall of Fame, was born today in 1934

---

9 Tuesday

Goin' Home

Goin' home
not to Triangle Bar
not to Gene McCarthy
not to Wheelock Parkway
not to Ramsey County welfare
not to Saint Paul schools

---

10 Wednesday

Goin' home
to walking Como Park
to Grand Avenue
to the Wilder Foundation
to inner College Macalester
late '60s wherever
I am
Marsha Drucker

---

11 Thursday
Veterans' Day

Minnesota State High School League
Girls' Volleyball Tournament

🐞 Adeline Whitford, co-founder of Women's City Club, was born today in 1878

November

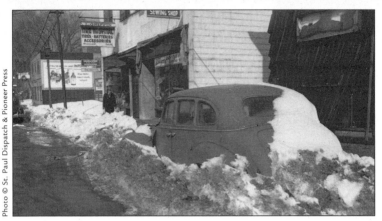

Car in front of Laurence Griffin Tires, 305 Selby Avenue in 1940

Photo © St. Paul Dispatch & Pioneer Press

12 Friday	Minnesota State High School League Girls' Volleyball Tournament

🍲 Brenda Langton, whole foods restaurant owner, was born today in 1957

13 Saturday	Saint Paul Farmers' Market
	Minnesota State High School League Girls' Volleyball Tournament

14 Sunday	Saint Paul Farmers' Market

November

November 11, 1859: The Athenaeum, a building designed for German educational lectures and social events, opens in Saint Paul.

Big Hair

Margaret Hasse

This fall, our son's chosen
to grow his hair out long.

He keeps his tresses clean,
Otherwise lets the fields lie fallow,

Doesn't cultivate with comb and brush.
One woman on Grand stares so long

at his hair, she trips over the curb.
Our mellow teen's unfazed,

But his friend shouts at her:
Why don't you just take a picture?

In winter, ropey knots and dreadlocks
raise a lion's mane around his face.

On myspace.com, he uses Bob
Marley's photo, not his own.

Now in hot spring, he scores his first job,
can't fit his 'do into the employee cap,

decides to have the wild bush
whacked, but declines the barber

whose shop attracts other young
black men with high style.

There's no escape for his father
who pulls out hair-trimming tools

inherited from his grandma.
Michael drapes a Batman cape,

sits on a kitchen stool so his dad can shear
the black mats that fall like Brillo pads.

The one now bald doesn't appear
to be the same boy: a soldier

could wear this chiseled head.
But look again, a softhearted youth

comes back thinking how to use
the surplus he raised and leaves behind.

Could it make a wig? he asks,
for someone like your mother

who got sick? I mask a smile,
imagine setting on her bare head

an ebony Rastafarian crown, bold
as shining gold bequeathed

from a grandson
she would have loved to hold.

⇨ "Who does not love a Minnesota winter, with its clear bracing air—its blue sky and its life-giving atmosphere? . . . Fear not then, the blast of coming winter." —*Saint Paul Minnesota Times,* November 20, 1854

S	M	T	W	T	F	S
31	1	2	3	4	5	6
7	8	9	10	11	12	13
14	15	16	17	18	19	20
21	22	23	24	25	26	27
28	29	30	1	2	3	4

15 Monday

16 Tuesday

🕸 William Kent Krueger, mystery writer, was born today in 1950

17 Wednesday
Eid al-Adha

18 Thursday

🕸 Janice Lynn Kuehnemund, rock musician, was born today in 1961

Mattocks Park in snow

19 Friday

20 Saturday   Saint Paul Farmers' Market

Universal Children's Day

21 Sunday   Saint Paul Farmers' Market

A 56-foot-high Saint Paul boxelder is listed in the Minnesota Big
Tree Registry.

Exploring the Fort Road Sewers

Greg Brick

Back in my younger and more foolish days, I spent a lot of time exploring the sewers under the Fort Road neighborhood of Saint Paul. The tunnels run under every street at an average depth of about thirty feet. These tunnels, which carry raw sewage, were dug out of the St. Peter sandstone bedrock with handpicks more than 100 years ago. Their floors are paved with brickwork. I once painstakingly measured the aggregate length of this sewer labyrinth on sewer maps and found it was thirty miles long—the length of the famous Carlsbad Caverns in New Mexico. The funny thing is, it's almost totally unknown to the public.

My motivation was simple curiosity about this strange netherworld of fermenting brickwork, and I kept a sewer diary to record my impressions. I wore plastic trash bags over my clothes, but even so, sometimes I had to discard what I had worn because it was caked with filth. I carried food, but the problem was finding a place clean enough in which to eat it. I usually explored alone because no one would go with me, and these ventures marked some of the loneliest moments of my life. I once jokingly referred to the sewer labyrinth as the Diamond mine, hoping to motivate squeamish friends to accompany me, holding out the prospect of finding wedding rings that had been flushed down the drain. Unfortunately, nobody was that stupid, and I never did find any rings.

Despite the sewers' eerie isolation, I wouldn't have cared to meet anyone down there anyway. In fact, what further unnerved me during my long solo expeditions was the ghostly reflection of flashlight beams from water surfaces onto the walls, which produced the momentary illusion that someone was approaching or retreating from me in the tunnels. After a while, you begin to hear voices in the dripping water.

It was a long time before I overcame my fear of sewer gas. Overall, the tunnels smelled vaguely like garlicky summer sausage. But there were pockets of better and worse. Lengthy dead-end passages, flooded with stagnant, blue-green septic pools, for example, were pretty overpowering. Laundromats overhead, with their sudsy downward discharges, provided a welcome olfactory oasis in the sewers below. And walking under Fort Road toward downtown, I could always tell when I passed Cossetta's, one of my favorite restaurants, owing to the pleasant, steamy aromas. Finally I would arrive under Seven Corners, where the passages branched out under the Loop.

1915 sewer cover on Hamline Avenue

I encountered rats, too—aplenty. One day, while strolling under one of the city's charity soup kitchens, I observed fresh pasta floating in the sewage. Following the stream, I came to a pipe vomiting pasta into the tunnel. Swarms of sleek, fat rats clustered about, feasting gluttonously. They parted ahead of me in the narrow passage when I approached, then closed the gap behind, squeaking in protest all the while. I actually welcomed comic relief like this, considering how perilously far I was from human aid.

There's very little graffiti in the tunnels, except for the initials of public works personnel, but I once encountered a very elaborate wall carving of a tree—carved *in relief!*—with intertwined branches, several feet high. It seemed symbolic of the labyrinth as a whole, with its endless, branching passages.

Subterranean Twin Cities (2009), published
by the University of Minnesota Press

▷ "Recreation and play means growth, progress, and development, all of which tend toward bettering social conditions."
—Eleanor Dowling, Christ Child Society, Saint Paul

S	M	T	W	T	F	S
31	1	2	3	4	5	6
7	8	9	10	11	12	13
14	15	16	17	18	19	20
21	22	23	24	25	26	27
28	29	30	1	2	3	4

22 Monday

23 Tuesday

🐞 W. A. Swanberg, award-winning biographer, was born today in 1907

24 Wednesday

25 Thursday
Thanksgiving Day

🐞 William Marvy, barber pole manufacturer, was born today in 1909

November

The Mississippi River as seen from Raspberry Island

26 Friday   Fourth Friday at the Movies
Buy Nothing Day
(www.buynothingday.org)

27 Saturday   Saint Paul Winter Farmers' Market

28 Sunday

November

Johnson High School moves into its current building—its third—
in the fall of 1963.

Native American Cathedral

J. Moreno Carranza

According to the *American Heritage College Dictionary*, a cathedral is "a principal place of authority, an important and authoritative gathering place." The great caves under the Mounds Park cliffs in Saint Paul can and should be seen as such a place, considering that they played such an important part in the lives of local Native Americans.

Before Europeans settled in the Mounds Park area and long after, the site had been regarded as sacred, steeped in myths and legends about the caves and their ceremonial use. Native Americans held council gatherings in one of the central caves under the Mounds Park cliffs. These councils were of great importance for the people surrounding the upper Mississippi River, for the members of these tribes did not necessarily look at each other as neighbors, but as emissaries using the same river, moving from place to place, taking a living from the same boundless territory.

Every so often, tribal chiefs from the surrounding native communities came together in the Central Cave to discuss problems between the tribes. These councils addressed matters of trade, peace accords, and even war pacts. War pacts were very important, because the more alliances you can build, the more revered, powerful, and feared your tribal council becomes. With this kind of power came the ability to negotiate tribal movements that meant better hunting, fishing, and trade opportunities.

As legend has it, the chiefs met at their rendezvous times in their central meeting place under the cliffs. The surrounding area was heavily wooded and covered with lush undergrowth, yet tribes never lost sight of their meeting place. For a long time, their cathedral, their meeting place, went undiscovered by non-Natives due to the inability of the local frontiersmen to understand and read Indian signs.

As the legend goes, at the top of the cliff, above the Native American cathedral, there was a huge tree with a large branch reaching out over the cliff. The Native Americans had taken the branch and secured it with sinew and twisted it, so that it pointed downward. This was the signal to other tribes that the meeting cave was at the bottom of that cliff.

When the caves were "discovered" by Europeans, their inability to understand and respect the cave's natural environment caused some people to misjudge its life-threatening properties. When people moved in to live in the caves, some of them died. Because of this, the caves were cordoned off behind chain-link fences, and abandoned. Now, signs are posted prohibiting entrance to the caves. It's a shame to let such a place as the Central Cave, a place of renowned past activity, pass into disuse.

On the Mythical Sighting of Chow Yun Fat in St. Paul

David Mura

She was working first
shift at Taco Bell
when out of Hong Kong
and the two-fisted guns
and that scene in the kitchen
where he rolled through flour
for dumplings and rose white
faced as the angel of death
or that night where pigeons
and candles in the chapel
scattered into cinematic
history, Chow Yun Fat
appeared at the driveby
window, waiting for
his two chaluppas
and a Diet Coke. If
Hmong was a word
among many she could
pronounce, if the Chinese
drove her people
into Laos and the CIA
and VC, if she was still
shifting off X and a little
high on chronic, no one
in the kitchen cared
when she squealed
like a white school girl
at the Backstreet Boys,
"It's him, it's him" after
the star of *The Killer*, the cat
the *LA Times* dubbed "the coolest
actor in the world," turned
onto Snelling and drove off.

Smiler

Dennis Kelly

"Hey kid," he coughed out at me from the mint green armchair, "I'll take it neat."

As he spoke, a rare shaft of late afternoon sun bounced at an odd angle through the dimly lit garden apartment and caught my great-uncle across the face. The mix of dusty light and smoke rising off his Chesterfield cigarette formed a sepia haze around his head. For an instant, his pallid complexion regained some youthful color reminiscent of the once-handsome Marine war hero. Ludwig was his real name, but he went by Smiler. If Smiler earned his name based on congeniality, it was a long-vanished attribute.

"Neat?" I asked.

"Christ, kid, what are ya, sixteen? And you ain't got a clue. I had been on three continents by the time I was your age. It means no ice. I got no time for watered-down drinks." Smiler's self observation was spot-on. At seventy, he was a broken-down alcoholic with terminal emphysema.

Smiler had recently drifted back to Saint Paul after a twenty-year absence and had proclaimed on his sister's doorstep, "This is the end of the line."

Grandma greeted the prodigal with a straight back and gnarled fists dug into her hips. "So aren't we the fortunate ones to end up with your pickled bag of bones," she said, blocking the threshold.

Smiler landed at the Gilbride Apartments, a rundown, red brick, three-story building on Snelling Avenue. Facing the noisy street, security bars on its windows, the place met Smiler's most significant needs: cheap, furnished, and near a liquor store.

He was a cranky cuss, but the demeanor of this tall gaunt man with a full shock of white hair was secondary to me. I needed a refuge from a mother on amphetamines and five younger siblings. Home life was a tinderbox, and everyone in it was a walking match. The only entrance requirement into the old man's place was my willingness to be on call, fake ID in hand, to shag his Haven Hill whisky and unfiltered cigarettes. And Smiler liked drinking companions, even when they were a bunch of delinquents.

On weekends, Smiler's place became party central. At times, we packed up to fifty kids in that one-bedroom apartment, spilling out into the hall and onto the sidewalk. There were only two rules: stay out of Gunnery Sergeant Smiler's chair and don't drink his booze. Many a night,

Smiler in his chair

he would be slumped deep in his chair, sound asleep, while a party raged around him. Other nights, the booze energized him to hold court and take us on fragmented journeys.

"The Germans gassed us in Somme, hit us with Big Bertha in Lyon, but we held 'em at Verdun and along the Hindenburg and took 'em at Belleau Wood." He'd wave the cigarette attached to his blue-veined hand, spreading smoke through the scene, enhancing his recollection. "Christ,

Illustration © Andy Singer

just boys, and getting hammered for what? So some jodi sonofabitch can steal your girl? Wilson and the Kaiser sipping Champagne over five million smoldering bodies, and I get to carry this goddam hackin' cough for the rest of my life." Raising his arm, he'd move it forward sharply in a mock salute. He'd lean back in his chair, eyes watery, hike his glass to signal a refill, and continue, "Kid, your grandma and I once swam across the river in October. Took a bonfire to thaw us out." As the thread of loneliness invariably wove its way through his accounts, he would abruptly clam up, pinch his cigarette, and stare steely-eyed into his unfinished story.

Thankfully, it was the landlord who found him that Friday—heart attack or something. The funeral at Saint Luke's was small, just immediate family and five of my friends who'd hung out at Smiler's whom I pressed to be pallbearers. As the incense burner swung over the casket, I removed a small military pin from my pocket: a spread-winged eagle perched on a globe, its eyes angry and its beak ready to strike, its talons gripping at the hemisphere. Smiler had unceremoniously given it to me a few weeks earlier. Removing a thick rubber band from his Don Diego Cigar box, he'd walked his long tobacco-stained fingers through the contents, pushing past old coins, a VFW poppy, a *Stevenson for President* button, and yellowed letters. Toward the bottom of the clutter, he chased the military pin into a corner, plucked it out, and held it up, like a prospector examining a gold nugget.

"Here, kid, this is for you," he said, holding the memento between his fingers. "It's taken me down this twisted road as far as it's gonna, and I come further than a lot of them boys. Some folks would say further than I should of." Seeing my face twist into a question, he sunk back in his chair and busied himself with the box.

My grandmother's muffled cry primed my tears, and I realized the pin had meant more than gratitude for booze running. It had signaled a passage for me as it had for Smiler, albeit a kinder one. He was my age when he joined the Marines, only to have his boyhood innocence stamped out and his manhood sculpted by war.

The service ended with a scratchy tape playing *Amazing Grace* as we proceeded to the back of the church. Walking alongside the casket, I threw off my teenage slouch, stood straight, and moved smartly. My friends, picking up on my new sense of purpose, fell in step behind me.

Semper Fi, Smiler.

November

November

November Paw and Ron Peterson

Not everyone in my family made it to Saint Paul. My parents were village people, until the villages were burnt down. Hiding in the jungle, their food was stolen; their friends and relatives starved. Our people, the Karen, were attacked because we have a different culture, language, and religion. My father was shot through his hand. It took a long time to heal.

Let me explain. My name is November Paw. My parents fled Burma (Myanmar), over mountains and a great river, before I was born in 1992. My entire life was in the Mae La refugee settlement in Thailand. Mae La is a large camp of 50,000 people. Our family of nine lived in a small bamboo house. The United Nations provided beans, rice, tea, and cooking oil for our survival, but the food was very boring. To add spices to our food, my brother Daniel snuck out of the camp to a job giving elephant rides to tourists. I went to a Karen school taught by the older children, and we all went to a Baptist church in the camp. My grandfather had been a pastor back in Burma.

My parents asked to live in America because there is freedom and good education. The day we arrived in Saint Paul my mother was happy, but she cried for all that was left behind. My oldest brother, Daniel, could not come to America because he was married. I remember my father became excited when he saw all the cars. But I was sick—starving, dizzy, tired. There was no food on our three-day journey to Minnesota, and for even more days the food I ate would not stay down.

Photo courtesy November Paw

November Paw in Minnesota

Photo courtesy November Paw

Hla/Paw family by their house in the Thai refugee camp.
Daniel is missing, November is on the left

Many people helped us when we arrived in August 2007 to be with my aunt in Saint Paul. On my first day of school, we rode a bus, but none of the Karen children knew what to do when we got there, so we waited on the sidewalk. Later some teachers came out and put us on another bus to the English-learning school. My friend Ron says I speak English well now. He says I am very smart.

My dad has a job in a food processing plant and my mother is learning English. She laughs and says she learns many words one day and they all go away the next. She has never gone to school before. She hopes the Karen in America will remember their language, hand-made clothes, and food. Rice is better here than in Thailand. But in winter, my face hurts as I walk up Rice Street in snow to the store. The wind is frightening and painful. I am learning how to stay warm.

I wonder, did you ever wake up in the night and be afraid for your life? Sometimes the Burmese military came into the camps and chased us into the forest. We had to be very quiet in the dark or we would be killed. I worry about that still.

Minnesota is a safe place. We each have our dreams and hopes. My parents want all of us children to have a good education and jobs someday, and they want to live in a house and not an apartment. I dream that I will be a nurse when I am older. And we all pray that the Karen people can someday have their own country, that the *myo dong* (genocide) will stop.

Joyous news! My brother Daniel and his wife and children have just come to America. They can live in our same apartment building! I will see Daniel's new baby for the first time. I can be an aunt!

Ta blit, Minnesota. Thank you.

December

The moon has landed
on earth, printing her
craters and hills, steamy
ponds and flat deserts
on this half-frozen maze
we call the Mississippi

Nora Murphy

261

⮩ December 4, 1928: "Dapper Dan" Hogan, a Saint Paul speakeasy owner and underworld figure, is fatally wounded when his car is bombed.

S	M	T	W	T	F	S
28	29	30	1	2	3	4
5	6	7	8	9	10	11
12	13	14	15	16	17	18
19	20	21	22	23	24	25
26	27	28	29	30	31	1

29 Monday

Saint Paul Almanac Reading Series

30 Tuesday

🐞 Gordon Parks, photographer, writer, and filmmaker, was born today in 1912

1 Wednesday

World AIDS Day

🐞 Ida Lusk Holman, leading suffragist, was born today in 1871

2 Thursday

Hanukkah begins

International Day for the Abolition of Slavery

Bouquets Wine Tasting

Holiday Bazaar

🐞 Evelyn Fairbanks, author of *Days of Rondo,* was born today in 1928

December

Sign reminding folks about thin ice this time of year

3 Friday

4 Saturday   Saint Paul Winter Farmers' Market

Holiday Flower Show begins

5 Sunday

Armenian Bedros Keljik arrives in Saint Paul in 1899 and
establishes an Oriental rug business.

Saint Paul Hotel

Chuck Tompkins

It's 5:15 p.m. in the entryway of the old Saint Paul Hotel. It's early winter, cold, and snowing. The lights across the street in Rice Park twinkle with the frost and people are rushing in to get warm and have the early evening cocktail at the famous bar where F. Scott Fitzgerald mulled over thoughts of *The Great Gatsby*. I just talked to the overworked, borderline frantic, new valet-parking operator, and he told me, "It will take a few minutes to get your car, we're really busy."

"Of course, no problem," I say. Linda and Cheri are in the lobby chatting, and I tell them it will be a while. I stand out in the cool entryway to be ready for the car and wait to see how long the "few minutes" will be.

The people stream in. I notice different perfumes, styles, faces red from the cold, smiles; the sound of laughter burbles and voices rise and fall like the tumbling water in a brook. The big brass revolving door is constantly going *swiiisssshhhhhhhh* as the people stream in. At 5:25 p.m., the valet sees me and says, "It shouldn't be too much longer; I'll come and get you." I say "Fine." Smile. I am enjoying the people. It is fun to be almost invisible as the people ebb and flow around you. The smiles, the hugs, tearful goodbyes. "I'll see you next week," and "It was so good to see you two again." Heartfelt, sincere, happiness-compressed-in-time feelings. I move over toward the corner for a bit more heat.

"You waitin' for number 368?"

"No."

I'm number 371, but we're getting close. It's 5:40 p.m. I turn and wave at Linda and Cheri. Linda smiles her beautiful radiant smile. I know she is sending me a message: "No worry, we've got lots of time." The guy beside me sees his car and runs out the door. "That's mine!"

Poor valet; he is now getting pretty frantic. Losing the appearance of being a "No problem" guy. Here he is with number 368 blocking the drive and no one is there to pick it up. I can see my breath in the cold entryway, but I am enjoying myself, and the lights are twinkling. I am immersed in a show. A show of life.

"Are you the one for number 371?"

"Yes I am."

Too bad. I give him a too-big tip. He smiles, relaxes, and leaves to find the owner of number 368. Me, I am sorry the show is over. I turn and wave at Linda and Cheri.

Early evening at the Saint Paul Hotel. One of the best plays in the Twin Cities. I hope when you're there, they can't get your car for you right away.

Como Lake community Christmas tree

The Como Lake Community Christmas Tree

Tom Haas

Between Thanksgiving and Christmas, something magical happens at Como Lake. Just off the side of the walking path stands a huge pine tree, and one by one, Christmas tree ornaments begin to appear on the branches. These are not the expensive, trendy decorations that you see for sale in matched, color-coordinated sets. No, some of these are the ragtag older ones used for years at grandma's house. Many appear to be homemade, perhaps a child's kitchen-table project. Some are what reflect the cultures of the people who have decided to share a bit of their traditions on the tree. As it gets closer to Christmas, more and more people add a decoration when they walk around the lake.

This community Christmas tree has no grand design, coordinated plan, or even matching colors. Somehow, though, each of the ornaments seems to fit in and play its role. Much like the people of Saint Paul, each of these decorations from different families and cultures comes together and forms a community. Every year, we walk around the lake at the holidays and enjoy the sense of community and the Como Lake community Christmas tree.

December

> "Fiction writers are the ones to insist that they don't know how they do what they do. Mostly because they don't like to be bothered with thinking about it." —Thomas Disch, science fiction writer

S	M	T	W	T	F	S
28	29	30	1	2	3	4
5	6	7	8	9	10	11
12	13	14	15	16	17	18
19	20	21	22	23	24	25
26	27	28	29	30	31	1

6 Monday

🐞 Victor Roehrich, Saint Paul's first city chemist, was born today in 1887

7 Tuesday

Muharram (Islamic New Year)

8 Wednesday

9 Thursday

🐞 Charles M. Flandrau, writer, was born today in 1871

Winter scene, Winona Street, on the West Side in 1930

10 Friday
International Human Rights Day

11 Saturday   Saint Paul Winter Farmers' Market

12 Sunday

December

The first Dutch elm disease in Minnesota is found in the
Highland Park neighborhood in early summer of 1961.

Revolt at the Midway
Discount Shopping Mall

Richard Broderick

The department's floor personnel—Bobbi, Tess, Shaun, Alice, and the stock boy, Luis—received word in that week's pay envelope, but rumors had been circulating for some time that the store was closing.

It was, after all, impossible to ignore how the shelves were not being restocked. "No mas," Luis would shrug, his palms turned upward, when one of the sales associates asked why a particular item—like those fleece-lined shoe inserts the old ladies liked so much—hadn't been replenished. "A little shipping problem," Mr. Beechner, the head buyer, had assured Alice, the oldest among them, when she'd worked up the nerve to ask. "Central's working on it," he said, then marched off in a rush. He was always in a rush.

But even though they all knew something was cooking, the news still came as a shock. In the break room that afternoon, Shaun stood transfixed, chewing his lower lip as he stared at the off-white sheet of company letterhead bearing the bad news. He was pale with shock. Everyone knew what was going through his mind; his partner, Allen, was sick—some said dying—and unable to work any longer. How were they going to pay the medical bills?

The gloom was finally broken by Angela, the pharmacy assistant. Waving her notice overhead, she declared, "Three weeks before Christmas! You'd think they'd have the decency to wait until after the holidays!"

"Honey," Tess rejoined, her blue-gray jowls wagging, "Ain't any good time to get fired!" That brought a flicker of a smile to Shaun's face, giving the others permission to chuckle.

"Least I won't have to listen to no more of them Christmas tapes," Luis declared. "I hear that 'bum-ba-bum-bum' song one more time, I swear I'm gonna puke!"

Soon they were all laughing and gleefully denouncing the store, its managers, the district executives who swooped through once a month for "spot" inspections the store president knew about in advance ("Hurry, everybody, hurry! They're going to be here in twenty minutes!"), the whole chain, and how the crooks and shirkers at the home office got all the goodies while the hard-working employees were left with the crumbs.

By the time Mr. Beechner became aware of the unusual noise coming from somewhere in the back of the store, Jacobi, the day custodian, had broken out a bottle of Seagram's 7 hidden in his cleaning closet and was passing it around—even Bobbi, with her pale round face and startled-looking eyes, took a pull.

"Thank you, Lord! Thank you for not making me work in his hellacious place anymore!" Tess cried out, her head tossed back and her eyes closed in ecstasy just as Mr. Beechner arrived at the swinging doors to the break room.

He peered for a moment through the cloudy plastic window, blinking with incomprehension, while the scene registered itself in his mind. He was about to burst in and reprimand everyone, reminding them that they were still employees, still expected to behave professionally, when a fresh round of mirth exploded in the break room. Bottle in hand, Jacobi was strutting back and forth, chest swelled with self-importance. With a shock, Beechner realized it was he who was being lampooned by this impersonation. Backing away from the door, he turned on his heels and stalked out into the merchandising area, pausing just long enough to straighten a rack of marked-down boys' winter jackets with an impatient flurry.

"Damn employees," he muttered to himself. "Can't get anything right!"

⇨ 1869: Saint Paul photographer Charles Zimmerman is struck by an icicle weighing several hundred pounds while he is making images of Minnehaha Falls. He is only slightly injured.

S	M	T	W	T	F	S
28	29	30	1	2	3	4
5	6	7	8	9	10	11
12	13	14	15	16	17	18
19	20	21	22	23	24	25
26	27	28	29	30	31	1

13 Monday

14 Tuesday

15 Wednesday

🕸 Carol Connolly, Saint Paul's poet laureate, was born today in 1934

16 Thursday

Ashura

December

Seven Corners winter trolley scene in 1950

17 Friday

🌸 Leona Scheunemann, Saint Paul Municipal Opera star, was born today in 1914

18 Saturday   Saint Paul Winter Farmers' Market

19 Sunday

> Sometimes the river
> doesn't like change.
> the water
> was crying when it came
> time to freeze.
> *Nora Murphy*

December

On December 13, 2008, an orangutan undergoes Como Zoo's
first Caesarean birth.

The Club

Collette DeNet

Saint Paul, Minnesota: Everyone's heard the tale of how it was built by drunken Irishmen who are responsible for the nonsensical layout of winding streets. Congruently, everyone who lives or has ever lived in Saint Paul knows that the one thing this city will never be without is its abundance of Irish pubs. My grandpa Roy was raised in the heart of this city where he brought up five children with the help of his lovely wife, Helen. Like many typical working men of Saint Paul, his three loves were family, friends, and O'Gara's Bar.

On the corner of Selby and Snelling avenues, the green awnings of O'Gara's are known to many. In the late 1940s, shortly following World War II, my grandpa chose this neighborhood bar as a meeting place for friends and fellow vets to unwind each Friday after a long work week. They'd share a few laughs, a few drinks, and memories from Pearl Harbor. Primarily Irish, it became a melting-pot of backgrounds and ideas.

As my dad and uncles grew, they, too, came to call the bar theirs on Friday nights. No matter how blustery, rainy, or muggy, they still made it out for a cold one. On the rare occasion that trips or vacations couldn't be avoided, there was always a phone call to the bar making sure everyone was in good spirits.

At the age of five I was already acquainted with the place my grandpa referred to as "The Club." I attended O'Gara's Santa Claus breakfast and sat on Santa's lap while my cousins chased each other around the room. I remember the sight of my grandpa sipping brandy gingers, surrounded by his aging circle of friends.

I remember squeezing into a booth after a softball game, slurping my club soda and listening to my grandpa regaling his friends with stories of Ireland. I longed for the day when I could sit on the bar stool beside him with stories of my own. I'd tilt my head and watch as he opened the can of ginger ale he'd brought from home and pour it into his tumbler of brandy. He never complained that they didn't serve ginger ale, he simply brought his own. The bartenders, along with the owners, Dan and Tim, never failed to make us feel welcome, and often before they knew it they'd be lost in the conversation. The topics amongst the boisterous crowd would inevitably lead back to varied opinions regarding politics, Cretin-Derham Hall sports, and good beer.

The grand age of twenty-one marked not only a milestone in my family, it was also a rite of passage. I, like my cousins and second cousins before

Tim O'Gara's Bar and Grill at Selby and Snelling avenues

me, was presented with my first beer and a walleye dinner at O'Gara's. My grandpa was sure to treat anyone sitting at our table. He could turn even the moodiest bar-goers into friends with his ebullient laugh.

Slowly, as is life, the rosy faces of that hearty group began to fade. Whether it was due to a stroke or lung cancer, one by one, their bar stools sat empty. The winter of 2007 brought the news that my grandpa had been diagnosed with cancer. I remember sitting at the bar the first Friday he was too sick to make it out. I knew then it wasn't good, because nothing kept him from his bar. Dan continued to send walleye dinners to his home each Friday.

His heart put up a good fight until he left us in the spring. I thought it would be too painful to set foot in my grandpa's bar without him, yet it has now become more a part of me than ever. No matter how unpredictable life is, I know that on any given Friday night I can walk into O'Gara's and find my family. I'll find cousins who've returned with amazing stories of China and South America. I'll find uncles offering free legal advice, and I'll find my dad, with a beer waiting for me.

⤷ 1971: Ebba Kirschbaum of Saint Paul is one of only two traditional midwives to renew her license with the Minnesota Board of Medical Practice. It is her last application.

DECEMBER

S	M	T	W	T	F	S
28	29	30	1	2	3	4
5	6	7	8	9	10	11
12	13	14	15	16	17	18
19	20	21	22	23	24	25
26	27	28	29	30	31	1

20 Monday

21 Tuesday

Winter Solstice

22 Wednesday

🐞 Frank B. Kellogg, statesman and Nobel Peace Prize winner, was born today in 1856

23 Thursday

🐞 Cecil Glickman, founder of Cecil's Deli, was born today in 1915

December

Gelatin silver print of night scene with snow,
Sixth Street looking east from Wabasha in 1904

24 Friday
Christmas Eve

Merry Christmas to all, and to all
A good night in wintry St. Paul.
When it's 20 below,
Read a book, drink some joe,
Be brave or (why not) go awol.
Garrison Keillor

25 Saturday
Christmas Day

Saint Paul Winter Farmers' Market

26 Sunday
Kwanzaa begins

Kwanzaa Family Celebration

Photo © Truman Ward Ingersoll

December

December 21, 1892: St. Peter Claver Church is founded to serve
the African American Catholic community of Saint Paul.

Christmas is One of the Best Holidays

Suad Arouni

Christmas is one of my favorite holidays—there are a lot of differences between Christmas in America and in my country, Sierra Leone. In America, all they do is exchange gifts and go to work, but in Sierra Leone people will start celebrating a week before Christmas. On Christmas Eve, people will do lots of grocery shopping and buy lots of meats and chicken because they like to cook fresh food in the morning. On the day of Christmas, all you can smell is the good smell of different aromas—yum, yum.

Christmas is so special for us in Africa, because you will meet new people and it is time to reconcile and a time of healing. That's why the best place people like to go is the beach with their small picnic baskets. They throw a mat on the sand and two or three other families will come and join them. Africans like to eat from the same bowl and like to share. I love to see little children running and playing soccer in the water while the old ladies will be in their traditional colorful gara cloth, and the old men will be in their ronkos, knee-length tunics woven of cotton. There will be lots of people in different costumes dancing and playing games and doing their traditional dances. The only difference about Christmas in Sierra Leone is that everybody is preparing the same dish—jollof rice, cassava leaf, and stew. In America you do have different choices of food from other countries.

At the Bar Where F. Scott Fitzgerald Drank Gin

Todd Boss

—even though I drank wine,
and then only half a glass—I felt I

owed it to myself and to the guests
who'd sat politely through the reading

—and to everyone in every
college and university 20th Century

American Literature class
throughout history—to get drunk

off my ass, just for the literary
symmetry of it, just for the laughs

and the high-society flap that would
surely ensue. I stood there outwardly

sober, but *within* I was disorderly
with the desire to be—to the very

rowdy, raunchy, reckless, and
innocent fiction of it—utterly true.

—*Commodore Hotel, 2008*

⇨ "You have to be funny about it and honest about it. You can't leave yourself out of that mix. You have to be honest enough to say, "'I'm that messed-up one in the family.'"
—Louie Anderson, Saint Paul native and comedian

S	M	T	W	T	F	S
28	29	30	1	2	3	4
5	6	7	8	9	10	11
12	13	14	15	16	17	18
19	20	21	22	23	24	25
26	27	28	29	30	31	1

27 Monday

🐞 Magdalena Rau, nurse and St. John's Hospital administrator, was born today in 1887

28 Tuesday

🐞 Anna Andahazy, ballet dancer and teacher, was born today in 1917

29 Wednesday

30 Thursday

December

Capital City Partnership hosts the Capital City Lights Program every holiday season

31 Friday
New Year's Eve

Fourth Friday at the Movies

1 Saturday
New Year's Day

2 Sunday

The 911 emergency telephone system is established in Saint Paul
in December 1982.

Weather

Maximilian Selim

The forty-fifth parallel runs through Saint Paul, Minnesota. This parallel is generally considered the halfway point between the equator and the North Pole. This is irrelevant to our everyday lives with the exception of one truth: it is the cause of our extremely unpredictable weather, a concept that consumes us. We talk about it with co-workers, we talk about it on dates, we analyze it on the TV, we use it as an excuse for being late, we complain about it, we use it to avoid awkward gaps in uncomfortable conversation, and most importantly, we live in it.

The winter brutalizes our morale. We naïvely think about it as a quarter of our year; in actuality, it tackles us without warning in November and its frostbitten fingers hang on tight until spring eventually stomps them off the ledge of late April. Leaving the house for any reason becomes a chore. You sit in your car, bundled up, and wait for the heat to kick in. Just as it does, it's inevitably time to get out again and return to the elements. All the while, your back is tight, your fingertips are numb, and the wind cuts against your cheeks. We pay an expensive energy bill. Weeks elapse without a "nice day." Months pass and the sun's warmth is only a distant memory of a luxury you foolishly took for granted.

But then in the summer? *Oh, man, that sun!* It beats down on you. You sweat while drying off, the occasional breeze from an oscillating fan is a frequent source of satisfaction, and a guy can't even have a few drinks and fall asleep in a pontoon without cooking himself twice over. We pay an expensive energy bill. The long day's heat creeps into the night and those winter nights sitting by the fire now seem like a luxury we foolishly took for granted.

Meanwhile, spring and fall, lovely as they are, find themselves squeezed tightly between the giants of winter and summer. Our well-groomed weather forecasters boldly predict it with laughable accuracy—or inaccuracy, for that matter. We indulge in criticizing them after the fact.

So why exactly do we go through this vicious cycle year after year? Why not move to that consistent climate? California? Miami? Ecuador? Is it possible that we enjoy this weather? Maybe the long cold winter makes us appreciate those "seventy-eight and sunny" days all the more. Perhaps the sweltering hot summer days make our winter hibernation oddly enjoyable. Deep down we all love criticizing the weather forecasters, right? It could be that our distinct seasons have an invigorating effect on our psyche. Or, most likely, the summer waves of sticky humidity, or that run of subzero days in January, are an even trade for all the awkward silences we avoid, thanks to our good friend, that forty-fifth parallel weather.

The Uptown

Patricia A. Cummings

In the drama of my family, the Uptown Theatre played a lead role. Sitting in the middle of the block at 1053 Grand Avenue, the theater began as the Oxford in 1921. In 1929, the Uptown was reborn as an "atmospheric theatre" with an Italian motif, stucco walls, faux balconies, stars and clouds on the ceiling, and a brightly lit marquee. In the 1950s, it was again remodeled in mid-century modern style. In 1976, the Uptown turned its lights out for the last time, to make way for a parking lot.

The Uptown's place in our family story began in the early 1930s. My dad, Verne Cummings, had started in the movie theater business as an usher when he was fifteen and worked his way up to a "plum" assignment as the manager of the Uptown. One of Dad's best managerial decisions was to hire Esther Lindgren as a cashier. They married on June 15, 1936.

My first memory of the Uptown was going to see Disney's *Bambi* when I was about four. I saw lots of movies—as many as three a week. Sometimes I got to sit in the projection booth with the operator. Often, I'd go with Dad to the theater in the morning, when he "did the books." In his office was a set of wooden cubbyholes—the repository for everything left behind in the auditorium. We got first pick of anything that wasn't claimed after thirty days, so we always had a colorful supply of mittens and scarves.

Described in an ad in 1929 as "Distinctly in a class by itself," the Uptown was a palace to my young eyes. There was a grand Ladies Lounge

Photo courtesy Patricia A. Cummings

The Uptown Theatre in the 1920s

upstairs with sofas and dressing tables and a maid in attendance. The doorman's job was to turn the wheel on the ticket box to grind out the tickets. He and the ushers wore uniforms with epaulets and lots of gold buttons. I always had a small-girl crush on one or another of them.

The Uptown was the first theater in Saint Paul to have air-conditioning. Down in the cavernous and spooky basement, an artesian well pumped cold water into a series of pipes. As the water fell from the pipes, huge fans blew through the rain to cool the air in the auditorium.

During World War II, Dad served in the Army in Europe. After the war, he chose to stay with the familiar and went back to the Uptown. We kids, now numbering three, resumed our three-movies-a-week routine.

When I was fourteen, I started working at the Uptown as the popcorn girl. I made the popcorn in a little upstairs room and carried it down to the candy counter. When the theater was remodeled in the 1950s, the clouds and stars disappeared, the Ladies Lounge became a utilitarian restroom, and Dad's office was moved downstairs. The popcorn machine was moved downstairs, too, and I worked behind the expanded candy counter.

At sixteen, I was promoted to the box office. Adult tickets cost twenty-five cents and kids got in for twelve cents. At the end of each shift, the cashiers had to reconcile ticket sales to the money taken in. Dad was a stickler for accuracy. More than once, I "padded the books" with some of my own change so that my numbers came out equal.

With the advent of television, the movie business declined and the Minnesota Amusement Company sold the Uptown to an independent owner who drastically cut Dad's salary. Dad decided it was time to develop a new career. While he studied for his license to become a real estate agent, Mother split the manager's job with him at the Uptown. By the late 1950s, Dad was ready to launch his new business. We all said good-bye to the Uptown with regret for the loss of this fixture in our lives, but also anticipation for the next step in our family's journey.

The Wilderness in the City

Gordy Palzer

Growing up in the West Seventh Street area of Saint Paul in the 1950s and 60s, in a family with no car, *could* have limited my adventure horizons, except that tucked away just out of sight, near its west end, lay Crosby Lake—and I was lucky enough to discover it in my teens, when any wildness oasis in the heart of Saint Paul seemed as rich in natural wonders as any of the great national parks out west!

I first set foot on Crosby Lake land in the late 1950s, when I was twelve years old and trailed my neighbor, Alex Hauwiller, on foot through a landfill just off Seventh Street on what was then Leland Street and followed a leaf-strewn trail to the lake's flooded shore. Some fifty feet out rested flood-remnant lumber that had perhaps once been the deck of a riverfront home—and so, because my neighbor wore hipboots and I did not, Alex carried me on his back to the platform, from which we fished with cane poles for several hours, catching a nice meal of perch, sunnies, and crappies.

My next magical visit to Crosby Lake came the following winter, when, amid gently falling snow, I followed my neighbor Alex again out onto the now-frozen lake, on my first-ever ice-fishing endeavor. The huge booming sounds of new ice forming underfoot froze me in my tracks, yet Alex walked fearlessly on, turning at last to assure me that the ice was safe and the rumbling sounds simply those of new ice forming beneath us. Again

Photo © Patricia Bour-Schilla

Crosby Lake pier in summer

that day, we took home a nice meal of fish, mostly crappies and even a few small northerns.

And so Crosby became the destination on weekends beyond number for similar fishing trips as well as exploratory hikes, and I came to know the entire layout of the abandoned farmland surrounding the lake, once owned by Thomas Crosby but now reduced to unmaintained, tax-delinquent city property. While Crosby was the site of many illegal beer parties and a drop-off site for many stolen cars, it was also a haven for wildlife, including an unbelievable variety of bird species. I learned to become a birder over years of hiking all about Crosby, and I learned about the little Crosby lake as well, which, though small, was unbelievably deep. I came to a deeper appreciation of the area's floodplain tree mix and the varying seasonal beauty that turned the area into a bejeweled gem of nature.

My brothers and I hiked Crosby even while Shepard Road was pushed westward above the lake area, the bridge piers for long-awaited I-35 were set in place, and the trusses and beams were thrown across them. We climbed with boyhood glee over all the heavy equipment parked there while that work progressed, and we even walked the catwalk underneath the bridge until it was padlocked! We could see that even the overhead presence of a busy commuter roadway and a booming freeway would not sully Crosby Lake's wildness, and we were further gladdened years later, when the City of Saint Paul realized the promise of Crosby's wildness and made it a city park, preserving its wild, undeveloped nature.

I am ecstatically reassured to know that Crosby Farm Park will continue to be there for new generations of young boys and girls looking for wildness in—of all places—the heart of our rivertown city!

The East Side—A Story of Tradition and Change

Tony Andrea

Follow the sounds of childhood laughter up and over the snowbanks and into Margaret Playground on the East Side. It is 1937, and as you near the hockey rink, you can see a small mob of adolescent boys and girls huddled together or sliding on the ice. They are joining the hockey goals into a small cage. Inside, giggling along with the others, are my grandmother and grandfather.

I am thankful my grandparents were caught in those hockey goals so many years ago. Because of them, we meet as a family every Friday night at their house. From across Johnson Parkway on a dark evening, you can see their house lit up and the cars of my family members parked outside. Inside, there's a din of laughter, shouting, and several simultaneous conversations. There will always be pizza, and my Italian father and my Greek grandfather drinking red wine. "How the heck are ya?" my grandpa will exclaim, and I go over, give him a big hug, and kiss the top of his bald head.

Like many, I hold onto what I consider the essence of the East Side. I also fear that time will bring about the end of those things we hold dear. Whether it's the old brick structures of the Hamm's Brewery or simple Friday night family customs, we worry about having to say good-bye to those things we consider traditions.

But if there's one crucial thing I have learned about the East Side of Saint Paul, it's that our story is just as much about how we have learned to adapt to change as about the traditions we keep. European settlers first flourished in the area around what's now known as Phalen Creek. The ravine became home to so many Swedish immigrants that it was known as Swede Hollow. Later, Irish, Italians, and Mexicans lived there as well. Homes were tucked wherever there was space, and outhouses were built over the creek. The hollow was basically a slum, but it was also a place that new Americans could call home. Someday they would move "up on the street," as the Swedes did before them. Today, if you walk across from Yarusso's and look down into the hollow, you may be able to hear the faint echoes of Italian songs, concertinas, and the rustle of grape vines blowing in the breeze.

In time, the Hamm's Mansion rose like a castle above the hollow. Even though his brewery empire made him rich, Theodore Hamm remained on the East Side instead of joining fellow financial giants on Summit Hill.

December

Above the hollow, businesses like the Harvester Works, the Gypsum Company, 3M, Whirlpool, and the railroads eventually became important employers and contributors to the development and character of the neighborhood. Immigrants established new communities like Railroad Island. While the old and new immigrants were sometimes at odds, each gained their footing and could not survive without one another.

In time, the clip-clop of the horses' hooves was replaced by the whine of streetcars and the putter of automobiles. Payne Avenue became the East Side's main drag, with restaurants, bakeries, delis, and clothing stores offering anything you needed.

When the Great Depression came, my grandma said so many people shared in the experience of being poor that no one realized how poor they actually were! President Roosevelt became a hero who put people back to work with such efforts as the Civilian Conservation Corps.

Many East Siders went off to fight World War II, while those staying home held scrap drives and took over the positions vacated by soldiers. When the war ended, the East Side saw a boom of prosperity and babies. This period of growth and development lasted until the 1980s, when production and manufacturing facilities began to shut down. Many who had worked on the East Side for most of their lives were forced to look for jobs elsewhere. Structures like the Whirlpool building became vast, empty husks. Traditional East Siders who remained began to see new waves of immigrants.

It was East Siders like Bruce Vento who welcomed these newcomers. Vento identified with the challenges facing Hmong immigrants, and in true East Side manner, he tried to ensure not only their inclusion but their success as members of the East Side community.

Ying's Corner Express Foods

In time, improvements in the economy and the initiative of community members brought about revitalization on the East Side. New businesses were invited in, and projects like the Phalen Corridor and natural habitat restoration created a rebirth. Today, the Bruce Vento

December

Nature Sanctuary has re-created a setting similar to what our ancestors first saw along Phalen Creek. To the north, Lake Phalen is another success story: once the victim of development, it now stands as one of the most beautiful and accomplished natural restoration projects anywhere.

Old-timers may mourn the loss of the East Side's smaller shops, but newer markets have sprouted up to take their place. At Ying's Corner Express Foods on Seventh and Kennard, Ying is always there with a smile, sending you off with your groceries and a happy heart. You can find similar experiences awaiting you at Chiang Mai Deli & Foods on Maryland, the *mercados* on Payne, and Pastor Hamilton's Barbeque on Seventh.

Some things have disappeared, never to return. Hamm's mansion is gone and the brewery's free, fresh water no longer flows. Martin Lumber has finally closed its doors, and the Viaduct, with its long wooden bar, no longer rests below the Earl Street Bridge. Even with the loss of favorite places and traditions, new ones appear, and they are just as valuable and important to the continuing history and vibrancy of the East Side. If the poorest of immigrants could make Swede Hollow sing on the coldest winter nights, then we, too, can create new traditions. Even when change erases the East Side's older buildings, streets, structures, and people, the neighborhood lives on in the hearts of those who believe in it.

There may come a Friday when we no longer meet at my grandparents' house on Johnson Parkway and when I no longer kiss my grandpa's bald head. But we have been blessed with memories and must look forward to making new ones. We should smile when we see other families celebrating East Side traditions of their own.

So do your part in holding onto the East Side, create new traditions, visit the local businesses, and get to know its workers and owners. And the next time you are at Ying's, tell him I said hi.

Chiang Mai Deli & Foods on the East Side

December

Search for a Home for the UGM Sign

Jewel Hill Mayer

At the corner of Seventh and Wacouta in Lowertown once stood the Union Gospel Mission. Late nineteenth-century predecessors of the mission included the Western Seamen's Friend Society, which moved along the Great Lakes route, establishing missions; Bethel Houses (Bethel means "house of God"); a mission at the bottom of Jackson Street that operated out of a houseboat, providing food and housing to men who worked on the Great Lakes; and the Society for the Relief of the Poor.

The houseboat burned in 1900, prompting a search for a large facility that could house transients, homeless men, alcoholics, and other "down-and-outers" of society. Who would have guessed this would become an organization that reached out to thousands of men and women in all walks of life?

The Union Gospel Mission opened its first permanent home in 1910, an imposing five-story building at 235 East Seventh Street. For approximately seventy years in that location, and elsewhere today, the mission's motto has been "Where the doors never close." The Bethel Hotel section was always full of men who could receive "soap, soup, and salvation"—though not necessarily in that order. They had to attend a religious service in the beautiful red chapel, then shower and eat a simple supper in the basement restaurant before earning a night's sleep on one of the cots.

In the early years, a rectangular sign extended about ten feet from the outside of the building between the fourth and fifth floors, proclaiming simply, GOD IS LOVE. This sign, with neon lights inside it, was purple, a beacon to all the traffic coming from the north. As cattle-laden trucks lumbered toward

Union Gospel Mission sign

Photo © Minnesota Historical Society

the South Saint Paul stockyards, the sign announced UNION GOSPEL MISSION, JESUS SAVES, BETHEL HOTEL. From the east, where street traffic came off Lafayette Road or from the East Side on Seventh Street, drivers read UNION GOSPEL MISSION, GOD IS LOVE, BETHEL HOTEL.

I was fascinated by everything about the mission—I tutored boys there in the 1970s—and I fell in love with that sign. I saw the north side of it whenever I drove into town from my home in Roseville. When I learned in 1981 that the mission had found a new home and the building at Seventh and Wacouta was to be razed, I called the salvage company and asked if I could have the sign. The owner said, "Okay, if you move it." And on a beautiful, cold day, November 22, 1981, I became the proud owner of the Union Gospel Mission sign. With the generous help of Dick Hoffman of Hoffman Electric, his two trucks, two cranes, and two men, that sign was moved to my house in Roseville.

What a sight! They picked up the sign with a huge crane, carefully raised it over my carport, and set it gently down lengthwise along the side of my house. It stretched from the front post on my carport to the back edge of my house. The neon lights were long gone; still, it was beautiful to me. My youngest son, fourteen at the time, was in the basement working with his friend Jay. Ordinarily quite interested in complex undertakings, they refused even to come upstairs and watch.

For the next several months, I tried very hard to find a permanent home for the sign. My house was on the market, and I planned to go to Florida for a few months to be a starving writer. (My mother said I was successful at half of that!) I sent out feelers to numerous places where I thought the sign might fit. The new mission over on Lafayette Road seemed a logical one. But the new superintendent let it be known that he had no interest in the sign or anything else I proposed. (I suspect that he had read the Oliver Towne column in the old *Saint Paul Dispatch* that had described my search and my appeal to art lovers to call me about the sign. Towne also wrote about some girls at school teasing my son about the sign: they had asked if and when we were going to hold services at our house. Andrew responded, "We're having a service of sacrifice. We're going to sacrifice a virgin; would you like to volunteer?" That stopped those questions!)

A friend suggested that I contact the Landmark Center, saying, "Wouldn't it look great in the cortille down there?" Oliver Towne suggested, among others, a spot beside the Indian in the City Hall/Courthouse on Kellogg.

Finally, having exhausted all possibilities, the closing on my house and my move-out looming, I made the heart-rending call to the salvage company.

I still think often of my beautiful sign, and I hope and trust that it is resting in peace.

Letter From United

Patricia Kirkpatrick

Of course I heard voices in the night,
saw visions,
felt the presence of dying,
that white, fringed place.
Shallow breath, narrow entrance—
the door to death opened.
Then came steroids
and their lack of inhibition.
There was terror. I admit it.

Just before I learned the news
I realized all you have meant to me
and I thought I had too much feeling
to continue to see and spend time with you.
Then they told me I had a brain tumor
and it had to come out. Damage had happened.
Seizure and aura, the grey dome of the growth
or a cathedral lit at the top where the cross is. Flora wrote
so much of life we find in the funniest places.

Boundaries. Love.
Bone, cutting, and stitches.
More blood than the surgeon had ever ordered.
I knew I needed your help
for the children, the family I might have to leave.

I am writing to say I can make the changes.
I am writing to say I have been opened and closed.
I am writing to say that today when the nurse came
to change my dressing,
she glanced up and said, "Oh, look, is that snow?"
We looked out the window and saw it together,
first flakes,
those white, fringed birds
flying,
the first snow of the new season.

Saint Paul Listings

Events

Health and Fitness Events

Coffee Houses and Tea Shops

Restaurants

Theater

Music Venues

Dance Venues

Art Galleries

Bookstores

Museums

Historical Sites and Tours

Food Co-ops

Sports

Events

JANUARY

**Downtown Saint Paul
Winter Farmers' Market**

Saturdays, 9 a.m.–1 p.m.
290 East Fifth St.
651.227.8101
www.stpaulfarmersmarket.com
*Local growers sell their fresh foods
directly to you.*

Holiday Flower Show

Continues through Jan. 18
Marjorie McNeely
Conservatory, Como Park
651.487.8200
www.comozooconservatory.org

Minnesota RollerGirls (Bout)

Jan. 2
Roy Wilkins Auditorium

651.265.4800
www.mnrollergirls.com
*The Minnesota RollerGirls are part of
the Women's Flat Track Derby Association (WFTDA), a national governing
body for female-only, skater-owned,
flat-track roller derby leagues. The Minnesota RollerGirls league was founded by
the Donnelly sisters in August 2004 and
has grown from 6 original members to a
current roster of 80 skaters, 8 referees
and coaches, and countless volunteers.
Great spectator sport!*

**Minnesota Boychoir
Winter Concert**

Jan. 3, 1–3 p.m.
Landmark Center
651.292.3225
www.landmarkcenter.org

Photo © Patricia Bour-Schilla

*2009 Winter Carnival snow sculpture third-place winner, "Chinese New Year"
(Dragon) by Johnathan Baller, Curt Cook and Joseph Hauwiller*

Hear the lovely sounds of over 100 boys aged 7–18.

Saint Paul Almanac
Reading Series
Jan. 4, 7–8:30 p.m.
Black Dog Cafe
651.785.6268
www.saintpaulalmanac.com
Selected writers curate readings around a theme they have chosen and invite other writers and artists to perform with them.

Land O' Lakes Kennel
Club Dog Show
Jan. 8–10
Saint Paul RiverCentre
651.265.4800
www.rivercentre.org
Come watch over 2,000 dogs strut their stuff.

The Saint Paul Chamber
Orchestra
Stravinsky Festival
Jan. 8, 9, 14, 16, 23, 24
Various locations and times
651.291.1144
www.thespco.org

Saint Paul Winter Carnival
Jan. 21–31
Downtown Saint Paul
651.223.4700
www.winter-carnival.com
Lots of winter events: parades, ice skating, ice sculpture, coronation, medallion hunt.

Global Hot Dish Variety Show
Jan. 23
Minnesota History Center
345 West Kellogg Blvd.
651.259.3000

www.mnhs.org
Entertainment featuring a jug band, a balloon artist, a Hmong comedian, Austrian alphorn players, and regional dances from Mexico in a classy, quirky 90-minute, family-friendly variety show.

Winter Carnival Orchid Show
Jan. 23–24
Marjorie McNeely
Conservatory, Como Park
651.487.8200
www.comozooconservatory.org

Saintly City Cat Show
Jan. 23–24
Saint Paul RiverCentre
651.265.4800
www.rivercentre.org
More than 300 felines compete to be crowned the Feline King and Queen of the Saint Paul Winter Carnival.

Fourth Friday at the Movies
Jan. 29
Golden Thyme Coffee Café
651.645.1340
Social hour at 6:30 p.m. and film at 7 p.m.

Minnesota Opera
Roberto Devereux by Gaetano Donizetti
Jan. 30, Feb. 2, 4, 6, 7
Ordway Center for the Performing Arts
612.333.6669
www.mnopera.org
Never betray your Queen. This bel canto masterpiece centers on the tragic love affair between Queen Elizabeth and Robert Devereux, Earl of Essex.

Marjorie McNeely Conservatory Winter Flower Show

Winter Flower Show
Jan. 30–Mar. 21
Marjorie McNeely Conservatory,
Como Park
651.487.8200
www.comozooconservatory.org

FEBRUARY

Downtown Saint Paul Winter Farmers' Market
Saturdays, 9 a.m.–1p.m.
290 East Fifth St.
651.227.8101
www.stpaulfarmersmarket.com
Local growers sell their fresh foods directly to you.

Winter Flower Show
Jan. 30–Mar. 21
Marjorie McNeely Conservatory,
Como Park
651.487.8200
www.comozooconservatory.org

Minnesota Opera
Roberto Devereux by Gaetano
Donizetti

Jan. 30, Feb. 2, 4, 6, 7
Ordway Center for the
Performing Arts
612.333.6669
www.mnopera.org
Never betray your Queen. This bel canto masterpiece centers around the tragic love affair between Queen Elizabeth and Robert Devereux, Earl of Essex.

Saint Paul Almanac Reading Series
Feb.1, 7–8:30 p.m.
Black Dog Cafe
651.785.6268
www.saintpaulalmanac.com
Tou SaiKo Lee curates a reading around a theme he has chosen and invites other writers/artists to perform with him.

Saint Paul Chamber Orchestra
Feb. 5, 8:00 p.m., and Feb. 7,
2 p.m.
The Music Room, SPCO Center
651.291.1144
www.thespco.org

Chamber music series: Boccherini, Leclair, and Borodin.

Minnesota RollerGirls (Bout)

Feb. 6
Roy Wilkins Auditorium
651.265.4800
www.mnrollergirls.com
The Minnesota RollerGirls are part of the Women's Flat Track Derby Association (WFTDA), a national governing body for female-only, skater-owned, flat-track roller derby leagues. The Minnesota RollerGirls league was founded by the Donnelly sisters in August 2004 and has grown from 6 original members to a current roster of 80 skaters, 8 referees and coaches, and countless volunteers. Great spectator sport!

Urban Expedition: Korea

Feb. 7, 1–3 p.m.
Landmark Center
651.292.3225
www.landmarkcenter.org
Travel to Korea without leaving Saint Paul. Celebrate the culture of Korea with authentic cultural performances by area musicians and performers.

Saint Paul Chamber Orchestra

Feb. 12 and 13, 8 p.m.
Ordway Center for the Performing Arts
651.291.1144
www.thespco.org
Dawn Upshaw sings Bach and Bartók.

Saint Paul Chamber Orchestra

Feb. 13, 9:30 and 11:30 a.m.
Ordway Center for the Performing Arts

651.291.1144
www.thespco.org
Ordway family series: The Inside Out Concert.
Tickets to this series are given away by random drawing. Visit www.thespco.org/target for more information.

Vietnamese Tet New Year Festival

Date to be announced
Saint Paul RiverCentre
651.265.4800
www.vietnam-minnesota.org
Vietnamese music, dancing, contests, food, and celebration. Free admission.

Scottish Ramble

Feb. 13–14
Landmark Center
651.292.3225
www.landmarkcenter.org
Scottish music, dancing, food, and celebration.

Saint Paul Chamber Orchestra

Feb. 19, 8:00 p.m., and
Feb. 21, 2 p.m.
The Music Room, SPCO Center
651.291.1144
www.thespco.org
Chamber music series: Dvořák and a world premiere.

Minnesota State High School League Girls' Hockey Tournament

Feb. 24–27
Xcel Energy Center
763.560.2262
www.mshsl.org

Fourth Friday at the Movies
Feb. 26
Golden Thyme Coffee Café
651.645.1340
Social hour at 6:30 p.m. and film at 7 p.m.

World of Wheels
Feb. 26–28
Saint Paul RiverCentre
651.265.4800
www.rivercentre.org
Come view over 300 hot rods, race cars, customized motorcycles, and antique vehicles.

Saint Paul Chamber Orchestra
Feb. 27, 8 p.m.
Ordway Center for the Performing Arts
651.291.1144
www.thespco.org
English classics.

Global Hot Dish Variety Show
Feb. 27
Minnesota History Center
345 West Kellogg Blvd.
651.259.3000
www.mnhs.org

Entertainment featuring a jug band, a balloon artist, a Hmong comedian, Austrian alphorn players, and regional dances from Mexico in a classy, quirky 90-minute, family-friendly variety show.

Urban Expedition: Colombia
Feb. 28, 1–3 p.m.
Landmark Center
651.292.3225
www.landmarkcenter.org
Travel to Colombia without leaving Saint Paul. Celebrate the culture of Colombia with authentic cultural performances by area musicians and performers.

MARCH

Downtown Saint Paul Winter Farmers' Market
Saturdays, 9 a.m.–1p.m.
290 East Fifth St.
651.227.8101
www.stpaulfarmersmarket.com
Local growers sell their fresh foods directly to you.

Winter Flower Show
Jan. 30–Mar. 21
Marjorie McNeely Conservatory,

Photo © Landmark Ceter

Mexico Urban Expedition at the Landmark Center

Como Park
651.487.8200
www.comozooconservatory.org

Saint Paul Almanac
Reading Series
Mar. 1, 7–8:30 p.m.
Black Dog Cafe
651.785.6268
www.saintpaulalmanac.com
Carol Connolly, Saint Paul Poet Laureate, curates a reading around a theme she has chosen and invites other writers/artists to perform with her. We suspect the theme may be Irish in nature.

Minnesota State High School League Boys' Wrestling Tournament
Mar. 3–6
Xcel Energy Center
763.560.2262
www.mshsl.org

Saint Paul Chamber Orchestra
Mar. 5, 8 p.m.
Saint Paul's United Church of Christ
651.291.1144
www.thespco.org
Ruggero Allifranchini plays Bruch's violin concerto.

Minnesota RollerGirls (Bout)
Mar. 6
Roy Wilkins Auditorium
651.265.4800
www.mnrollergirls.com
The Minnesota RollerGirls are part of the Women's Flat Track Derby Association (WFTDA), a national governing body for female-only, skater-owned, flat-track roller derby leagues. The Minnesota RollerGirls league was founded by the Donnelly sisters in August 2004 and has grown from 6 original members to a current roster of 80 skaters, 8 referees and coaches, and countless volunteers. Great spectator sport!

Minnesota Opera
La bohème by Giacomo Puccini
Mar. 6, 7, 9, 10, 11, 12, 13, 14
Ordway Center for the Performing Arts
612.333.6669
www.mnopera.org
La bohème may be the world's most popular opera, and for good reason—it's the quintessential portrait of romance, high-spirited friendship, and idealistic pursuit of love and art.

Urban Expedition: Israel
Mar. 7, 1–3 p.m.
Landmark Center
651.292.3225
www.landmarkcenter.org
Travel to Israel without leaving Saint Paul. Celebrate the culture of Israel with authentic cultural performances by area musicians and performers.

Minnesota State High School League Boys' Hockey Tournament
Mar. 10–13
Xcel Energy Center
763.560.2262
www.mshsl.org

Saint Paul Chamber Orchestra
Mar. 13, 8 p.m.
Saint Paul's United Church of Christ

651.291.1144
www.thespco.org
Celebrating composer Robert Schumann.

Irish Music and Dance Association (IMDA) Day of Irish Dance

Mar. 14
Landmark Center
651.292.3225
www.landmarkcenter.org
Irish food, lively music, Irish dancing, and art vendors.

Saint Patrick's Day Parade

Mar. 17
Downtown Saint Paul
651.256.2155
www.stpatsassoc.org
Once the biggest parade in Saint Paul and still very big.

IMDA Saint Patrick's Day Celebration

Mar. 17, 10 a.m.–5 p.m.
Landmark Center
651.292.3225
www.landmarkcenter.org

Saint Patrick's Day Irish Ceili Dance

Mar. 17, 7–10 p.m.
CSPS Hall, 383 Michigan St.
651.290.0542
www.minnesotafolkfestival.org
Learn the steps of the Irish, because everyone is Irish on St. Paddy's day.

Western Collegiate Hockey Association (WCHA) Men's Tournament

Mar. 18–20
Xcel Energy Center

763.560.2262
www.xcelenergycenter.com

Fourth Friday at the Movies

Mar. 26
Golden Thyme Coffee Café
651.645.1340
Social hour at 6:30 p.m. and film at 7 p.m.

NCAA Division I Men's Ice Hockey Championships

Mar. 26–27
Xcel Energy Center
763.560.2262
www.xcelenergycenter.com

Global Hot Dish Variety Show

Mar. 27
Minnesota History Center
345 West Kellogg Blvd.
651.259.3000
www.mnhs.org
Entertainment featuring a jug band, a balloon artist, a Hmong comedian, Austrian alphorn players, and regional dances from Mexico in a classy, quirky 90-minute, family-friendly variety show.

Spring Flower Show

Mar. 27–May 2
Marjorie McNeely Conservatory, Como Park
651.487.8200
www.comozooconservatory.org

APRIL

Downtown Saint Paul Farmers' Market

Apr. 24 through Nov. 21
Saturdays, 6 a.m.–1 p.m.
and Sundays, 8 a.m.–1 p.m.

651.227.8101
www.stpaulfarmersmarket.com
Local growers sell their fresh produce directly to you.

Spring Flower Show
Mar. 27–May 2
Marjorie McNeely Conservatory, Como Park
651.487.8200
www.comozooconservatory.org

Saint Paul Chamber Orchestra
Apr. 2 and 3, 8 p.m.
Ordway Center for the Performing Arts
651.291.1144
www.thespco.org
Adès and Berlioz. Thomas Adès conducts.

Saint Paul Chamber Orchestra
Apr. 3, 9:30 a.m. and 11 a.m.
Ordway Center for the Performing Arts
651.291.1144
www.thespco.org
Ordway family series: I am inspired by . . . Tickets to this series are given away by random drawing. Visit www.thespco.org/target for more information.

Minnesota RollerGirls (Bout)
Apr. 3
Roy Wilkins Auditorium
651.265.4800
www.mnrollergirls.com
The Minnesota RollerGirls are part of the Women's Flat Track Derby Association (WFTDA), a national governing body for female-only, skater-owned, flat-track roller derby leagues. The Min-
nesota RollerGirls league was founded by the Donnelly sisters in August 2004 and has grown from 6 original members to a current roster of 80 skaters, 8 referees and coaches, and countless volunteers. Great spectator sport!

Saint Paul Almanac Reading Series
Apr. 5, 7–8:30 p.m.
Black Dog Cafe
651.785.6268
www.saintpaulalmanac.com
Desdemona curates a reading around a theme she has chosen and invites other writers/artists to perform with her.

Saint Paul Chamber Orchestra
Apr. 10, 8 p.m.
Saint Paul's United Church of Christ
651.291.1144
www.thespco.org
Zehetmair plays Beethoven's violin concerto.

Minnesota Opera
Salome by Richard Strauss
Apr. 10, 15, 18, 20, 24
Performing Arts
612.333.6669
www.mnopera.org
The final revival of this scandalously erotic opera retells the biblical story of obsession and vengeance.

Urban Expedition: Ghana
Apr. 11, 1–3 p.m.
Landmark Center
651.292.3225
www.landmarkcenter.org
Travel to Ghana without leaving Saint

Paul. Celebrate the culture of Ghana with authentic cultural performances by area musicians and performers.

27th Annual Minneapolis–Saint Paul International Film Festival

Mid-April/dates to be announced
612.331.7563
www.mspfilmfest.org
The largest film festival in the Upper Midwest. Over 150 films from more than 50 countries. Various locations.

Saint Paul Conservatory for the Performing Arts

Apr. 18, 1–3 p.m.
Landmark Center
651.292.3225
www.landmarkcenter.org

Fourth Friday at the Movies

Apr. 23
Golden Thyme Coffee Café
651.645.1340
Social hour at 6:30 p.m. and film at 7 p.m.

Saint Paul Art Crawl

Apr. 23–25
Downtown Saint Paul
651.292.4373
www.artcrawl.org
More than 200 artists open their studios to the public.

Saint Paul Chamber Orchestra

Apr. 24, 10:15 a.m. and 11:15 a.m.
The Music Room, SPCO Center
651.291.1144
www.thespco.org
Start the Music! *Pounding Percussion: meet the percussion family. Tickets to this series are given away by random drawing. Visit www.thespco.org/target for more information.*

Saint Paul Chamber Orchestra

Apr. 24, 29, 30, and May 1, 8 p.m.
Various locations
651.291.1144
www.thespco.org
Dennis Russell Davies conducts. Dawn Upshaw, soprano.

Saint Paul Chamber Orchestra

Apr. 29 and May 1, 8 p.m.
The Music Room, SPCO Center
651.291.1144
www.thespco.org
Marimba festival.

Festival of Nations

Apr. 29–30 and May 1–2
Saint Paul RiverCentre
651.647.0191
www.festivalofnations.com
Over 90 ethnic groups share the foods, crafts, and traditions that form the mosaic of American culture.

MAY

Downtown Saint Paul Farmers' Market

April 24 through November 21
Saturdays, 6 a.m.–1 p.m.
and Sundays, 8 a.m.–1 p.m.
651.227.8101
www.stpaulfarmersmarket.com
Local growers sell their fresh produce directly to you.

Spring Flower Show

Mar. 27–May 2
Marjorie McNeely Conservatory, Como Park

St. Paul Farmers' Market

651.487.8200
www.comozooconservatory.org

Festival of Nations

Apr. 29–30 and May 1–2
Saint Paul RiverCentre
651.647.0191
www.festivalofnations.com
Over 90 ethnic groups share the foods, crafts, and traditions that form the mosaic of American culture.

Como Memorial Japanese Garden

May 1–Sept. 30
Marjorie McNeely Conservatory, Como Park
651.487.8200
www.comozooconservatory.org
Como opens its beautiful outdoor Japanese garden during these months.

Saint Paul Almanac Reading Series

May 3, 7–8:30 p.m.
Black Dog Cafe
651.785.6268
www.saintpaulalmanac.com
Deborah Torraine curates a reading around a theme she has chosen and invites other writers/artists to perform with her.

Cinco de Mayo Festival

May 7–8
District del Sol
651.222.6347
www.districtdelsol.com
Celebrate with live music, food, children's area, community wellness village, parade, vendors.

Living Green Expo

Dates to be announced
10 a.m.–5 p.m.
State Fairgrounds
651.215.0218
www.livinggreen.org
Environmental fair, workshops, live music, food, kids' activities.

Saint Paul Chamber Orchestra

May 8, 10:15 a.m. and 11:15 a.m.
The Music Room, SPCO Center
651.291.1144
www.thespco.org
Start the Music! *Tickets to this series are given away by random drawing. Visit www.thespco.org/target for more information.*

Saint Paul Chamber Orchestra
May 8, 8 p.m.
Saint Paul's United Church of Christ
651.291.1144
www.thespco.org
Bach's The Art of Fugue.

Summer Flower Show
May 8–Oct. 3
Marjorie McNeely Conservatory,
Como Park
651.487.8200
www.comozooconservatory.org
Roses, statice, geraniums, Asiatic lilies, heliotrope, New Guinea impatiens, petunias, and caladiums bloom throughout the season.

**Minnesota Bonsai
Society Bonsai Show**
May 8–9
Marjorie McNeely Conservatory,
Como Park
651.487.8200
www.comozooconservatory.org

**Saint Paul Civic Symphony
Mother's Day Celebration**
May 9
Landmark Center
651.292.3225
www.landmarkcenter.org
Bring your mother to enjoy music at the Landmark.

Saint Paul Chamber Orchestra
May 13 and 15, 8 p.m.
The Music Room, SPCO Center
651.291.1144
www.thespco.org
Marimba festival.

Saint Paul Chamber Orchestra
May 14, 8 p.m. and May 16, 2 p.m.
The Music Room, SPCO Center
651.291.1144
www.thespco.org
Chamber music series: Mozart, Beethoven, and more.

Bulb Sale
May 15
Marjorie McNeely Conservatory,
Como Park
651.487.8200
www.comozooconservatory.org

Minnesota Dance Festival
Dates to be announced
Fitzgerald Theater
651.290.1221
www.balletminnesota.org
Variety of dance performances.

Saint Paul Chamber Orchestra
May 27, 28, 29
Ordway Center for the Performing Arts
651.291.1144
www.thespco.org
Joshua Bell returns as featured violin soloist and director of the orchestra.

Fourth Friday at the Movies
May 28
Golden Thyme Coffee Café
651.645.1340
Social hour at 6:30 p.m. and film at 7 p.m.

**Flint Hills International
Children's Festival**
May 29–30

Ordway Center for the Performing
Arts and Rice Park
651.224.4222
www.ordway.org
*Parade, performances, dancing, inter-
national foods, and hands-on workshops
for children.*

JUNE

Downtown Saint Paul Farmers' Market

Apr. 24 through Nov. 21
Saturdays, 6 a.m.–1 p.m.
and Sundays, 8 a.m.–1 p.m.
651.227.8101
www.stpaulfarmersmarket.com
*Local growers sell their fresh produce
directly to you.*

Saint Paul (Seventh Place) Farmers' Market

June–Sept.
Tuesdays and Thursdays
Seventh Place, 10–2 p.m.
651.227.8101
www.stpaulfarmersmarket.com
*Local growers sell their fresh produce
directly to you.*

Summer Flower Show

May 8–Oct. 3
Marjorie McNeely Conservatory,
Como Park
651.487.8200
www.comozooconservatory.org
*Roses, statice, geraniums, Asiatic lilies,
heliotrope, New Guinea impatiens, petunias, and caladiums bloom throughout
the season.*

Music in Mears Park

Thursdays, June 3, 10, 17, 24,
6–9 p.m.
Mears Park
221 East Fifth St.
651.291.9128
www.musicinmears.com
*Enjoy the sounds of summer in the beau-
tiful outdoors.*

Saint Paul Chamber Orchestra

June 5, 10:30 a.m.
The Music Room, SPCO Center
651.291.1144
www.thespco.org
Xplorchestra! *Family concert.
Tickets to this series are given away by
random drawing. Visit www.thespco.
org/target for more information.*

Grand Old Day

June 6
Grand Avenue, Dale to Fairview
651.699.0029
www.grandave.com
*Sporting events, parade, family fun area,
teen battle of the bands, live music,
festival gardens, and over 140 outdoor
food and merchandise vendors.*

Saint Paul Almanac Reading Series

June 7, 7–8:30 p.m.
Black Dog Cafe
651.785.6268
www.saintpaulalmanac.com
*Tish Jones curates a reading around a
theme she has chosen and invites other
writers and artists to perform with her.*

Saint Paul Chamber Orchestra
Jun. 11, 10:30 a.m. and 8 p.m.
Ordway Center for the Performing Arts
651.291.1144
www.thespco.org
Schumann's Spring Symphony.

Twin Cities Jazz Festival
June 17–19
Mears Park
www.hotsummerjazz.com
One of the best outdoor concerts of the year. Bring your lawn chair.

Solstice Film Festival
Dates to be announced
Fitzgerald Theater
10 East Exchange St.
651.290.1496
www.solsticefilmfest.org
Get off the couch and experience a film festival unlike any other. Five days of film at downtown venues, with outdoor music and parties at local restaurants.

Music and Movies, *District del Sol*
Thursdays, June 17 to Aug 5.
June 17 and 24, 6:30 p.m.
Parque Castillo
149 Cesar Chavez Rd.
651.222.6347
www.districtdelsol.com
Youth activities at 6:30 p.m., music at 7 p.m., and movies at dusk.
Beer, food, and gift vendors. Come and go as you please. No coolers, but bring your lawn chair.

Back to the 50s Car Show
June 18–20
Minnesota State Fairgrounds
651.641.1992

www.msra.com
Over 10,000 cars registered last year, over 300 vendors and crafters, over 350 swappers, plus 50s dances Friday and Saturday nights.

Fourth Friday at the Movies
June 25
Golden Thyme Coffee Café
651.645.1340
Social hour at 6:30 p.m. and film at 7 p.m.

JULY

Downtown Saint Paul Farmers' Market
Apr. 24 through Nov. 21
Saturdays, 6 a.m.–1 p.m.
and Sundays, 8 a.m.–1 p.m.
651.227.8101
www.stpaulfarmersmarket.com
Local growers sell their fresh produce directly to you.

Saint Paul (Seventh Place) Farmers' Market
June–Sept.
Tuesdays and Thursdays
Seventh Place, 10–2 p.m.
651.227.8101
www.stpaulfarmersmarket.com
Local growers sell their fresh produce directly to you.

Summer Flower Show
May 8–Oct. 3
Marjorie McNeely Conservatory, Como Park
651.487.8200
www.comozooconservatory.org
Roses, statice, geraniums, Asiatic lilies, heliotrope, New Guinea impatiens, pe-

tunias, and caladiums bloom throughout the season.

Music in Mears Park
Thursdays, July 1, 8, 15, 22, 29, 6–9 p.m.
Mears Park
221 East Fifth St.
651.291.9128
www.musicinmears.com
Enjoy the sounds of summer in the beautiful outdoors.

Music and Movies, *District del Sol*
Thursdays, July 1, 8, 15, 22, 29, 6:30 p.m.
Parque Castillo
149 Cesar Chavez Rd.
651.222.6347
www.districtdelsol.com
Youth activities at 6:30 p.m., music at 7 p.m., and movies at dusk.
Beer, food, and gift vendors. Come and go as you please. No coolers, but bring your lawn chair.

Boom Bap Village
July 1–2
651.353.7497
www.boombapvillage.com
Nationwide, youth-organized event promoting positivity through hip-hop art forms: breakdancing, rapping, DJing, and aerosol arts.

Taste of Minnesota
July 2–4
Harriet Island and Downtown
651.772.9980
www.tasteofmn.com
Includes four music stages, many food vendors, and fireworks every night.

Hmong International Sports Tournament and Freedom Festival
July 3–4
Como Park
651.266.6400
Largest Hmong community sporting event in the nation. Volleyball, soccer, kato, and tops tournaments; food, retail, and music.

Saint Paul Almanac Reading Series
July 5, 7–8:30 p.m.
Black Dog Cafe
651.785.6268
www.saintpaulalmanac.com
Selected writers curate readings around a theme they have chosen and invite other writers and artists to perform with them.

Nine Nights of Music Series
July 6, 13, 20, and 27
Minnesota History Center
345 West Kellogg Blvd.
651.259.3000
www.mnhs.org
Every Tuesday in July and August. Bring a lawn chair and pack a picnic or purchase food from the Café Minnesota terrace grill. In case of rain, concerts will be held inside the History Center.

Dragon Festival and Dragon Boat Races
July 10–11
Lake Phalen
651.646.7717
www.dragonfestival.org
Asian cultural festival with performances, food vendors, and dragon boat races with paddlers following the drumbeats.

Highland Fest

July 16–18
Highland Village
651.699.9042
www.highlandfest.com
Three-day outdoor festival. Food, art vendors, and live entertainment on two stages. Fireworks Friday and Saturday.

Rondo Days

July 17
Rondo Days are a central gathering time for celebrating the unique heritage of Saint Paul's historic Black community. The festival remembers Rondo with a senior citizens' dinner, one-day festival, famous drill team competition, parade, music, food, and art.

Rice Street Festival

July 22–24
651.285.4101
www.ricestreetfestival.org
Celebrate Rice Street. Parade on Thursday, July 22, begins at 6:30 p.m.

Fourth Friday at the Movies

July 30
Golden Thyme Coffee Café
651.645.1340
Social hour at 6:30 p.m. and film at 7 p.m.

Car Craft Summer Nationals

Dates to be announced
Minnesota State Fairgrounds
877.413.6515
www.carcraft.com
Showcases over 4,000 street machines and muscle cars.

AUGUST

Downtown Saint Paul Farmers' Market

Apr. 24 through Nov. 21
Saturdays, 6 a.m.–1 p.m.
and Sundays, 8 a.m.–1 p.m.
651.227.8101
www.stpaulfarmersmarket.com
Local growers sell their fresh produce directly to you.

Saint Paul (Seventh Place) Farmers' Market

June–Sept.
Tuesdays and Thursdays
Seventh Place, 10–2 p.m.
651.227.8101
www.stpaulfarmersmarket.com
Local growers sell their fresh produce directly to you.

Summer Flower Show

May 8–Oct. 3
Marjorie McNeely Conservatory, Como Park
651.487.8200
www.comozooconservatory.org
Roses, statice, geraniums, Asiatic lilies, heliotrope, New Guinea impatiens, petunias, and caladiums bloom throughout the season.

Nine Nights of Music Series

Aug. 3, 10, 17, 24, and 31
Minnesota History Center
345 West Kellogg Blvd.
651.259.3000
www.mnhs.org
Every Tuesday in July and August. Bring a lawn chair and pack a picnic or

Rondo Days

purchase food from the Café Minnesota terrace grill. In case of rain, concerts will be held inside the History Center.

Music in Mears Park

Thursdays, Aug. 5, 12, 19, 26, 6–9 p.m.
Mears Park
221 East Fifth St.
651.291.9128
www.musicinmears.com
Enjoy the sounds of summer in the beautiful outdoors.

Music and Movies, *District del Sol*

Thursday, Aug. 5, 6:30 p.m.
Parque Castillo
149 Cesar Chavez Rd.
651.222.6347
www.districtdelsol.com
Youth activities at 6:30 p.m., music at 7 p.m., and movies at dusk.
Beer, food, and gift vendors. Come and go as you please. No coolers, but bring your lawn chair.

Circus Juventas

Dates to be announced
651.699.8229
www.circusjuventas.org
Youth performers create a spectacular Cirque du Soleil-like show. Afternoon and evening shows.

Irish Fair

August 13–15
Harriet Island
952.474.7411
www.irishfair.com
Upper Midwest's largest Irish festival. Lots of music, dance, history, food, and theater. Free.

Japanese Lantern Lighting Festival

Aug. 15, 4 p.m.–dusk
Marjorie McNeely Conservatory, Como Park
651.487.8200
www.comozooconservatory.org
Lanterns float in the Japanese garden ponds to celebrate Obon, the Japanese

festival honoring ancestors. Japanese food and entertainment.

Minnesota State Fair

Aug. 26–Sept. 6
Minnesota State Fairgrounds
651.288.4400
www.mnstatefair.org
The biggest state fair in the Midwest. Lots of food on sticks.

Fourth Friday at the Movies

Aug. 27
Golden Thyme Coffee Café
651.645.1340
Social hour at 6:30 p.m. and film at 7 p.m.

SEPTEMBER

Downtown Saint Paul Farmers' Market

Apr. 24 through Nov. 21
Saturdays, 6 a.m.–1 p.m.
and Sundays, 8 a.m.–1 p.m.
651.227.8101
www.stpaulfarmersmarket.com
Local growers sell their fresh produce directly to you.

Saint Paul (Seventh Place) Farmers' Market

June–Sept.
Tuesdays and Thursdays
Seventh Place, 10–2 p.m.
651.227.8101
www.stpaulfarmersmarket.com
Local growers sell their fresh produce directly to you.

Summer Flower Show

May 8–Oct. 3

Marjorie McNeely Conservatory,
Como Park
651.487.8200
www.comozooconservatory.org
Roses, statice, geraniums, Asiatic lilies, heliotrope, New Guinea impatiens, petunias, and caladiums bloom throughout the season.

Minnesota State Fair

Aug. 26–Sept. 6
Minnesota State Fairgrounds
651.288.4400
www.mnstatefair.org
The biggest state fair in the Midwest. Lots of food on sticks.

Selby Avenue JazzFest

Sept. 11, 11 a.m. –7 p.m.
Corner of Selby and Milton
www.selbyareacdc.org
Outdoor festival celebrating jazz music. Bring the whole family. Delicious food, including lots of southern cuisine. Local artisans and businesses too.

Payne-Arcade Business Association (PABA) Festival

Sept. 10
Parade runs on Payne between Rose and York streets
Sept. 11–12
Annual Torch Light Parade
651.771.5477
Sponsored by the Payne-Arcade Avenue Business Association (PABA).

Saint Paul Almanac Book Release Party

Sept. 16, 6 p.m.–8 p.m.
Black Dog Cafe
651.785.6268

www.saintpaulalmanac.com
Book release party for the 2011 Saint Paul Almanac. Get your book signed by authors and hear writers read their work.

Annual Twin Cities Black Film Festival
Sept. 17–19
Various locations in Saint Paul
www.tcbff.com
Opening and closing night premieres, panel discussions, festival parties, 25 independent film projects, plus much more.

Fourth Friday at the Movies
Sept. 24
Golden Thyme Coffee Café
651.645.1340
Social hour at 6:30 p.m. and film at 7 p.m.

OCTOBER

Downtown Saint Paul Farmers' Market
Apr. 24 through Nov. 21
Saturdays, 6 a.m.–1 p.m.
and Sundays, 8 a.m.–1 p.m.
651.227.8101
www.stpaulfarmersmarket.com
Local growers sell their fresh produce directly to you.

Saint Paul Almanac Reading Series
Oct. 4, 7–8:30 p.m.
Black Dog Cafe
651.785.6268
www.saintpaulalmanac.com

Selected writers curate readings around a theme they have chosen and invite other writers and artists to perform with them.

Saint Paul Art Crawl
Oct. 8–10
Downtown Saint Paul
651.292.4373
www.artcrawl.org
More than 200 artists open their studios to the public.

Fall Flower Show
Oct. 9–Nov. 28
Marjorie McNeely Conservatory, Como Park
651.487.8200
www.comozooconservatory.org

Saint Paul Oktoberfest
Oct. 9–10
197 Geranium Avenue West
www.saintpauloktoberfest.org
A fun, free event on Rice Street at the corner of Rose and Geranium. A family-oriented festival featuring live music for dancing and listening as well as a wide array of German foods and refreshments.

Zoo Boo
Oct. 16–17 and Oct. 22–24, 5–7:30 p.m.
Como Park Zoo
651.487.8200
www.comozooconservatory.org
Annual Halloween dress-up family festival.

Fourth Friday at the Movies
Oct. 29
Golden Thyme Coffee Café

651.645.1340
Social hour at 6:30 p.m. and film at 7 p.m.

Dia de los Muertos Family Fiesta
Oct. 30
Minnesota History Center
345 West Kellogg Blvd.
651.259.3000
www.mnhs.org
Lots of calaveras, jollity, and costumes.

Great Pumpkin Festival
Oct. 31
Landmark Center
651.292.3225
www.landmarkcenter.org
An autumn celebration for the whole family, including costume contests, music, and art projects.

NOVEMBER

Downtown Saint Paul Farmers' Market
Apr. 24 through Nov. 21
Saturdays, 6 a.m.–1 p.m.
and Sundays, 8 a.m.–1 p.m.
651.227.8101
www.stpaulfarmersmarket.com
Local growers sell their fresh produce directly to you.

Fall Flower Show
Oct. 9–Nov. 28
Marjorie McNeely Conservatory, Como Park
651.487.8200
www.comozooconservatory.org
Sunken Garden closed for mid-show change, November 1–5.

Saint Paul Almanac
Reading Series
Nov. 1, 7–8:30 p.m.
Black Dog Cafe
651.785.6268
www.saintpaulalmanac.com
Selected writers curate readings around a theme they have chosen and invite other writers and artists to perform with them.

Minnesota State High School League Girls' Volleyball Tournament
Nov. 11–13
Xcel Energy Center
763.560.2262
www.mshsl.org

Capital City Lights
Mid-Nov.–Mar.
Downtown Saint Paul
651.291.5600
www.capitalcitypartnership.com
Come downtown and enjoy the holiday lights in winter.

Fourth Friday at the Movies
Nov. 26
Golden Thyme Coffee Café
651.645.1340
Social hour at 6:30 p.m. and film at 7 p.m.

Minnesota Hmong New Year
Dates to be announced
Saint Paul RiverCentre
651.265.4800
www.rivercentre.org
Celebrate the Hmong New Year with dance, food, music, entertainment, and more.

DECEMBER

Downtown Saint Paul
Winter Farmers' Market
Saturdays, 9 a.m.–1p.m.
290 East Fifth St.
651.227.8101
www.stpaulfarmersmarket.com
*Local growers sell their fresh foods
directly to you.*

Bouquets Wine Tasting
Dec. 2
Marjorie McNeely Conservatory,
Como Park
651.487.8200
www.comozooconservatory.org

Holiday Bazaar
Dec. 2–4
Landmark Center
651.292.3225
www.landmarkcenter.org
*More than 80 exhibits featuring local
artists' work and gift items.*

Holiday Flower Show
Dec. 4–Jan.18
Marjorie McNeely Conservatory,
Como Park
651.487.8200
www.comozooconservatory.org

Saint Paul Almanac
Reading Series
Dec. 6, 7–8:30 p.m.
Black Dog Cafe
651.785.6268
www.saintpaulalmanac.com
*Selected writers curate readings around a
theme they have chosen and invite other
writers and artists to perform with them.*

Kwanzaa Family Celebration
Dec. 26
Minnesota History Center
651.259.3000
www.mnhs.org
*Annual Kwanzaa celebration with crafts,
stories, and music for all ages.*

Photo © Patricia Bour-Schilla

Capital City Lights

Health and Fitness Events

Teri J. Dwyer

JANUARY

Jan. 17: Frigid 5

The Frigid 5 is a 5K and 10K race circling the State Fair grounds with shorter races (¼ mile and ½ mile) for the kids. The Fair's booths and wide-open roadway look quite different covered in snow.
www.tslevents.com

Jan. 23: Saint Paul Winter Carnival's Half Marathon and 5K

The "Coolest Race on Earth," **Saint Paul Winter Carnival's Half Marathon and 5K** start and end downtown. The courses follow the Mississippi River for midportions of each race.
www.winter-carnival.com

Twin Cities Bicycling Club (TCBC) Winter Warm-up, Think Spring, We Don't Need No Stinkin' Winter, and Fridays on the Bike

TCBC members are unwilling to hang up their bikes just because of a little snow and cold. Join them for their winter events each month.
www.mtn.org/tcbc

FEBRUARY

Feb. 13–2nd Annual Valentine's Day Hearts are Running 5K & 1.5 Mile

Family & Friends Fun Walk
Part of series of holiday-themed races around Como Lake.
www.charitieschallenge.org

TCBC events (see January)
www.mtn.org/tcbc

MARCH

March 14: St. Pat's Irish Traditions 5K
Part of series of holiday-themed races around Como Lake.
www.charitieschallenge.org

March 21: Saint Patrick's Day Human Race

For more than three decades, Saint Patrick's Day Human Race running and walking events have signaled start of spring racing season. 8K run, 5K run/walk, and youth runs from ¼ to ½ mile.
www.tslevents.com

TCBC events (see January)
www.mtn.org/tcbc

APRIL

Apr. 3: Challenge Obesity 5K
Sponsored by Charities Challenge. First in summer series at Como Lake. "Run, Race Walk," "Fitness Walk," and "Walk By My Side" 2.5K.
www.charitieschallenge.org

April 4: Easter Sunday Rise 'n Shine 5K

Part of series of holiday-themed races around Como Lake.
www.charitieschallenge.org

Apr. 11: Running of the Pigs

Fun, festive 5K loop course in front of Midway Stadium, home of Saint Paul Saints. Includes ¼-mile and ½-mile youth runs. Stay for catered lunch afterward. www.tslevents.com

Apr. 19: 3rd Annual Joe Plant Memorial Living the Dream 5K Run & Walk

Running and walking event at Lake Phalen honoring Joe, an avid runner who died unexpectedly at 24 of an undiagnosed congenital heart condition. www.charitieschallenge.org

April Saturday: Saint Paul Parks' Annual Spring Parks Clean-Up

Annual event hosted by Saint Paul Parks and Recreation to clean up trash in city parks and recreation centers. Usually held on a Saturday in April. www.stpaul.gov/depts/parks

TCBC events (see January)

www.mtn.org/tcbc

MAY

May 2: Friends of the Orphans 2nd Annual Cinco de Mayo 5K Run/Walk

Low-key event benefiting Friends of the Orphans at Highland Park, with starts and finishes by Highland Pool. www.friendsoftheorphans.org

May 8: Menudo 5K

Cinco de Mayo celebration each spring on weekend closest to May 5 includes **Menudo 5K**. www.districtdelsol.com/cinco. html

May 3: Walk for Animals

Hosted by Humane Society, this walk kicks off national "Be Kind to Animals Week" at Como Park. www.animalhumanesociety.org

May 9: Mother's Day 5K
Part of series of holiday-themed races around Como Lake.
www.charitieschallenge.org

May 31: Challenge Hearts & Minds 5K

Sponsored by Charities Challenge. Second in summer series at Como Lake. "Run, Race Walk," "Fitness Walk," and "Walk By My Side" 2½ K. www.charitieschallenge.org

May 31: Mississippi 10-Miler

Long-standing race sponsored by Minnesota Distance Running Association (MDRA). Course is out and back along Mississippi River, starting and ending at Summit Avenue and East Mississippi River Boulevard. www.runmdra.org

TCBC events (see January)

www.mtn.org/tcbc

JUNE

June 6: Grand Old Day on the Go! Races

8K in-line skate, 8K run, 5K run/ walk and youth run events (¼ mile and ½ mile)—kick off Grand Old Day, largest one-day music, food, and entertainment festival in the United States.
www.tslevents.com

June 5: Challenge Cancer 5K

Sponsored by Charities Challenge. Part of summer series at Como Lake. "Run, Race Walk," "Fitness Walk," and "Walk By My Side" 2½ K.
www.charitieschallenge.org

June 6: Walk on the Wild Side

5K run/walk at Como Lake benefiting Dakota Communities, organization providing services to people with disabilities.
www.dakotacommunities.org

June 12: Lederhosenlauf 5K Run & 1-Mile Health Walk

Part of Deutsche Tage Weekend Festival at Germanic-American Institute. Race takes runners on loop around Saint Paul Cathedral. Special prizes for German-themed costumes.
www.gai-mn.org

June 20: Father's Day 5K

Part of series of holiday-themed races around Como Lake.
www.charitieschallenge.org

June 26: Time to Fly 10K and 5K

Races sponsored by Children's Cancer Research Fund on Harriet Island. Include 2K and 1K kids' runs.

www.childrenscancer.org/news _details_events_timetofly.html

TCBC events (see January)
www.mtn.org/tcbc

JULY

July 4: Langford Park Races

Very low-key races (runners choose 2- or 4-mile option) with 50¢ entry fee since 1974. Two-mile loop through Saint Anthony Park beginning and ending at Langford Park.

July 4: 3rd Annual Free to Run 4 Miles

Part of series of holiday-themed races (this one at Harriet Island).
www.charitieschallenge.org

July 10: Challenge Diabetes 5K

Sponsored by Charities Challenge. Part of summer series at Como Lake. "Run, Race Walk," "Fitness Walk," and "Walk By My Side" 2½ K.
www.charitieschallenge.org

July 17: Highland Fest 5K

Low-key, family-friendly fun run showcasing annual Highland Fest. Course is out and back along the Mississippi River.
www.highlandfest.com

July 25: Rice Street Mile

Starts at intersection of Rice Street and Front Avenue to kick off annual Rice Street Festival parade. Course is flat and point to point, one of shortest running

races in Saint Paul.
www.ricestreetfestival.com

TCBC events (see January)
www.mtn.org/tcbc

AUGUST

Aug. 4–25: MDRA Cross-Country Runs

Since 1974, MDRA has sponsored cross-country races every Wednesday evening in August at Como Park. Open to all ages and abilities.
www.runmdra.org

Aug. 14: Minnesota Half Marathon and 5K (Half Marathon—in-line skate or run, 5K run)

Formerly known as Saint Paul Inline Marathon. Skaters and runners race along beautiful Mississippi River, ending in Mears Park.
www.minnesotahalfmarathon. com

Aug. 22: Minnesota State Fair Milk Run 5K

Participants receive admission ticket to fair and coupon for free malt!
www.mnstatefair.org

Aug. 22: 5th Annual Saint Paul Triathlon

Sprint and international distance, including Clydesdale and Athena Divisions.
www.vacationsports.com

Aug. 28: Challenge Arthritis 5K

Sponsored by Charities Challenge. Part of summer series at Como Lake. "Run, Race Walk," "Fitness Walk," and "Walk By My Side" 2½ K.
www.charitieschallenge.org

TCBC events (see January)
www.mtn.org/tcbc

SEPTEMBER

Sept. 5: Saint Paul Classic Bike Tour

Rare opportunity to bike on streets free from car traffic. Family-friendly event offers 15- or 30-mile tour of Saint Paul.
www.spnec.org

Sept. 5: Sharing Life Walk/Run (3 miles)

Lake Phalen all-ages event with special races and games for kids. Supports organ donation education and raises money for families undergoing transplants.
www.sharinglife.org

Sept. 18: West Fest Jalapeno Hustle 5K

Race showcasing the West Side. Family-friendly; includes Chile Chase free for runners 10 or younger.

Sept. 19: MMRF Race for Research

5K Walk/Run raises money and awareness for multiple myeloma, an incurable blood cancer. Held at Lake Phalen.
www.mmrfrace.org

Sept. 26: Dream Mile

Includes 10K and 5K runs and 5K fun walk around Lake Phalen. Part of national fundraiser aiding child welfare projects funded by Vibha in India and United States; 10 percent of proceeds donated to local chapter of Big Brothers Big Sisters of the Greater Twin Cities.
wiki.vibha.org

TCBC events (see January)

www.mtn.org/tcbc

OCTOBER

Oct. 3: Twin Cities Marathon

5K and family events on Saturday before Sunday's big race. Races start and end near State Capitol.
www.twincitiesmarathon.org

Oct. 10: Paul Mausling Cross-Country Run (4K and 6K)

Named after former Saint Paul resident and graduate of Macalester College Paul Mausling. Cross-country race for runners of all ages and abilities at Como Park.
www.tslevents.com

Oct. 16: Halloween Hustle

5K Run/Walk and Kid's Fun Run on Harriet Island sponsored by the Junior League of Saint Paul.
www.jlsp.org

Oct. 30: Halloween Fearless 5K & 1.5-Mile Fun Run

Part of series of holiday-themed races around Como Lake.
www.charitieschallenge.org

TCBC events (see January)

www.mtn.org/tcbc

NOVEMBER

Nov. 7: Rocky's Run

Cross-country race offers runners a chance to run same course used by U of M men's and women's cross-country teams at Les Bolstad University Golf Course. 8K and 5K races benefit scholarship named for Rocky Racette.
www.tslevents.com

Nov. 21: Turkey Run

Tradition for Sunday before Thanksgiving. Family-friendly fun run circles Como Lake, starting and ending at Como Elementary School.
www.tslevents.com

Nov. 25: Giving Thanks 5K

Part of series of holiday-themed races around Como Lake.
www.charitieschallenge.org

TCBC events (see January)

www.mtn.org/tcbc

DECEMBER

Dec. 25: 5th Annual Joyful 5K Christmas Day

Part of series of holiday-themed races around Como Lake.
www.charitieschallenge.org

TCBC events (see January)

www.mtn.org/tcbc

ALL-YEAR SAINT PAUL ACTIVITIES

Saint Paul Hiking Club

Meets regularly throughout city. Everyone welcome. Check newspaper recreation/events calendar for current hike locations and contact information.

SEASONAL ACTIVITIES

Rowing

Minnesota Boat Club offers classes, camps, and events to rowers of all ages and abilities from its headquarters on Raspberry Island across from downtown.
www.boatclub.org

Star Swim Team

Programs for swimmers of all ages and abilities in summer at Highland Park Pool.
www.starswimteam.net

WINTER ACTIVITIES

Cross-Country Skiing

City grooms trails at **Como, Phalen, and Highland** golf courses each winter.

Tuesday Night Lessons

Lessons in classic and skate skiing through Saint Paul Parks and Recreation.
www.stpaul.gov/depts/parks

Ice-Skating Rinks

Outdoor ice-skating rinks located throughout the city. Amenities vary.
www.stpaul.gov/depts/parks
www.capitalcitypartnership.com

Key:

4K (2.5 miles)
5K (3.1 miles)
6K (3.75 miles)
8K (4.97 miles)
10K (6.2 miles)
Half Marathon (13.1 miles)
Marathon (26.2 miles)

Illustration © Andy Singer

Minnesota fun

Coffee Houses and Tea Shops

Amore Coffee

917 Grand Ave.
651.222.6770
www.amorecoffee.com
Locally owned coffee house featuring award-winning coffee and authentic Italian gelato. Warm, friendly environment.

Black Dog Coffee and Wine Bar

308 Prince St.
651.228.9274
www.blackdogstpaul.com
Sandwiches, soups, salads, pizza. Exhibits and events featuring the local arts, music, and peace communities.

Blue Cat Coffee and Tea

151 Cesar Chavez St.
651.291.7676
Snappy drinks. Happy cats. Get your paws on a cup. Donations welcome.

Bread and Chocolate

867 Grand Ave.
651.228.1017
www.cafelatte.com/bread_
chocolate.html
Coffee, sandwiches, and fresh-baked goods, including the best brownies in the city!

Brewberry's Coffee Place

475 Fairview Ave. South
651.699.1117
A neighborhood shop with a café-like setting where you can enjoy all-natural soups, sandwiches, frappes, ice cream, and free Wi-Fi.

Café Juliahna

879 Smith Ave. South
651.450.7070
Organic bakery and café roasting its own fair trade coffee. Family friendly with free Wi-Fi.

Cahoots Coffee Bar

1562 Selby Ave.
651.644.6778
Cool art. Lots of seating; backyard patio reminiscent of European dives.

Coffee Bené

53 Cleveland Ave. South
651.698.2266
www.coffeebene.com
Organic fair trade coffee from master roasters, fresh baked goods, and sandwiches made from their own bakery. Décor includes double fireplace, fine rugs, and leather easy chairs.

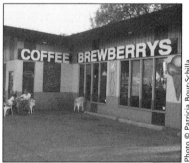

Sandwiches and ice cream too

The Coffee Grounds

1579 Hamline Ave. North
651.644.9959
www.thecoffeegrounds.net
Featuring free live music four days a week, open mike, storytelling, and community knitting and beading groups.

Coffee News Cafe

1662 Grand Ave.
651.698.3324
www.myspace.com/
coffeenewscafe
A friendly neighborhood place serving liberal portions to liberal minds.

Cosmic's Coffee

189 Snelling Ave. North
651.645.0106
www.myspace.com/
cosmicscoffee
Internet coffee shop.

Dunn Brothers Grand Avenue

1569 Grand Ave.
651.698.0618
www.dunnbrosgrand.com
The original Dunn Brothers featuring great coffee and monthly live music. Close to Macalester College.

The EDGE Coffee House (originally Prairie Star)

2399 University Ave. West
651.641.1656
High ceilings, artsy feel. Free computer and Wi-Fi. Old-time music jam on Saturday mornings, 9 a.m. until they stop.

Executive Coffee and Tea

180 Fifth St. East, Suite 266
651.228.9820
Certified Jamaican Blue Mountain and kona coffee available daily.

A Fine Grind Coffeehouse

2038 Marshall Ave.
651.645.9700
www.afinegrind.com
A real, down-to-earth neighborhood coffee house where friends and neighbors gather. Lots of workspace, great music.

Fresh Grounds

1362 West Seventh St.
651.224.2348
www.freshgroundscoffee.com
Coffee. Community. Conversation. Cause.

Gig's (formerly Buzz Coffee)

80 Snelling Ave. North
651.644.3421

Ginkgo Coffeehouse

721 Snelling Ave. North
651.645.2647
www.ginkgocoffee.com
Serving only the highest-quality coffee, tea, smoothies, and food. Live music. Story hour. Family-friendly.

Ginkgo Coffee & Smoothie Bar

St. Joseph's Hospital
69 West Exchange St.
651.232.3084
www.ginkgocoffee.com/location.
htm
Located inside the historic St. Joseph's hospital. Coffee, fresh pastries, and smoothies. Two seating areas and a fireplace.

Ginkgo Coffee Bar & Deli

Garden View Medical Building
(next to Children's Hospital)
347 Smith Ave. North
651.220.6200
A coffee bar and deli with homemade sandwiches and other fresh, healthy food.

Global Village

508 Jackson St.
612.968.0333
www.liftkids.org
The purpose of Global Village is to increase social responsibility, peace and justice. Welcoming to people of all ages, Global Village provides a meeting place, coffee, tea, free Wi-Fi and more.

Golden Thyme Coffee Café

921 Selby Ave.
651.645.1340
A community hub offering special drinks named after jazz legends, fresh pastries, homemade soups (including a great gumbo), sandwiches, and entrées. Owners Stephanie and Mychael Wright serve up warm hospitality. Meeting rooms also available.

Grumpy Steve's Coffee

215 Wabasha St. South
651.224.1191
www.wabashastreetcaves.com
Coffee, tea, Italian sodas, beer and wine, fresh-made Belgian waffles, smoothies, and sandwiches. "You may come in grumpy, but you sure won't leave that way."

J & S Bean Factory

1518 Randolph Ave.
651.699.7788
www.jsbeanfactory.com
Full-service roastery and coffee shop. Now featuring the Obama Blend. Great space that supports artists, musicians, and the community.

Java Train Cafe

1341 Pascal St. North
651.646.9179
www.javatraincafe.com
Family-friendly coffee house serving Izzy's ice cream. Play areas for kids, including a real train.

Jerabek's New Bohemian Coffeehouse and Bakery

63 Winifred St. West
651.228.1245
www.jerabeks.com
Coffee house, bakery, deli, and gifts. Specializing in Old World pastries since 1906.

Kopplin's Coffee

490 Hamline Ave. South
651.698.0457
www.kopplinscoffee.com
For true brewing connoisseurs. Good taste: superior beans and great baristas.

Lady Elegant's Tea Room

2230 Carter Ave.
651.645.6676
www.ladyeleganttea.com
An English cottage tea room with a Victorian touch where the world waits while you have tea. Offering three-, four-, and six-course themed tea events all year 'round.

Mad Hatter Coffee Cafe and Teahouse

943 West Seventh St.

In Saint Paul, we love the stuff

651.227.2511
Friends, food, and philosophy by the cup.

Midway Café
1342 Thomas Ave.
651.645.6466
Popular neighborhood hangout.

Nina's Coffee Café
165 Western Ave. North
651.292.9816
A café in a beautiful historic building made famous by F. Scott Fitzgerald. Features readings by local writers.

Pat & Mike's Lobby Shoppe
85 Seventh Place East and 401 Robert St.
651.292.8888 and 651.726.7777
Coffee bar, lunch, and gift shop.

Polly's Coffee Cove
1382 Payne Ave.
651.771.5531
Convenient and quiet. Boxed lunches. Off-street parking. Delivery service available.

Rudies Coffeehouse
1169 West Seventh St.
651.291.1963
An edgy little coffee shop specializing in Thai coffee and online gaming.

St. Paul Corner Drug
240 Snelling Ave. South
651.698.8859
www.stpaulcornerdrug.com
A pharmacy with 5-cent coffee at the old-fashioned soda fountain in front of the shop. Ice cream too. A favorite local hangout.

Steep Brew Coffee Shop
101 Fifth St. East, Suite 296
651.221.9859
www.store.sbcoffeeshop.com
The oldest coffee shop in downtown Saint Paul, making the Skyway homier.

The Tea Garden
1692 Grand Ave. and 101 E. Fifth Street (Skyway level, US Bank Building)
651.690.3495 abd 651-493-8943
www.teagardeninc.com
Specializing in bubble tea (a delightful drink with sweet, chewy tapioca bubbles in the bottom).

TeaSource
752 Cleveland Ave. South
651.690.9822
www.teasource.com
Tea shop with large variety of extraordinary teas.

White Rock Coffee Roasters
769 Cleveland Ave. South
651.699.5448
www.whiterockcoffee.com
A legend since 5 a.m. Roasts coffee from all over the world. Free Wi-Fi and access to hard-wired terminals for people without laptops.

Restaurants

128 Café

128 Cleveland Ave. North
651.645.4128
www.128cafe.net
Cozy atmosphere with changing menu that highlights fresh, seasonal ingredients. Sunday brunch available. $$

Abu Nader Deli and Grocery

2095 Como Ave.
651.647.5391
Small deli serving satisfying falafel sandwiches and other Middle Eastern delights made from scratch. $

Asian Express

1151 Clarence St.
651.771.1409
Newly opened restaurant. Sparse décor. Features pho. $

Babani's Kurdish Restaurant

544 Saint Peter St.
651.602.9964
www.babanis.com
Saint Paul's first (maybe only) Kurdish restaurant. Friendly, warm place. $

Barbary Fig

720 Grand Ave.
651.290.2085
Chic location featuring North African and Southern France–inspired cuisine. $$

Barrio Tequila Bar

One of Saint Paul's newest restaurants across from picturesque Mears Park. Owner/Chef Tim McKee is the 2009 Best Chef Midwest James Beard Award Winner. Tequila, of course, plus tacos, enchiladas, seafood, chicken, ribs, steak, $–$$

Black Bear Crossings on the Lake

1360 North Lexington Pkwy.
651.488.4920
www.blackbearcrossings.com
Cafeteria-style breakfasts and lunches along with coffee shop. Great for meetings. Right on Como Lake. $

Black Dog Coffee & Wine Bar

308 Prince St.
651.228.9274
www.blackdogstpaul.com
Nice digs and great Lowertown location. $

Black Sea

737 Snelling Ave. North
651.917.8832
www.blacksearestaurant.com
Turkish. Run by Ali and Sema. Neighborly, cozy, delicious, and comfortable. No debit or credit cards. $

Blondies Café

454 Snelling Ave. South
651.204.0152
www.blondiescafe.com
Fun, cozy atmosphere offering a variety of sandwiches, soups, and homemade desserts. Nice place to sit with free Wi-Fi. Open for breakfast and lunch only. $

The Blue Door Pub

1811 Selby Ave.
651.493.1865

Bon Vie at 518 Selby Avenue

www.thebdp.com
Features Juicy Blucys (cheese-stuffed burgers). $

Boca Chica Restaurante Mexicano and Cantina
11 Cesar Chavez St.
651.222.8499
www.bocachicarestaurant.com
Authentic Mexican cuisine with patio. Mariachi music every fourth Saturday of the month. $ (lunch) $$ (dinner)

Bon Vie
518 Selby Ave
651.287.0112
www.apieceofcakebakery.net
Bistro breakfast-and-lunch café with menu changing twice weekly. $

The Bulldog Lowertown
237 East Sixth St.
651.221.0750
www.thebulldoglowertown.com
Pub grub and home-style entrées like Tater Tot Hotdish. $

Brasa Premium Rotisserie
777 Grand Avenue
651.224.1302

651.224.1628 (take-out)
A new restaurant in Saint Paul. Organic, local ingredients featuring chicken and slow-cooked pork dishes. Dine in or take out. Patio. $

Café BonXai
1613 University Ave. West
651.644.1444
www.cafebonxai.moonfruit.com
Hmong-owned fusion restaurant. Famous for their Fireside Steak. $

Café Juliahna
879 Smith Ave. South
651.450.7070
Family-friendly, organic coffee shop, bakery, and café. Vegetarian sandwiches and soups. Free Wi-Fi. Live music Fridays and Saturdays. $

Cafe Latté
850 Grand Ave.
651.224.5687
www.cafelatte.com
Cafeteria-style gourmet soups, salads, and sandwiches. Features a great variety of fresh desserts. $

Café Minnesota

Minnesota History Center
345 West Kellogg Blvd.
651.651.259.3000
www.minnesotahistorycenter.org
*Self-serve café. Outdoor patio and free
Wi-Fi. Breakfast and lunch only. $*

Caffe Biaggio

2356 University Ave.
651.917.7997
www.cafebiaggio.com
*Italian bistro. Delicious. $ (lunch) $$
(dinner)*

Casper's Cherokee Sirloin Room

886 Smith Ave. South
651.457.2729
www.cherokeesirloinroom.com
*A Saint Paul classic featuring steaks,
seafood, and spirits. $$*

Casper and Runyon's Nook

492 Hamline Ave. South
651.698.4347
www.crnook.net
Classic neighborhood bar and grill. $

Cat-Man-Do

1659 Grand Ave.
651.528.7575
www.thecatmando.com
*Himalayan cuisine. Yummy curries,
chhoylas, samosas, naan. Patio.*

Cecil's Delicatessen, Bakery, and Restaurant

651 Cleveland Ave. South
651.341.0170
Delicatessen Phone:
651.698.6276
Restaurant Phone: 651.698.0334
*Best Reubens in town. Delivery
available. $*

Chatterbox Pub

800 Cleveland Ave. S
651.699.1154
www.chatterboxpub.net
*All-day breakfast. Many entrées. Play
vintage Atari, Nintendo, and Sega
Genesis games while you eat. $*

Cheeky Monkey Deli

525 Selby Ave.
651.225.0819
www.cheekymonkeydeli.com
Soups, salads, cheese, beer, and wine. $

Cheng Heng

448 University Ave. West
651.222.5577
*Cambodian. Modest surroundings,
great food. $*

Christo's

214 Fourth St. East
651.224.6000
www.christos.com
*Greek food in the restored Union
Depot. Lunch buffet. $*

Coffee News Café

1662 Grand Ave.
651.698.3324
*A real neighborhood place with great
desserts and 17 varieties of coffee
roasted on site $*

Cossetta Italian Market and Pizzeria

211 West Seventh St.
651.222.3476
*A Saint Paul landmark. Great Italian
food and gourmet shop. $*

Dari-ette Drive In

1440 Minnehaha Ave. East
651.776.3470

Seasonal April–October
Car-hops who really, truly come to your car! Homemade malts, cherry Cokes, burgers, fries, onion rings, and pizza burgers! Underlying flavor is Italian. Owned and operated for over fifty years by an East Side Italian family, Dari-ette offers traditional sauce, pasta, meatball sandwiches, hot dagos, even fried peppers! Topping it all off, fresh banana malts! $

Day by Day Café
477 West Seventh St.
651.227.0654
www.daybyday.com
Good for breakfast, all day long. $

Degidio's
425 West Seventh St.
651.291.7105
www.degidios.com
Italian cuisine with family recipes and affordable prices. Classic Saint Paul eatery. $

Destiny Café
995 University Ave. West
651.649.0394
Located inside Sunrise Market. Hmong deli and sit-down restaurant. Great kow poon (curry noodles). $

Dixie's on Grand
695 Grand Ave.
651.222.7345
www.dixiesongrand.com
Southern comfort food, casual dining, and live music. $$

Downtowner Woodfire Grill
253 West Seventh St.
651.228.9500
www.downtownerwoodfire.com
Meats and vegetables grilled over oak. Cozy in winter. $$

East Side Thai
879 Payne Ave.
651.776.6599
Tiny place with great Thai food and pho. $

Eden Pizza
629 Aldine St.
651.646.7616
www.edenpizza.com
Opened by lovers of cooking and poetry. $

Egg & I
2550 University Ave. West
651.647.1292
www.eggandimn.com
Breakfast and lunch served all day. Famous for kamikaze cakes. $

El Burrito Mercado
175 Cesar Chavez Blvd.
651.227.2192
www.elburritomercado.com
Satisfying, inexpensive Mexican taquer'a inside a West Side supermercado. $

Everest on Grand
1278 Grand Ave.
651.696.1666
www.everestongrand.com
Nepalese. Terrific curries and momos (dumplings) bring the taste of the Himalayas to Minnesota. $$

Fasika
510 Snelling Ave. North
651.646.4747

Forepaughs

www.fasika.com
Ethiopian fare with a variety of stewed, curried, and charbroiled meats. Vegetarian entrees too. $

Flamingo
490 Syndicate St. North
651.917.9332
East African-Eritrean cuisine. Fabulous. $

Forepaughs
276 Exchange St. South
651.224.5606
www.forepaughs.com
Victorian mansion built by its namesake in 1870. French cuisine with some Asian and classic American flavors. $$

Fuji Ya
465 North Wabasha St.
651.310.0111
www.fujiyasushi.com
Authentic Japanese restaurant with nice happy hour menu. $$

Glockenspiel
605 West Seventh St.
651.292.9421
www.Glockenspielrestaurant.com
Saint Paul's German restaurant with extensive drink listing. $

Grand Ole Creamery
750 Grand Ave.
651.293.1655
www.grandolecreamery.com
Yummy homemade ice cream with handmade, malted waffle cones. $

Grandview Grill
1818 Grand Ave.
651.698.2346
Gleaming '50s-decor malt shop. $

Great Waters Brewing Company
426 Saint Peter St.
651.224.2739
www.greatwatersbc.com
Brew pub and restaurant with award-winning beers and year-round patio. $

Happy Gnome
498 Selby Ave.
651.287.2018
www.thehappygnome.com
Pub with over 44 taps, eclectic seasonal menus, and outdoor seating. $$

Highland Grill
771 Cleveland Ave. South
651.690.1173
www.highlandgrill.com
Neighborhood restaurant serving sophisticated comfort food with a flair. Good sweet potato fries and fun staff. $

Ho Ho Gourmet Restaurant
1985 Old Hudson Rd.
651.731.0316
www.hohogourmetrestaurant.com
Chinese restaurant featuring buffet and à la carte items. Great chicken wings and roast duck. $

Il Vesco Vino Bar Napoletano

242 West Seventh St.
651.222.7000
www.ilvescovino.com
Artful appetizers, wood-fired pizzas, authentic pastas, and a patio. $$

India House

758 Grand Ave.
651.293.9124
www.indiahousesaintpaul.com
Fresh Indian food. Daily lunch buffet. $

Italian Pie Shoppe & Winery

1670 Grand Ave.
651.221.0093
www.italianpieshoppe.com
Established in 1976. Award-winning pizzas. Lots of online and dine-in specials. $

Izzy's Ice Cream Café

2034 Marshall Ave.
651.603.1458
www.izzysicecream.com
Artisan ice cream with inspired, quirky flavors. $

Jay's Café

791 Raymond Ave.
651.641.1446
www.jays-café.com
Yum, yum. Attractive. Half-price bottle of wine Wednesdays. $ (breakfast/lunch) $$ (dinner)

Jerabek's New Bohemian Coffeehouse and Bakery

63 Winifred St. West
651.228.1245
www.jerabeks.com
Best soups ever. Fresh pastries. Cozy. Saint Paul at its finest. Vegan options. $

Key's Café

767 Raymond Ave.
500 Robert Street North
651.646.5756 or 651.222.4083
www.keyscafe.com
Great staff and food. Family restaurant since 1973. $

Khyber Pass Cafe

1571 Grand Ave.
651.690.0505
www.khyberpasscafe.com
Afghan. Delicious and friendy. Lunch buffet available. $$

Kim Huoy Chor

1664 University Ave. West
651.642.1111
www.yourchineserestaurant.com
Cambodian-Chinese restaurant. Pick-up, delivery, and buffet options. $

Kolap Restaurant

601 Dale St. North
651.222.2488
www.kolaprestaurant.com
Cambodian cuisine. $

Krua Thailand

432 University Ave. West
651.224.4053
Thai; great curries. $

Lao Thai Family Restaurant

501 University Ave.
651.224.5026
Traditional Lao-Thai cuisines like raw beef laab and chicken laab. Great pad thai and chicken wings. $

La Cucaracha

36 Dale St. South
651.221.9682
www.lacucaracha
restaurante.com

Mexican. Family-owned since the 1960s. $$

La Grolla
452 Selby Ave.
651.221.1061
www.lagrollastpaul.com
*Great ambience and lovely food. Patio.
$ (lunch) $$ (dinner)*

Lee's & Dee's Barbeque Express
161 North Victoria St.
651.225.9454
Good ribs and catfish. $

The Lexington
1096 Grand Ave.
651.222.5878
www.the-lexington.com
*A classic restaurant featuring steaks,
seafood, and traditional favorites. $$*

The Liffey Irish Pub
175 West Seventh St.
651.556.1420
www.theliffey.com
*Irish pub with outdoor patio. $ (lunch)
$$ (dinner)*

The Little Oven
1786 Minnehaha Ave. East
651.735.4944

The Liffey Irish Pub patio

www.thelittleoven.com
*Italian. Very reasonable. Great deals
on takeout pizza. $*

Little Szechuan
422 University Ave. West
651.222.1333
www.littleszechuan.com
*Authentic Szechuan cuisine. Menu
offers dishes for adventurous eaters as
well as conservative ones. $*

Loto Life Café
Galtier Plaza
380 Jackson St.
651.209.777
www.lotolifecafe.com
*David Fhima's restaurant on Mears
Park. Bakery, deli, wine bar, wine
store, restaurant, and retail shop.
Outdoor seating. $, $$*

Luci Ancora
2060 Randolph Ave.
651.698.6889
www.ristoranteluci.com
*Italian with fresh foods, handmade
recipes, and experienced chefs. $$*

The M St. Café
Saint Paul Hotel
350 Market St.
651.228.3855
www.mstcafe.com
*Upscale; à la carte items as well as
European-style sideboard servings. $,
$$*

Magnolia's Family Restaurant
1081 Payne Ave.
651.774.3333
Traditional American comfort
food. $

Mai Village

394 University Ave. West
651.290.2585
*Re-creation of a traditional
Vietnamese restaurant. Great
ambience. $, $$*

Malina's Sports Bar

691 Dale St. North
651.488.7622
*Bar with late-night offerings of great
papaya salad, beef laab, and chicken
wings. $*

Mancini's Char House

531 West Seventh St.
651.224.7345
www.mancinis.com
*Saint Paul all the way. Great food and
entertainment in a unique lounge. $$,
$$$*

Mango Thai Restaurant

610 Selby Ave.
651.291.1414
www.mangothaimn.com
Good Thai food. $

Meritage

410 St. Peter St.
651.222.5670
www.meritage-stpaul.com
*Seasonal New American cuisine with
French influences. Patio. $$*

Mickey's Dining Car

36 West Seventh St.
651.222.5633
www.mickeysdiningcar.com
*On National Register of Historic
Places. Thirties Art Deco architecture.
Open 24 hours a day, 365 days a
year. $*

Mirror of Korea

761 Snelling Ave. North
651.647.9004
www.mirrorofkorea.com
*A solid Korean restaurant, family-
owned. Good menu options. $*

Moscow on the Hill

371 Selby Ave.
651.291.1236
www.moscowonthehill.com
*Russian food and drinks. Nice
backyard patio. $, $$*

Muddy Pig

162 Dale St. North
651.254.1030
www.muddypig.com
*Neighborhood bar and grill. Huge
sandwiches! $*

Muffuletta

2260 Como Ave.
651.644.9116
www.muffuletta.com
*Bistro offering seasonal ingredients;
wine list tended by a sommelier.
Outdoor seating. $ (lunch) $$
(dinner)*

Nina's Coffee Café

165 Western Ave. North
651.292.9816
*Great neighborhood hangout on
Cathedral Hill. Free Wi-Fi. Hosts
occasional literary readings. $*

Ngon Vietnamese Bistro

799 University Ave. West
651.222.3301
www.ngonbistro.com
*Vietnamese cuisine with French fusion.
Great ambience. Patio. Extensive
drinks list. $*

Obb's Sports Bar & Grill

1347 Burns Ave.
651.776.7010
www.obbsbar.com
*Large portions of home-cooked meals,
Friday night Lenten fish fries, quick,
thoughtful service/servers, and roses
on Valentine's Day. $*

Pad Thai Grand Café

1659 Grand Ave.
651.690.1393
*Fresh, homemade Thai food, casual
dining, quick service. $*

Padelford Packet Boat Co., Inc.

Harriet Island
651.227.1100
www.riverrides.com
*Prime rib dinner cruises every Friday.
$$*

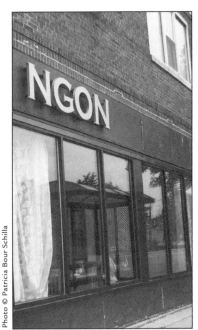

Ngon Vietnamese Bistro

Palace's Pizza

1373 Maryland Ave.
651.771.3535
*Good pizzas as well as Southeast Asian
fares like pho and laab. $*

Pappy's Chicago Style Eatery

1783 E. Maryland Avenue
651.771.5531
*Philly cheese steaks, gyros, burgers,
Italian beef, and the ubiquitous
Chicago dog. Serve yourself, stand in
line to order, get your drink, and wait
for just a short bit. It's worth it. All the
trimmings included.*

Pastor Hamilton's Bar-B-Que

1154 East Seventh St.
651.772.0279
www.pastorhamilton-bbq.com
*One-of-a-kind Saint Paul eatery.
Great ribs. Proceeds benefit youth
college fund. $*

Patrick McGovern's Pub

225 West Seventh St.
651.224.5821
Pub food and drinks. $

Pazzaluna

360 Saint Peter St.
651.223.7000
www.pazzaluna.com
*Critically acclaimed Italian cuisine
in hip atmosphere. Dinner only.
Complimentary valet parking. $$*

Pizza Luce

1183 Selby Ave.
651.288.0186
www.pizzaluce.com
*Unusual, tasty pizzas; vegan options.
Delivery available. Great taps. $*

Pop!!

6 West Sixth St.
651.228.1002
www.poprestaurant.com
Stylish décor and eclectic menu offering American, Mexican, and Swedish meatball dishes. $

Porky's Drive-In

1890 University Ave. West
651.644.1790
The best onion rings. Classic car-watching hangout on summer weekends. $

Punch Neopolitan Pizza

704 Cleveland Ave. South and
769 Grand Ave.
651.696.1066 or 651.602.6068
www.punchpizza.com
Great gourmet pizzas cooked fresh in a wood-burning oven. $

Que Nha Vietnamese Restaurant

849 University Ave. West
651.290.8552
Vietnamese food including unique items like goat curry and rice steamed in an earthen pot. $

Ray's Mediterranean Restaurant

1199 West Seventh St.
651.224.3883
www.raysmediterranean.com
Features Greek and Italian foods. $

Red's Savoy Inn and Pizza

421 East Seventh St. or 520
White Bear Ave. North
651.227.1437 or 651.731.1068
www.theoriginalredssavoypizza.com
Great variety of pizza. $

Ristorante Luci

470 Cleveland Ave. South
651.699.8258
www.ristoranteluci.com
Romantic bistro featuring Italian cuisine. $$

River Boat Grill

Harriet Island riverfront
105 Harriet Island Rd.
651.290.2363
www.riverboatgrill.com
Eat with a great view of the Mississippi. $

Ruam Mit Thai Cafe

475 Saint Peter St.
651.222.7871
www.ruam-mit-thai.com
Convenient downtown location. Lunch buffet. $

Russian Tea House

1758 University Ave. West
651.646.4144
Borscht, piroshki, cabbage rolls, real Russian tea. Open 11–3, Tuesday–Friday. $

Saigon Restaurant

704 University Ave.
651.225.8751
Vietnamese cuisine with pho, broken rice dishes, banh mi sandwiches and more. $

St. Clair Broiler

1580 St. Clair Ave.
651.698.7055
www.stclairbroiler.com
Traditional American fare like burgers, sandwiches, and buttermilk fried chicken. $

St. Paul Cheese Shop

1573 Grand Ave.
651.698.3391
Deli sandwiches and delicious sweets.
$

St. Paul Grill

The Saint Paul Hotel
350 Market St.
651.292.9292
www.stpaulhotel.com
Classic American entrées and drinks.
$$$

Saji-Ya

695 Grand Ave.
651.292.0444
www.sajiya.com
Japanese restaurant and bar with teppenyaki grill. $$

Sakura

350 Saint Peter St.
651.224.0185
www.sakurastpaul.com
Japanese staples along with shabu shabu. $$

Salut Bar Américain

917 Grand Ave.
651.917.2345
French inspired. Steaks, seafood, patio. $$

Señor Wong

111 Kellogg Blvd. East
651.224.2019
www.senorwong.com
Menu includes foods from Mexico, Korea, Vietnam, Thailand, and China.
$

Serlin's Café

1124 Payne Ave.
651.776.9003
Classic step-back-in-time feel. All-American. Great breakfast options. $

Shamrock Grill

995 West Seventh St.
651.228.9925
A real pub. Music too. $

Shish Café

1668 Grand Ave.
651.690.2212
Mediterranean Grill and Café. Includes full breakfast menu. Open 7 a.m. to 11 p.m. daily. $

The Strip Club

378 Maria Ave.
651.793.6247
www.domeats.com
Features menu items like wild rice crepes. Great view of the downtown skyline. $$

Supatra's Thai Cuisine

967 West Seventh St.
651.222.5859
www.supatra.com
Thai cuisine with lunch specials. $

Tanpopo Noodle Shop

308 Prince St.
651.209.6527
www.tanpoporestaurant.com
Simple and elegant Japanese food. $

Taste of Thailand

1669 Selby Ave.
651.644.3997
www.tasteofthailand.net
Traditional Thai food. $

Taste of Thailand III
1753 Old Hudson Rd.
651.774.6905
Lots of curry options and unique egg rolls. $

Tavern on Grand
656 Grand Ave.
651.228.9030
www.tavernongrand.com
Famous for walleye. $$

Tavern on the Avenue
825 Jefferson Ave.
651.227.6315
www.tavontheavenue.com
Karaoke on Thursdays and Saturdays. $

Tay Ho Restaurant
302 University Ave. West
651.228.7216
Chinese, Vietnamese. Delicious banh mi sandwiches. $

The Tea House
1676 Suburban Ave.
651.771.1790
www.ourteahouse.com
Great Chinese restaurant hidden on the East Side. Menu items reminiscent of California dim sum. $

Thai Bazil
704 University Ave. West
651.225.8080
Delicious and reasonably -priced Thai cuisine. $

Trieu Chau Restaurant
500 University Ave. West
651.222.6148
Outstanding soups and tasty sandwiches. Nice service. $

Trattoria da Vinci
400 Sibley St.
651.222.4050
www.trattoriadavinci.com
Italian. Romantic. $$

Trotter's Cafe & Bakery
232 Cleveland Ave. North
651.645.8950
www.trotterscafe.com
Dinner menu includes American cuisine as well as Tuscany Chicken and West African Potato Stew. Fresh baked goods. $

W. A. Frost & Company
Dacotah Building
374 Selby Ave.
651.224.5715
www.wafrost.com
A favorite destination since 1975. Incomparable ambiance and Old World character. Fireplaces, charming bar, European-style garden patio. $$, $$$

Yarusso's
637 Payne Ave.
651.776.4848
www.yarussos.com
Italian classic since 1933. Stop by for the sauce, stay for the bocce ball. Restaurant currently under reconstruction. Check website for ordering information. $

Theater

Actors Theater of Minnesota
350 St. Peter St., Suite 254
651.290.2290
www.actorsmn.org.
Professional theater company offering annual season at the Lowry Lab Theater in downtown Saint Paul.

Anodyne Theatre
825 Carleton St.
651.646.8242
Anodyne Theatre produces conventional and unconventional works and continues community building by supporting emerging performing artists.

Commedia Beauregard
354 Warwick St.
651.797.4967
www.cbtheatre.org

Commedia Beauregard presents classic and modern works from around the world translated into English and made accessible to modern audiences.

Dreamland Arts
677 Hamline Ave. North
651.645.5506
www.dreamlandarts.com
Gathering place for creative expression through the arts that builds a healthy community.

Gremlin Theatre
2400 University Avenue West
651.228.7008
www.gremlin-theatre.org
Small professional theater focusing on a wide range of styles and works in an intimate, urban venue.

Gremlin Theatre at 2400 University Avenue West

Photo © Patricia Bour-Schilla

The Historic Mounds Theatre
1029 Hudson Rd.
651.772.2253
www.moundstheatre.org
*Home to Starting Gate Productions.
Provides Dayton's Bluff and Saint
Paul's East Side, as well as the
larger Twin Cities community, with
engaging, live entertainment. Owned
and operated by Portage for Youth, a
nonprofit, after-school and summer
enrichment program for young women.*

History Theatre
30 East Tenth St.
651.292.4323
www.historytheatre.com
*Nonprofit professional theater in
downtown devoted to creating and
producing plays about Minnesota, the
Midwest, and the diverse American
experience.*

In the Basement Productions
P.O. Box 65861
www.itbp.org
*Working out of the Fourth Street
Theatre, this nonprofit company
produces original, classic, and
contemporary works emphasizing the
unique talents and contributions of its
artists.*

Lex-Ham Community Theater
1184 Portland Ave.
651.644.3366
www.LexHamArts.org
*Offers variety of ways for novice
and experienced theater lovers and
performers to become involved:
Shakespeare Reading Series, acting
classes, and main stage theater
productions throughout the year.*

Lowry Theater
16 West Fifth St.
651.227.2464
www.wegottabingo.com
*Professional dinner theater presenting
interactive comedies.*

Lowry Lab Theater
350 St. Peter St.
651.644.1890

**Minnesota Jewish
Theatre Company**
P.O. Box 16155
651.647.4315
www.mnjewishtheatre.org
*Telling stories of our common search
for identity in a multicultural world.
Igniting your mind by touching your
heart (even if you're not Jewish!).
Performances located at Hillcrest
Center Theater, 1978 Ford Parkway.*

Nautilus Music-Theater
308 Prince St., Suite 250
651.298.9913
*Supports the creation, development,
and production of new operas and
music theater pieces, working with
writers, composers, performers, and
directors. Works-in-progress presented
in program of monthly rough-cuts.
Occasional full productions.*

Park Square Theatre
20 West Seventh Place
651.291.7005
www.parksquaretheatre.org
*Professional theater in downtown
Saint Paul producing balance of
familiar favorites and fresh new
stories.*

Penumbra Theatre Company

270 North Kent St.
651.224.3180
www.penumbratheatre.org
*Minnesota's only professional
African American theater company,
performing at the Martin Luther King/
Hallie Q. Brown Center in the heart
of the Selby-Dale neighborhood*

Skylark Opera

Landmark Center, Suite 414
75 West Fifth St.
651.292.4309
www.skylarkopera.org
*Founded in 1980 and offering a
wide-ranging repertoire of opera,
operetta, and musical theater. Stresses
accessibility by performing works in
English in intimate venues at moderate
prices.*

Starting Gate Productions

P.O. Box 16392
651.645.3503
www.startinggate.org
*Performing at the Mounds Theatre
in the Dayton's Bluff neighborhood,
this small professional theater
group produces primarily classic and
contemporary dramas and comedies.*

SteppingStone Theatre
for Youth Development

55 North Victoria St.
(corner of Portland and Victoria)
651.225.9265
www.steppingstonetheatre.org
*SteppingStone Theatre is Saint
Paul's premier youth-centered arts*

*organization, creating high-quality,
affordable family entertainment that
feeds the mind.*

Teatro del Pueblo

209 Page St. West, Suite 208
Saint Paul, MN 55107
651.224.8806
www.teatrodelpueblo.org
*A fun-loving, hard-working theater
company devoted to Latino issues,
artists, and culture. Teatro serves
many communities across the state
with educational residencies, touring
shows, and Annual Political Theater
Festival.*

The Theatrical Music Company

152 Hurley Ave. East
651.554.7794
*Focus of this innovative, award-
winning performance ensemble is on
reimagining how music tells stories.*

Upright Egg Theatre Company

300 Broadway, Studio 306
651.292.0179
uprightegg@gmail.com
*Small, sprightly theater company
performing original plays in Lowertown
several times a year.*

Music Venues

Arnellia's
1183 University Ave. West
651.642.5975
www.arnellias.com
The 'Legendary Club Apollo' of Minnesota. Great music, great culture.

Artists' Quarter
408 St. Peter St.
651.292.1359
www.artistsquarter.com
Located in the basement of the historic Hamm Building in downtown Saint Paul—a subterranean classic vibe. There isn't a better place in the Twin Cities to listen to jazz.

Dubliner Pub
2162 University Ave. West
651.646.5551
No- frills bar offering a smorgasborg of beer, whiskey, and scotch.

Ginkgo Coffeeshop
721 Snelling Ave. North
651.645.2647
www.ginkgocoffee.com
Corner coffee café, offering fair trade and organic products and a diverse mix of music and clientele.

Half Time Rec
1013 Front St.
651.488.8245
www.halftimerec.com
Your neighborhood nightclub, with the only indoor bocce courts in the city!

Hat Trick Lounge
134 East Fifth St.
651.228.1347
www.robincommunications.com/
hat_trick_lounge.htm
Classic saloon, offering rock and roll, blues, country, folk, jazz, pop. Every night's a surprise!

Minnesota Music Café
499 Payne Ave.
651.776.4699
www.minnesotamusiccafe.com
Where the food Is great and the music is cooking!

O'Gara's Bar & Grill
164 Snelling Ave. North
651.644.3333
www.ogaras.com
Since 1942, a place of nostalgia, charm, and good humor. Great music, good food, and wonderful people-watching!

Saint Paul Chamber Orchestra
408 Saint Peter St., Third Floor
651.291.1144
www.thespco.org
America's premier chamber orchestra.

Shamrock Grill
995 West Seventh St.
651.228.9925
Serving American fare with to-die-for juicy lucys!

Station 4
201 West Fourth St.
651.298.0173
www.station-4.com
Cult music.

Tavern on the Avenue
825 Jefferson Ave.
651.227.6315
www.tavontheavenue.com
*Classic rock and roll, rhythm, blues
and soul. No cover!*

Turf Club
1601 University Ave. West
651.647.0486
www.turfclub.net
*A dim and gritty atmosphere, often
called "the best remnant of the '40s."
Good music, good company.*

Station 4

Photo © Patricia Bour-Schilla

Dance Venues

Sunday Night Social Dances
Half Time Rec
1013 Front St.
651.488.8245
www.halftimerec.com
8–11 p.m. Band varies weekly.
Usually couples dancing. Dance lesson
before the dance. $5.

Swing Night on Thursdays
Wabasha Caves
215 Wabasha St. South
651.224.1191
www.wabashastreetcaves.com
Doors open at 6 p.m. Lesson at 6:15.
Live music, 7–9 p.m. Remember the
password(s): Gus sent me. All-ages
event. $7.

Third Saturdays
Argentine Tango
Black Dog Coffee & Wine Bar
308 Prince St.
651.228.9274
www.blackdogstpaul.com
Lesson at 7.30, dance at 8 p.m.
Beginners welcome.

Tuesdays Clogging
Oddfellows' Hall
(Corner of Hampden and
Raymond avenues.)
651.644.9549
tanby@aol.com
Alcohol free. Dancing begins at 8 p.m.

Wednesday Ceili Dancing
and Lessons
The Dubliner
2162 University Ave. West
651.646.5551
7–9 p.m. Lesson at beginning of
dance. Free.

Wednesday Ceili Dancing
and Lessons
The Conway Recreation Center
2090 Conway St.
7–8:45 p.m. Alcohol free. Lesson at
beginning of dance. Free.

Art Galleries

Art Resources Gallery
494 Jackson St.
651.292.8475

AZ Gallery
308 Prince St.
651.224.3757
www.theazgallery.org

Catherine G. Murphy Gallery
College of Saint Catherine
2004 Randolph Ave.
651.690.6637
www.stkate.edu/gallery/

Colors of Art
180 East Fifth St.
Suite 220
651.379.5083

Evoke Gallery
355 Wabasha St. North
Suite 140
651.224.6388
www.evokegallery.com

Grand Hand Gallery
619 Grand Ave.
651.312.1122
www.thegrandhand.com

9th Street Entry Gallery
Rossmor Building
500 North Robert St.
651.638.6527
www.bethel.edu/galleries

Olson Gallery
CLC Building, second floor
3900 Bethel Drive
651.638.6527
www.bethel.edu/galleries

Raymond Avenue Gallery
761 Raymond Ave.
651.644.9200

Water and Oil Art Gallery
506 Kenny Rd.
651.774.2260
www.waterandoil.com

Photo © Patricia Bour Schilla

AZ Gallery in Lowertown

Bookstores

Common Good Books

165 Western Ave. North
651.225.8989
www.commongoodbooks.com
Open daily, 10 a.m.–10 p.m., except
Sunday (closes at 8 p.m.).

Hmong ABC

298 University Ave. West
651.293.0019
hmongabc@hmongabc.com
The first Hmong bookstore in town.
Also sells handmade crafts, clothing,
and jewelry.

Lee's Books

375 Wabasha St. North
651.225.9118

Micawber's Books

2238 Carter Ave.
651.646.5506
www.micawbers.com
St. Anthony Park bookstore open
Monday–Friday, 10 a.m.–8 p.m.,
Saturday, 10 a.m.–6 p.m., Sunday,
11 a.m.–5 p.m.

Midway Books

1579 University Ave. West
651.644.7605
www.midwaybook.com
Rare, used, and out-of-print books,
along with an eclectic array of
memorabilia.

Red Balloon Bookstore

891 Grand Ave.
651.224.8320
www.redballoonbookshop.com
The perfect place to bring a child.
Reading hours, signings, terrific
selection of hand puppets.

Sixth Chamber Used Books

1332 Grand Ave.
651.690.9463
www.sixthchamber.com
Coupons offered on their website.

Museums

American Association of Woodturners Gallery of Wood Art

222 Landmark Center
75 West Fifth St.
651.484.9094
www.woodturner.org
Spectacular wood art.

Gibbs Museum

2097 West Larpenteur Ave.
651.646.8629
www.rchs.com
Re-creates experience of pioneer and Dakotah life. Closed mid-Nov. to mid-Apr.

The Goldstein Museum of Design

University of Minnesota

241 McNeal Hall
1985 Buford Ave.
612.624.7434
www.goldstein.che.umn.edu/
U of M's design, textile, and fashion museum.

Jackson Street Roundhouse

193 East Pennsylvania Ave.
651.228.0263
www.mtmuseum.org
Working railroad museum.

Minnesota Children's Museum

10 West Seventh St.
651.225.6000
www.mcm.org
Lots of fun for kids of all ages.

Twin City Model Railroad Museum

Minnesota History Center

345 Kellogg Blvd. West
651.259.3000 or 800.657.3773
www.mnhs.org
Rotating exhibits. Extraordinary library.

Minnesota Museum of American Art

50 Kellogg Blvd. West, Suite 341
651.266.1030
www.mmaa.org
Gallery is closed, museum is working to secure a permanet site. See website for updates and how you can help.

Raptor Center

University of Minnesota
1920 Fitch Ave.
612.624.4745
www.raptor.cvm.umn.edu
Check out the hawks, eagles, falcons, and owls.

Science Museum of Minnesota

120 Kellogg Blvd. West
651.221.9444
www.smm.org
Includes Omnimax Theater and traveling exhibits. Underground parking.

The Schubert Club's Museum of Musical Instruments

Lower level and second floor of
302 Landmark Center
75 West Fifth St.
651.292.3267
www.schubert.org
Mon–Fri. 11 a.m.–3 p.m., Sun. 1–5 p.m. Free.

Twin City Model Railroad Museum

1021 East Bandana Blvd., Suite 222
Suite 222
651.647.9628
www.tcmrm.org
State-of-the-art miniature railroad. Ages 5 and up: $4. Free parking!

Historical Sites and Tours

Alexander Ramsey House
265 South Exchange St.
651.296.8760
www.mnhs.org/ramseyhouse
Victorian-era home of Alexander Ramsey, completed in 1872. Guided hourly tours, Fridays and Saturdays, 10 a.m.–3 p.m; Sundays, noon–3 p.m.. Closed Jan. 2 to May 31.

Assumption Church
51 West Seventh St.
651.224.7536
Roman Catholic Church built in 1871. On National List of Historic Places. Guided or self-guided tours.

Cathedral of Saint Paul
239 Selby Ave.
651.228.1766
www.cathedralsaintpaul.org
Construction completed in 1915. Guided tours Mondays, Wednesdays, and Fridays, 1 p.m.

Governor's Residence
1006 Summit Ave.
651.297.2161
www.admin.state.mn.us/govres
Limited public tours.

Historic Fort Snelling
Highways 5 and 55 (near the HHH Airport)
612.726.1171
www.mnhs.org/fortsnelling
Open May through October.
Reconstructed 1820s military post. Costumed guides and demonstrations.

James J. Hill House
240 Summit Ave.
651.297.2555
www.mnhs.org/hillhouse
Red sandstone residence completed in 1891. Art gallery and tours. Tours: $8 adults, $6 seniors.

Julian H. Sleeper House
66 Saint Albans St. South
651.225.1505
www.julianhsleeperhouse.com
Nine exhibition rooms from the Gilded Age. Includes President James A. Garfield's memorabilia. Tours by appointment.

Minnesota Korean War Veterans' Memorial
State Capitol Grounds
www.mdva.state.mn.us/KoreanWarPlaqueDedication.htm
Dramatic sculpture honoring troops who fought in Korea.

Minnesota State Capitol
75 Rev. Dr. Martin Luther King Jr. Blvd.
651.296.2881 (tours)
www.mnhs.org/statecapitol
Cass Gilbert's masterpiece. Guided tours on the hour. Free.

Minnesota Vietnam Veterans' Memorial
State Capitol Grounds
www.mvvm.org
Granite memorial recognizing and honoring the 68,000 Minnesotans who

served in Vietnam, of whom 1,077 were killed and 40 are still missing.

Old Muskego Church

Luther Seminary
2481 Como Ave.
651.641.3456
www.luthersem.edu/events
First church built by Norse immigrants in America. Erected in 1844 in Wisconsin and moved to Luther Seminary in 1904. Self-guided or guided tours on request.

Ramsey County Courthouse and Saint Paul City Hall

15 Kellogg Blvd. West
651.266.8500
www.co.ramsey.mn.us
Built in 1932; art deco architecture. "Vision of Peace" statue designed by Carl Milles is three stories high and sculpted from

onyx. *Self-guided tours and tours by appointment, 8 a.m.–4:30 p.m.*

Roy Wilkins Memorial

State Capitol Grounds
Honors Minnesota native and civil rights leader Roy Wilkins. Designed by Curtis Patterson.

Saint Paul Public Central Library

90 West Fourth St.
651.266.7000
www.stpaul.lib.mn.us
Italian Renaissance Revival building built in 1917. A jewel in the city's crown.

Wabasha Street Caves

215 Wabasha St. South
651.292.1220
www.wabashastreetcaves.com
Swing dancing, tours. Cave tours Thursdays, 5 p.m., Saturday and Sundays, 11 a.m., $22 per person.

Food Co-ops

Mississippi Market Food Co-ops:

1500 West Seventh St.
651.690.0507
www.msmarket.coop
New location and large, shiny new facility.

622 Selby Ave.
651.310.9499
www.msmarket.coop
Superb deli and attractive layout. Café, tiny outdoor park.

Hampden Park Food Co-op

928 Raymond Ave.
651.646.6686
www.hampdenparkcoop.com
Now expanded. Working member discounts, friendly staff, great prices, strong neighborhood feel, terrific soups.

New Mississippi Market on West Seventh

Sports

Bocce Ball
Half Time Rec
1013 Front Ave.
651.488.8245
www.halftimerec.com
Also weekly dart and pool leagues.

Minnesota RollerGirls
Roy Wilkins Auditorium,
RiverCentre
175 Kellogg Blvd. West, Suite 501
651.265.4899
www.mnrollergirls.com

Minnesota State High School League
2100 Freeway Blvd.
Brooklyn Center
763.560.2262
www.mshsl.org

Minnesota Swarm
317 Washington St.
888.MNS.WARM
www.mnswarm.com
Lacrosse

Minnesota Wild
317 Washington St.
651.222.WILD (box office)
www.wild.com
Hockey

Saint Paul Curling Club
470 Selby Ave.
651.224.7408
www.stpaulcurlingclub.org
Grab a pitcher of beer and pull up a chair at the viewing windows. The perfect cheap date.

Saint Paul Saints
1771 Energy Park Dr.
651.644.6659
www.saintsbaseball.com
Saint Paul's own minor league baseball team. A great way to spend a summer evening.

Saint Paul Bicycle Racing Club
www.spbrc.org
Bringing all levels of racers together.

Contributors' Biographies

Abenet Amare is from Ethiopia. He didn't know how to write a good story, but with a lot of help from his teachers, Ms. Sevald and Ms. Lind (they help him a lot), now he can write about anything. He became a good writer because he started writing at home or somewhere else when nobody was around. He thinks he can write a book because he can't stop once he starts.

Annelia Anderson attends St. Anthony Park Elementary School, and she is eleven years old. She had fun writing about the O'Shaughnessy theater because she performed her first *big* show there. She didn't have to do much research, because she remembered it all. Thanks for reading her writing.

Kirk Anderson grew up in a loving, stable, small-town Midwestern middle-class family, a difficult start for a professional cynic. Over time and with great determination, he was able to nurture his underdeveloped angst and rage through his parents' controlled exposure of him to the real world. From these unlikely beginnings, Kirk turned himself around and flowered into the fully maladjusted, paranoid professional pessimist that he is today.

Tony Andrea is a travel videographer, educator, and proud East Sider. While his travels have brought him on many unique adventures, he claims that the more he travels, the deeper his roots grow into the East Side of Saint Paul. Furthermore, he is always available to help his hometown in any way he can!

Suad Arouni is from Sierra Leone, and misses Christmas picnics on the beach with her family and friends.

Ashanti Austin is a writer for Nonprofit Newsletter Partnership, a subsidiary of Twin Cities Local Initiatives Support Corporation. She is also the marketing and community outreach coordinator at Sibley Bike Depot in Saint Paul. She is a recent transplant from California, where she grew up, worked, and taught critical reading and writing on race, gender, sexuality, and class as a teaching assistant at University of California–San Diego in the Dimensions of Culture Program. Ashanti has found a home in Minnesota teaching women how to fix their bicycles for Women and Transgender Night at Sibley. She is obsessed with underground hip-hop culture, loves dancing, graphic novels, and everything African Diaspora.

Shalaya Avant likes to dream. Shalaya attends Saint Paul Public Schools.

Amanda Baden is eleven years old and she lives in Saint Paul and attends St. Anthony Park Elementary School. She is in sixth grade. She has a cat and a dog. Her favorite kind of writing is poetry.

Elen Bahr is a self-proclaimed Saint Paulite, grant writer, and aspiring children's book author. Elen and her family live in the Summit-University neighborhood, where she bakes pies, grows beautiful gardens, coordinates her neighborhood block club, and would never, ever dream of trading love for a street grid system.

Carolen Bailey was hired as a police woman in 1961 in Saint Paul and retired in 1991 as a lieutenant, the first woman to pass the same test as male officers. She was a pioneer in sexual assault and domestic violence work, was appointed Minnesota Assistant Commissioner of Public Safety (1992–1997), and served as president of Minnesota and the International Association of Women Police.

Aleli Balagtas prudently does not ski downhill. Occasionally, she cross-country skis—at Como Park, of course. Sometimes she writes. More often, she has good ideas for writing that she soon forgets, in the confusion of getting kids to soccer games at the right times.

Paul Bartlett and his wife, Linda, trekked their way through Wisconsin in the 1990s and plopped down here in Minnesota. They came from the land of cheese—and a beer and a bratwurst, please—to live with the Nordics. They couldn't be happier. Paul is a quirky guy; he's a lifelong Democratic activist, pens many, many political letters to the editor (all around the country), and so loves our new president that he sports a Barack Obama "rising sun" tattoo on his right arm.

Marjorie (Weaver) Bednarek enjoys writing poems and stories with a nostalgic touch. She has published letters to editors of various publications and written stories for *Antique Week Newspaper* and *Yesterday's Magazette*. Thanks for the opportunity to appear in the *Almanac*!

Kenneth ("Kenny") A. Blumenfeld's head went into the clouds during early childhood, and he has spent most of his life fighting to keep it there. He recently earned a Ph.D. from the University of Minnesota, where he studied Minnesota's extreme and hazardous weather. Kenny's presentations on tornado history almost always include at least one defeathered chicken as a visual aid.

Todd Boss is the poet laureate of Nina's Café on Cathedral Hill, which was named for the madame who once ran a brothel there. Todd doesn't drink gin unless F. Scott or Nina is buying.

Patricia Bour-Schilla has lived in Saint Paul all her life. She enjoys being with friends and family and spends her free time bicycling, hiking, and photographing. Her best friend is her partner, Larry.

Greg Brick, a native of Saint Paul, teaches geology at local colleges. His latest book, *Subterranean Twin Cities*, was published by the University of Minnesota Press in 2009. His work has been featured in *National Geographic Adventure* magazine as well as on the History Channel.

Richard Broderick has lived in Saint Paul for the past twenty-one years. The author of three books of poetry and prose, the recipient of a Minnesota Book Award, and co-founder of The Twin Cities Daily Planet, an award-winning online community newspaper, he currently serves as president of the Macalester-Groveland Community Council.

Frank Brown has greeted people each and every day for the last twelve years with the saying "Another day, another blessing." When he says this, he is giving all thanks to his Lord. Frank believes in what he calls the "4Ps": "patience, perseverance, persistence, and prayer," because nothing can come about without God.

Mary Legato Brownell, who grew up in Saint Paul, now lives outside Philadelphia and teaches in a nearby independent school. She's received study seminar grants from the National Endowment for the Humanities, the Leeway Foundation, Mid-Atlantic Arts Council, and Pennsylvania Council of the Arts. She has been published in *American Poetry Review*, *Pivot*, *Comstock Review*, *GSU*, *Margie*, *Wind*, *InkPot*, and other journals. She was awarded first honors by the W. B. Yeats Society of New York, finalist and honorable mention by the *Comstock Review*, "Discovery"/*The Nation* (2006), and others.

Deacon J. Moreno Carranza is a native Texan and adopted son of Saint Paul. He attended the University of Houston and St. Mary's Seminary and was ordained a deacon in 1978. He worked in corporate America through the 1980s and then created his own enterprise, Accent Resources, Inc. All along, his interest in Native American culture never waned. Currently, he is connected with Native American Ventures, directing the creation, marketing, and sale of Native American arts and crafts.

John Lee Clark can often be found roaming downtown, sometimes with his wife and three sons in tow. He is a widely published poet whose first collection of poems is *Suddenly Slow* (Handtype Press, 2008). He also edited the definitive anthology *Deaf American Poetry* (Gallaudet University Press, 2009).

Mariela Consuela Cole is twelve years old. Her birthday is September 4, 1997. She has an older sister, Marisa, and an older brother, Diamonte. In her life, Mariela has had four dogs, eight cats, two hamsters, and three fish. She has gone to two different schools, Pratt and St. Anthony Park. She thanks you for reading her life story.

Carol Connolly, Saint Paul's first poet laureate, was appointed by Mayor Chris Coleman. Her family has lived in Saint Paul for six generations. She has been a political candidate, political and human rights activist, journalist, and poet. Her book of poems, *Payments Due*, now in its fifth printing, was published by Minnesota Villages and Voices, a small press founded by poet Meridel LeSueur. Currently, Carol is a columnist for *Minnesota Law & Politics*, and for ten years she has curated and hosted the monthly Readings by Writers series at the historic University Club of Saint Paul, presented by Public Art Saint Paul/ Everyday Poems for City Sidewalk.

D. D. Costandine is an artist and writer who loves her fair city and the interesting nooks and crannies that are waiting to be explored. Deborah is continuing her studies at Adler Graduate School in hopes of becoming an art therapist in the near future.

Barbara Cox lives in the Mac-Groveland area with her husband, Joe, and her three young children. She has the kind of zeal for the city often found in those raised in the suburbs. Her favorite spots in the city include Mattocks Park, the River Road bike trail, and Candyland.

Kira Cronin-Hennessy moved from New York State to Minnesota five years ago. She has this to say: it's different. For one thing, it's a lot colder. Also, there are a lot more parades and a lot fewer hills. She likes it at the Half-Price Bookstore because she gets a strange feeling of security with books all around her. When she sees a book that she has read, she smiles because she knows another child is going to be able to enjoy that same book.

Molly Culligan's life has revolved around Saint Paul. Act I: Third of six in the John and Margaret Culligan family. Act II: Motherhood. Act III: Actor, dancer, director, producer, writer, editor, poet, coach. Peace work figures large. She presents readings of her poetry on life, death, and the tango. She performs as Meridel Le Sueur and other writers.

Patricia Cummings grew up in Nativity Parish. After graduating from St. Catherine's College, she taught English, married, and had three children. Pat then spent twenty-five years in the field of philanthropy, most recently as the executive director of the Phillips Foundation. Now retired, Pat spends much of her time volunteering in the community and writing.

Captain Bob Deck grew up following his father from air force base to air force base. In 1975, after graduating from Highland Park High School, he hired on as a barge deckhand on the Upper Mississippi in Saint Paul. He has written a book about his adventures, *Deck on Deck—Towboating in the Twin Cities*. These days, he teaches elementary school and works the Padelford Packet boats.

Collette DeNet was born and raised in Saint Paul. Do not be fooled by the spelling of her last name: it does not rhyme with her first name (the 't' is silent). This bright young twenty-four-year old is an avid Guinness drinker and travel enthusiast. She also has a deep love for acoustic '70s ballads and Irish folk songs. If you ever need to find her, she is probably walking around Como Lake with her dogs singing a cheesy '70s ballad.

Louis DiSanto never thought of being a zookeeper after graduating from UW-River Falls in 1972 with a degree in journalism. But after several jobs as a writer-photographer and many résumés, a civil service exam led him to a position at Como Zoo in 1985. For the next twenty years, Louis took care of creatures great and small, becoming skilled with a hose and shovel. Now retired, Louis enjoys making photographs and writing children's stories, some inspired by his zoo experiences.

Norita Dittberner-Jax is the author of two collections of poetry, *What They Always Were* and *The Watch*. She has won a number of awards for her work. A lifelong resident of Saint Paul, Norita is crazy about the city.

Marsha Drucker misses Saint Paul and currently lives in Ohio.

Teri J. Dwyer has been a fitness enthusiast all her life. She's been lucky enough to parlay her recreation passion into a great excuse to not grow up. As a freelance sports and health & fitness writer, she's made a career out of going outside to play.

Tina Dybvik boards the bus in Lowertown Saint Paul. Her work has appeared in *Iron Horse Literary Review* and *Lake Country Journal*, and she occasionally sounds off in the *Downtown St. Paul Voice*. Visit her website at www.TinaDybvik.net

Pamela Espeland moved to Minnesota for college and has never left. She is the author of many books and has been a freelance writer for most of her life. She writes about jazz for MinnPost.com, JazzPolice.com, and bebopified.blogspot.com. Pamela and her husband, John, a photographer, have an exuberant little dog named Carmen.

Janaly Farias is a GED and ABE student at the Area Adult Learning Center in Gaylord. Although born in the United States, she lived in Mexico during her middle childhood. Janaly works at Michael Foods/MN Pullet (producers of eggs and egg products) and enjoys drawing, listening to all types of music, spending time with friends, and playing soccer, tennis, and volleyball. She wants to get a baccalaureate degree so she can have a professional career. She is interested in being an interpreter.

Daniel Gabriel's life and writings span the globe, but after watching his two boys grow up in Saint Paul, he knows where his deepest roots now lie. Speaking of lying, if you prefer fiction to reality, check out his short story collection, *Tales From the Tinker's Dam*, at local independent bookstores.

Joyce Garcia grew up in Northern Minnesota like Mowgli in *The Jungle Book*, running through the trees. Although not as flexible as she once was, she still dreams that dream.

Heatherjo Gilbertson is a local photographer who owns Personal Image Photography studio in Lowertown. Saint Paul has always been near and dear to her heart. She enjoys the history and culture of the city and its residents. One of her favorite past times is capturing the charm and beauty of the city in photographs.

Connie Goldman's long career has focused on the changes and challenges of aging. Her message on public radio, in print, and in person is clear—make any time of life an opportunity for new learning, creative pursuits, self-discovery, spiritual deepening, and continued growth. Her presentations are designed to inform, empower, and inspire.

Adán González moved to Saint Paul from Guatemala three years ago. He really appreciates the quiet and safety in Minnesota, as well as how nice and helpful people are. However, he really misses his two daughters, who are still living in Guatemala. In the future, he would like his daughters to be fluent in English. He is looking forward to visiting them and teaching them to read English, using his story from *Saint Paul Almanac*.

Tom Haas was born and raised in Saint Paul. When is he not busy with his dream job, working in a cubicle in a corporate tower, he loves to write for fun. When he is not writing, he loves to ride his bike and of course walk around Como Lake.

Andrew Hall is fifteen years old and a sophomore at Highland Park Senior High School. Andrew only writes occasionally but wishes he did so more often.

Carol Hall is a senior, a freelance writer, and a lifelong resident of Minnesota. Her column, "Good Memories," has appeared in *Minnesota Good Age* magazine since 2004. Previously, she contributed columns and articles to a number of local publications and edited her husband's college textbook, *Integrated Project Management*. In her younger years, Carol earned a BA in journalism from the U of M while working as a stewardess for that "magic carpet of the Corn Belt," Northwest Airlines.

Evan Hall is a reader, writer, talker, and a player who likes basketball. Evan is ten years old and a student at Expo Elementary.

Moira Harris, an art historian, enjoys viewing and writing about public art, permanent and ephemeral. Her interests range from murals and sculpture in Minnesota to painted cars, dragon boats, and donkey carts elsewhere. She was born in Minneapolis but has lived mainly in Saint Paul.

Margaret Hasse is twice blessed, with degrees in English, one from Stanford University and one from the University of Minnesota. She loves living in the Mac-Groveland neighborhood, where every block has at least one writer and many avid readers of poetry and other literary work. The titles of her three collections of poetry are *Stars Above, Stars Below*; *In a Sheep's Eye, Darling*; and *Milk and Tides*.

Mike Hazard, aka Media Mike, is a Bush Artist Fellow. He earns a living working as an artist in the schools and makes a good life writing poems, essays, and film scripts. For more, visit his website at www.thecie.org. Mike is part of the Saratoga Studio A.M. Sunday Writers.

Marlin L. Heise is an old, technology challenged, one-speed bicyclist who loves heat and sunshine. Home is western Minnesota, Stuttgart, Oslo, Sheffield, Bangkok, Hong Kong, Vientiane, Luang Prabang, Phnom Penh, and Saint Paul—when it is hot and sunny. He thanks the University of Minnesota for his Scandinavian, German, history, and library classes.

Jim Heynen no longer teaches full-time at St. Olaf, where he was writer-in-residence for many years. He *is not retired* but instead is trying to write sort of full-time, and therefore is not necessarily available for rides to the airport, instant walking dates, coffee at any old time, dog sitting, garden watering, reading rough drafts of the memoir you just finished, or listening to hardships of the heart. You're always welcome, however, to ask him for samples of what he has been writing.

Jennifer Holder's passions are writing and traveling. During the school year, she and her husband live in China, where she does freelance writing and also teaches English at a specialist foreign language school. She enjoys returning to her home in Saint Paul semiannually.

Lonnie Howard fell in love with a poet in 2000. The relationship didn't work out, but she discovered the poet within. She grew up in Saint Paul and still visits often, but she has lived for many years in Santa Fe, New Mexico, where a wild gray fox who comes into the garden at night is currently one of her muses.

Ed Howell was born and raised in the Boston area, the son of immigrant parents. Well, actually, they were from Canada, but you get the idea. He currently resides in the Lowertown area of Saint Paul.

Matt Jackson is thirty and has lived in Saint Paul his whole life. He owns rental property and so has a lot of free time. He spends it eating pho on University, drinking beer on Selby, and reading in the sun on Grand Avenue, accompanied by a cup of Earl Grey. Drop by and say hello.

Ann Iverson is a poet and artist who grew up in Saint Paul. She is the author of *Come Now to The Window* (Laurel Poetry Collective) and *Definite Space* (Holy Cow! Press). She is the dean of learning at Dunwoody College.

Katie Ka Vang is a Hmong American performance artist/actor/playwright/poet. She has performed on stages locally (Pillsbury House Theater, Center for Hmong Arts and Talent, Pangea World Theater, Mu Performing Arts, Intermedia Arts, Exposed Brick Theater, The Loft) and at conferences nationally in Florida, Wisconsin, and New York. She was a recipient of a Jerome Foundation Naked Stages grant, for which she used her poetry to create her first solo performance art piece *5:1 Meaning of Freedom; 6:2 Use of Sharpening*, directed by Laurie Carlos. She was also awarded an Artist Initiative poetry grant through the Minnesota State Arts Board, with which she produced her first chapbook. As a new recipient of a Jerome Travel and Study grant, she will be interviewing Hmong dancers and choreographers for her next one-woman show. She's currently working on a play as part of Mu Performing Art's New Eyes Festival and will be holding workshops in creative drama through Center for Hmong Arts and Talent.

Kim Kankiewicz writes fundraising and marketing materials for nonprofit organizations and launched the Minnesota Bookshelf blog (www.minnesotabookshelf.com), dedicated to Minnesota books and readers, in 2009. She has written for Nebraska Public Radio, Denver's alternative weekly paper, and other publications. Her family moved to the Twin Cities in 2007.

Linda Kantner is a Honda Rebel–riding writer who gets her kicks riding too fast and living to tell the story. She will publish her memoir, *As Told To Me,* if there is any justice in the world.

Karen Karsten is a life coach and continues to live in downtown Saint Paul, even though it is rumored that Minneapolis is much more exciting. She has come to consider reality as just one option for explaining the world, loves words, and delights in helping others find their own power.

Garrison Keillor is the host and writer of *A Prairie Home Companion,* the author of many books, including the Lake Wobegon novels and *Daddy's Girl,* and the editor of *Good Poems* and *Good Poems for Hard Times.* His most recent publication is *77 Love Sonnets.* His syndicated column, "The Old Scout," is seen in papers coast to coast. A member of the Academy of American Arts and Letters, he lives in Saint Paul.

Dennis Kelly grew up in Saint Paul hopping trains on the Short Line, vaulting the fence at the State Fair, playing outdoor hockey at Dunning Field, and shooting pool at Sarge's Billards.

Patricia Kirkpatrick lives in Saint Paul and teaches at Hamline University, where she edits poetry for *Water-Stone Review.* Her book of poetry is *Century's Road.* Recent poems have appeared on Saint Paul sidewalks through the Everyday Poem Project and in the anthology *The Poets' Guide to Birds.*

Hannah Kroonblawd spends nine months out of each year in Nebraska, two months in Idaho, and whatever time is left over in Minnesota. She misses the state of loons and lakes dreadfully at times, but knows that the land of sky blue waters will always be home.

Kathryn Kysar is the author of *Dark Lake,* a book of poetry, and the editor of *Riding Shotgun: Women Write About Their Mothers.* She grew up riding her banana bike around the Midway neighborhood and now rides a mountain bike with her children in the Highland Park area. Find out more about her work at www.kysar.com.

Andrea Taylor Langworthy knows if she ever loses her column gigs for the *Rosemount Town Pages* and *Minnesota Good Age* newspapers, she can always write stories about the cast of characters she met in her nearly thirty years of selling cars in the Twin Cities area.

Keng Lee lives in Saint Paul. He is a very nice person. He went to high school at Highland Senior High.

Maxine Lightfoot was born in Indiana, and her full name is Maxine Indiana Lightfoot. She lives in Saint Paul and attends St. Anthony Park Elementary School. Her favorite color is turquoise, and if she had three wishes, they would be world peace, no animals would become extinct, and mosquitos wouldn't bite. She is the oldest child in her family.

Steven Lukas moved to Minnesota from Nebraska in 1971 with his wife, Dianne. After a career as a CPA and chief financial officer for several medical device companies in the Twin Cities, he transitioned into semiretirement and teaches various graduate level courses in business. He enjoys writing, motorcycles, winter, and time with his family at their cabin on the North Shore.

Angela Mack at seven years old loved Wonder Woman. Her mom bought her a Wonder Woman swimsuit with gold bracelets and a cape. Angela believed she could fly. She dove from the couch to the loveseat and landed on her feet. Her flying powers got stronger, so she started jumping from the top of the bunk bed, making perfect landings. As her powers grew, so did her courage. She climbed onto the third floor window ledge. She could feel the wind blowing her cape, letting her know she was ready for take off: 3, 2, 1 . . . just then, her mom grabbed her, yelling "*Girl, you cannot fly!*"

Rick Mantley is a native of Denver by way of Los Angeles. He now calls the city of Saint Paul home. He writes, edits newspaper copy, videotapes, facilitates, and is a student of all the vagaries of human nature. He was delighted to be asked to contribute a piece to the *2010 Saint Paul Almanac* partly because doing so was a labor of love and a paean to a city he has become quite attached to.

Donna Martin is a retired purchasing agent who has found great joy in documenting the Bernier Family Century Farm life stories, using vignettes to capture the essence of our ancestors' heritage, beginning when Cyrille Bernier purchased and cleared land in 1890 and continuing on to current seventh-generation farmers.

Michael Maupin is a former educator, writer, and managing editor of *Minnesota Law & Politics* magazine. He has lived in Indianapolis, Washington, DC, Garmisch-Partenkirchen, Iowa City, London, and Glasgow, but he calls Saint Paul home.

Jewel Hill Mayer was born and raised in Mississippi and came to Minnesota as a young bride in 1952. She considers herself a native. (Yah! You betcha!) She writes poetry, essays, novellas, and songs—accompanying herself on the autoharp—and is quite active in City Passport for people over fifty, living life to the fullest.

Rose McGee is a member of Women Who Really Cook. Her business, Deep Roots Gourmet Desserts™, features her own creations, Sweet Potato Pie and Mango Cobbler. She sells her products on select Saturdays at the Midtown Global Market and previously at the Minneapolis Farmers Market. Her sweet potato pies were among ten Minnesota foods selected by Minnesota State Senator Amy Klobuchar for her reception in Washington, DC, during the 2009 Presidential inauguration. She is currently writing a delightful novel, *Can't Nobody Make A Sweet Potato Pie Like My Mama,* a tribute to the history of the sacred dessert and an homage to the legacy of magnificent bakers embodied by her deceased grandmother.

James McKenzie got his first Saint Paul library card five years ago, when he retired here to the south from Grand Forks about the same time he began volunteering at the Center for Victims of Torture (CVT). He bikes to coffee shops every day, as far into the winter as possible, where he works on the great American autobiography.

David Mura has written three books of poetry: *Angels for the Burning, The Colors of Desire*, and *After We Lost Our Way*. He recently published a novel, *Famous Suicides of the Japanese Empire*. If you don't know who Chow Yun Fat is, go rent *The Killers* or *Hardboiled*.

Nora Murphy was born at St. Joe's Hospital in downtown Saint Paul, was raised in Minneapolis, and now lives in Highland Park, just a few blocks from where her mom grew up. Check out Nora's latest book, *Knitting the Threads of Time,* a knitting memoir and cultural history of women's fiber arts, at www.nora-murphy.com. Nora is part of the Saratoga Studio A.M. Sunday Writers. They meet every other Sunday morning in a small studio above a garage in Saint Paul

New Foundations Writers worked together as a group to write their poem. New Foundations is a nonprofit organization located on Saint Paul's East Side that provides permanent, supportive, affordable housing and comprehensive on-site services for homeless dually diagnosed adults in recovery and their families.Together they create a housing community where adults achieve education and employment goals, strengthen families, build relationships, and contribute to the community. .

Suzanne Nielsen strived for years to become Klondike Kate, and to this day practices sultry solos in the shower. In addition, she vied for Mudonna's role for the Saints, but her height was a disadvantage. Today, Nielsen accepts her fate as a writer arguing with her characters and inevitably surrendering to their desires.

Loren Niemi is a storyteller, poet, performer, public policy consultant, and trainer who either has a short attention span or multiple converging interests. He is also author of *The Book of Plots* and coauthor, with Elizabeth Ellis, of *Inviting the Wolf In: Thinking About Difficult Stories*. Loren is part of the Saratoga Studio A.M. Sunday Writers. They meet every other Sunday morning in a small studio above a garage in Saint Paul.

Tim Nolan is a lawyer and poet in Minneapolis where he lives with his wife, Kate, and three teenage kids. Years ago, Tim lived in various apartments in Saint Paul, including one above the Animal Medical Clinic at St. Clair and Snelling, from which he ventured out often to the Clo-Spin Laundry.

Gordy Palzer's quest to be a serious writer has continually been delayed by various calls to duty along the road of life. Over the years, he has kept his writing skills honed through the penning of countless personal letters and several published articles. Encouraged by having made it into *Saint Paul Almanac*, Gordy plans on further mining the rich mother lode of memories he has just scratched into with his piece on Crosby Lake.

November Paw (she was indeed born in November) is now a student at Roseville Area High School. She's taking many mainstream classes like physical science and algebra. Recently, she was honored as student of the trimester! This summer, in her spare time, she hopes to learn Spanish, piano basics, anatomy, and how to be a good badminton player.

Margery Peterson is a writer/artist who has created a life in Saint Paul for many years.

Ron Peterson has been coaching November Paw and her sister December to learn English rapidly, using Rosetta Stone. He is the former chief technology officer of Honeywell, a community organizer, a doting grandfather, and has written a science fiction novel, *Children's Chrysalis*.

Marcie Rendon, White Earth Anishinabe: Saint Paul was her first home in the urban area in the infamous Selby-Dale area of the late '60s, early '70s. American Indian Movement (AIM) and Marvin Gaye combined to raise her poetic awareness. Now the Sunday Saratoga poets help nudge her words onto the page. Marcie is published in many Native anthologies.

Steve Rouch has been creating images since 1971. He has been named master of photography and has won the Minnesota State Wedding album competition. He has had his work selected for a show at Epcot Center at Disneyworld. He has published three fine art photo books, a book of poetry, and a book of short stories. He is a singer-songwriter, performing around town, and holds a second-degree black belt in karate. Most important, he believes in being silly and marveling at the mystery and majesty of life.

Allison Rudolph is a ten year old who lives and plays in Saint Paul. On the weekends, you can find her at the History Center or munching on gumdrops at Candyland. She always has a smile on her face and an incredible zest for life. She has a love for creating art, writing, and playing her clarinet. Her favorite Saint Paul places are Carbone's on Randolph and Artscraps. Her dream is to one day be a writer.

Mary Kay Rummel's newest poetry book is *Love in the End* (Bright Hill Press, 2008.) Her other books of poetry are *The Illuminations* (Cherry Grove Collections, 2006), *Green Journey Red Bird* (Loonfeather Press, 2001), *The Long Journey Into North* (Juniper Press, 2000) and *This Body She's Entered* (New Rivers Press, 1989) She lives in Fridley.

Maximilian Selim evolved from an ambitious student to a struggling, unemployed writer/ filmmaker the moment he received his diploma from the University of Minnesota in spring of 2009. You may find Max at Dunning Field coaching the Saint Paul Central Baseball Team or playing for the Highland Park Amateur Baseball team in his spare time.

Jane Sevald, Saint Paul public school teacher, unprepared in September 2001 at forty-five to begin a career teaching English to teenage immigrants, will forever be grateful to Linda Kantner for giving her the courage to move away from the textbooks and embark on a journey of discovery with the students. Uncharted waters indeed!

Richard Shwe moved to Saint Paul with his wife and five sons in August 2008. Within his first year, he accomplished the three goals he had set for himself in English class: buy a car, move to a new apartment, and find a permanent job. In his free time, he enjoys spending time at the mechanic's, getting his car fixed.

Andy Singer is a four-armed, six-eyed alien with large horns and powerful jaws. In 1965, he came from the planet Neptor to observe the earth and make small drawings of everything he saw. His multiple arms have enabled him to be very prolific and his multiple eyes have enabled him to see things that most humans are unaware of. If you see him riding his bicycle around

Saint Paul, don't be intimidated by his appearance. He's really quite friendly. You can see more of his drawings and cartoons at www.andysinger.com.

Julia Klatt Singer gave up wearing a watch while in Barcelona two years ago and has managed to find a few hours tucked in between the couch cushions and hidden between the changing months of the calendar. She has donated all of them to poetry. Julia is part of the Saratoga Studio A.M. Sunday Writers. They meet every other Sunday morning in a small studio above a garage in Saint Paul.

Su Smallen's book *Weight of Light* was nominated for the Pushcart Press Editor's Book Award. Her many honors include the Jane Kenyon Poetry Prize. Su Smallen is a frequent contributor to Saint Paul's *Water-Stone Review* and teaches in the MFA programs of Hamline University.

Dennis Stern was a farm kid from western Wisconsin who moved here to teach seventh and eighth grade at St. Rose of Lima School in Roseville but he lost the job "because I was too liberal for the nuns and was dating one of the lay teachers." He has worked in advertising for *The Villager* and *Midway Monitor.* He and wife, Mary Lee, have three sons who love playing disk golf with their "old man."

Keith Sterner, a native of the East Side now living in Vadnais Heights, has a passion for family, nature, and the simple pleasures of life. He prefers the woods to the city, a storm to a clear sky, and a few close friends to a wide circle of friends. Always bring humor when you meet him.

Sain Thin arrived in Saint Paul on August 1, 2008, after living in a refugee camp in Thailand for three years. He has one beautiful daughter and a son who was born in April. He says that his son is good luck, since he was born the same day that Sain Thin got his first job in Minnesota.

Ellie Thorsgaard doesn't like tornadoes, but she still likes to bike. Ellie attends Saint Paul Public Schools.

Sebastian Tippett is ten years old and attends St. Anthony Park Elementary School. He has an older sister and a mom and a dad. He likes to play sports. He plays football, baseball, soccer, and tennis. He also likes hanging with friends and sometimes writing.

Chuck Tompkins, a frequent visitor to the Saint Paul Hotel, is an independent insurance agent, author, and pilot. He and his wife, Linda, fly his Citation II into the downtown Saint Paul airport frequently. Tompkins is also the author of *The Insurance Wars* (2004) (www.theinsurancewars.com), a business novel.

Deborah A. Torraine has worked as an theater artist in the San Francisco Bay Area, Washington, DC, and Minnesota. She is an award-winning short story author and has written five locally commissioned children's plays. Deborah's hobbies include making pudding out of bread and turning water into wine. Deborah speaks survivor French and Spanish. Her favorite sayings include "Nobody knows the trouble I've seen." But if you want to know what that trouble has been . . . buy the book.

Steve Trimble lives in the Dayton's Bluff neighborhood on Saint Paul's East Side. Steve has taught at local colleges and, while he has degrees in history, tries to write books and articles in a way that regular people will enjoy them—usually in local newspapers or in the *Ramsey County History* magazine. His house near Indian Mounds Park is filled with books and odd collections mostly garnered at garage sales.

Penny Ueltschi has lived in Saint Paul for most of her life, moving with her family from the East Side to Battle Creek to Highland Park, where she currently resides. Penny loves to write long letters to friends and family and is the official record keeper of family information.

Matthew Van Tassell resides in South Saint Paul. He enjoys spending time with his four children and fourteen grandchildren. He also spends time painting and writing. Since retiring from the army two decades ago, he has worked as a school bus driver. This has given him freedom, and it also pays the rent.

Robert Van Tassell knows the soul grows from life's experiences. His formal education was in art at the University of Minnesota and then commercial art training. Robert has learned we are all teachers and students simultaneously. Two life experiences left him with that awareness. The first was teaching printmaking to second and fifth graders; the second was an independent study doing impressionist painting in Paris. His motto is that each day we should all be born-again virgins, experience life, and acknowledge our curiosity.

Diego Vázquez, Jr., wrote his first poem crossing the border with his legal guardian during a snowstorm in the desert. He rose to prominence as a poet last year when his poem was stuck in cement on the sidewalks of Saint Paul. www.diegovazquezjr.com. He is also part of the Saratoga Studio A.M. Sunday Writers. They meet every other Sunday morning in a small studio above a garage in Saint Paul.

Kathleen Vellenga grew up where dry air and lack of trees made clothes dryers redundant. Having lived in Saint Paul most of her adult life, she now cherishes trees, rivers, lakes, and humidity—but a walk down her alley will reveal her clothesline is not empty. She regrets failing to point this out in her campaign brochures while serving in the Minnesota state legislature.

Camille Verzal lives in Saint Paul. She has been writing in the corporate world for years but longs to earn a living as a screenwriter, short story writer, or children's book author.

Greg Watson's poetry has appeared in numerous literary reviews, as well as Garrison Keillor's *The Writer's Almanac*. His most recent collections are *Things You Will Never See Again* and *The Distance Between Two Hands,* both published by March Street Press. A new book, *Not Elsewhere, But Here,* is forthcoming. Born in Saint Paul, he currently resides in Mac-Groveland.

Annie Wilder is one of Penny's many cousins on the Irish side of the family. Annie is the author of *House of Spirits and Whispers,* her account of living in a haunted house, and *Spirits Out of Time,* a collection of true family ghost stories.

Diane Wilson is a writer, walker, weeder, and waterer who claims to have taught her dog to whistle. *Spirit Car: Journey to a Dakota Past* was awarded a Minnesota Book Award in 2006 for creative nonfiction, memoir, and autobiography. Diane is part of the Saratoga Studio A.M. Sunday Writers. They meet every other Sunday morning in a small studio above a garage in Saint Paul.

Andreesa Wright attends Rochester Community College and is majoring in communication studies.

Alcides Andreas Xiong is a person who comes from nowhere. He is a wonderful person who makes all things seem happy, a person who came to the United States to be your friend. He is a person who came from a little town in Argentina to the best place in the world.

Chong Xiong was born in Ban Vinai refugee camp in Thailand. She came to the United States with her family in 2004 and lived in Rhode Island for a year and a half before moving to Minnesota. Although she enjoys the many support services that Minnesota offers for refugees, she misses ocean beaches, which are sorely lacking in Minnesota. In her free time, Chong enjoys going to the zoo and playing hide-and-seek with her children.

Lily Kaliea Yang used to live in California, but now she lives in Saint Paul. Lily attends Saint Paul Public Schools.

Try the *Saint Paul Almanac* Where's the Snowflake? Game

Find the ten snowflakes hidden on different pages
of the *Saint Paul Almanac*.

Email us the ten page numbers plus your name and email, and we will enter your name into a drawing for a Saint Paul Almanac cup and tee-shirt.

Email us at: game@saintpaulalmanac.com

Answers to the 2010 *Saint Paul Almanac* Coffee Shop Quiz, page 47

1. Amore Coffee

2. Coffee Bené

3. Cosmic's Coffee

4. A Fine Grind

5. Nina's Coffee Café

6. Mad Hatter Coffee Cafe and   Teahouse

7. Java Train Cafe

8. Cahoots Coffee Bar

9. Coffee News Cafe

10. Golden Thyme Coffee Café

11. Polly's Coffee Cove

12. The Coffee Grounds

13. Grumpy Steve's Coffee

14. Kopplin's Coffee

15. Executive Coffee and Tea

16. Midway Café

17. Steep Brew Coffee Shop

18. The EDGE Coffee House (Originally Prairie Star)

19. Café Juliahna

20. Brewberry's Coffee Place

21. Jerabek's New Bohemian

22. White Rock Coffee Roasters

23. Fresh Grounds

24. J & S Bean Factory

25. Dunn Brothers Grand Avenue

26. Bread and Chocolate

27. Ginkgo

28. Black Dog Coffee and
    Wine Bar

29. Gig's (formerly Buzz Coffee)

30. Blue Cat Coffee and Tea

31. St. Paul Corner Drug

2010 Year Planner

	JANUARY	FEBRUARY	MARCH
1	F NEW YEAR'S DAY	M	M
2	SA	T GROUNDHOG DAY	T
3	SU	W	W
4	M	TH	TH
5	T	F	F
6	W	SA	SA
7	TH	SU	SU
8	F	M	M INTERNATIONAL WOMEN'S DAY
9	SA	T	T
10	SU	W	W
11	M	TH	TH
12	T	F	F
13	W	SA	SA
14	TH	SU VALENTINE'S DAY CHINESE NEW YEAR	SU DAYLIGHT SAVING TIME BEGINS
15	F	M PRESIDENTS' DAY	M
16	SA	T MARDI GRAS	T
17	SU	W ASH WEDNESDAY	W ST. PATRICK'S DAY
18	M MARTIN LUTHER KING, JR., DAY	TH	TH
19	T	F	F
20	W	SA	SA SPRING EQUINOX
21	TH	SU	SU
22	F	M	M
23	SA	T	T
24	SU	W	W
25	M	TH	TH
26	T	F MAWLID AL-NABI	F
27	W	SA	SA
28	TH	SU PURIM	SU PALM SUNDAY
29	F		M PASSOVER BEGINS
30	SA		T
31	SU		W

2010 Year Planner

	APRIL		MAY		JUNE	
1	TH	APRIL FOOLS' DAY	SA	MAY DAY	T	
2	F	GOOD FRIDAY	SU		W	
3	SA		M		TH	
4	SU	EASTER	T		F	
5	M		W	CINCO DE MAYO	SA	
6	T		TH		SU	
7	W		F		M	
8	TH		SA		T	
9	F		SU	MOTHER'S DAY	W	
10	SA		M		TH	
11	SU		T		F	
12	M		W		SA	
13	T		TH		SU	
14	W		F		M	FLAG DAY
15	TH		SA		T	
16	F		SU		W	
17	SA		M		TH	
18	SU		T		F	
19	M		W	SHAVUOT	SA	JUNETEENTH
20	T		TH		SU	FATHER'S DAY
21	W		F		M	SUMMER SOLSTICE
22	TH	EARTH DAY	SA		T	
23	F		SU		W	
24	SA		M		TH	
25	SU		T		F	
26	M		W		SA	
27	T		TH		SU	
28	W		F		M	
29	TH		SA		T	
30	F		SU		W	
31			M	MEMORIAL DAY		

2010 Year Planner

	JULY	AUGUST	SEPTEMBER
1	TH	SU	W
2	F	M	TH
3	SA	T	F
4	SU INDEPENDENCE DAY	W	SA
5	M	TH	SU
6	T	F	M LABOR DAY
7	W	SA	T
8	TH	SU	W
9	F	M	TH ROSH HASHANAH
10	SA	T	F EID AL-FITR
11	SU	W	SA
12	M	TH RAMADAN BEGINS	SU
13	T	F	M
14	W	SA	T
15	TH	SU	W
16	F	M	TH
17	SA	T	F
18	SU	W	SA YOM KIPPUR
19	M	TH	SU
20	T	F	M
21	W	SA	T INTERNATIONAL DAY OF PEACE
22	TH	SU	W FALL EQUINOX
23	F	M	TH
24	SA	T	F
25	SU	W	SA
26	M	TH	SU
27	T	F	M
28	W	SA	T
29	TH	SU	W
30	F	M	TH
31	SA	T	

2010 Year Planner

	OCTOBER		NOVEMBER		DECEMBER
1	F	M	ALL SAINTS' DAY DAY OF THE DEAD	W	HANUKKAH BEGINS
2	SA	T		TH	
3	SU	W		F	
4	M	TH		SA	
5	T	F		SU	
6	W	SA		M	
7	TH	SU	DAYLIGHT SAVING TIME ENDS	T	MUHARRAM
8	F	M		W	
9	SA	T		TH	
10	SU	W		F	INTERNATIONAL HUMAN RIGHTS DAY
11	M INDIGENOUS PEOPLE DAY	TH	VETERANS' DAY	SA	
12	T	F		SU	
13	W	SA		M	
14	TH	SU		T	
15	F	M		W	
16	SA	T		TH	
17	SU	W	EID AL-ADHA	F	
18	M	TH		SA	
19	T	F		SU	
20	W	SA		M	
21	TH	SU		T	WINTER SOLSTICE
22	F	M		W	
23	SA	T		TH	
24	SU UNITED NATIONS DAY	W		F	CHRISTMAS EVE
25	M	TH	THANKSGIVING	SA	CHRISTMAS
26	T	F		SU	KWANZAA BEGINS
27	W	SA		M	
28	TH	SU		T	
29	F	M		W	
30	SA	T		TH	
31	SU HALLOWEEN			F	NEW YEAR'S EVE

Subscribe!

Three annual issues for $30

(price includes tax, shipping, and handling)

To order

www.saintpaulalmanac.com

mail: Subscriptions
Saint Paul Almanac
PO Box 16243
Saint Paul, MN 55116

If mailing, please fill out and send the info below.

. . . .

Begin with *2010 Saint Paul Almanac*

Check or money order enclosed

Charge: __ Visa __ MasterCard

_____

CARD NUMBER

_____

EXPIRATION DATE

_____

SIGNATURE OF CARDHOLDER

_____

MAILING ADDRESS

_____

EMAIL

For gift orders

_____

SHIP TO NAME

_____

MAILING ADDRESS

Notes